Praise for *Buying Real Estate without*

"This power-packed book gives you practical, proven tec... mediately to buy residential real estate."

—Brian Tracy, best-selling author of *The Psychology of Selling* and *Create Your Own Future*

"Even as a long-time coach of rental property owners, I'm overwhelmed with the number of innovative ways and examples Peter and David reveal of how to buy real estate. Equally important, they provide steps needed to have ongoing success."

—Jeffrey Taylor (Mr. Landlord), founder of MrLandlord.com and best-selling author of *The Landlord Kit*

"This step-by-step approach to investing in real estate without cash or credit is presented in a unique workshop format. Readers will reap the benefit of attending a three-day live presentation by experts, but will be able to do it at their own pace. In addition to being able to refer to the book as an ongoing resource, there are references to other books, web sites, and programs that can continue the learning curve."

—J. Kathleen Belville, Managing Partner, Fair Housing Department, Law Offices of Kimball, Tirey & St. John

"On my last property purchase I followed David and Peter's formulas exactly, and I saved about $30,000 compared to what I had been willing to pay for the property."

—Lee R. Phillips, Attorney/Asset Protection Speaker

"Peter and David are truly amazing mentors. As the owner of a large mortgage bank and a fellow investor, I have been fortunate enough to be involved with this organization. Over the past few years I have watched many clients achieve financial freedom through Peter and David's techniques. These guys do, while others just talk about it."

—Morgan Smith, Morgan Financial Inc.

CREATING CASH FLOW SERIES

BUYING REAL ESTATE
without
CASH *or* CREDIT

Peter Conti & David Finkel

WILEY

John Wiley & Sons, Inc.

Published by John Wiley & Sons, Inc., Hoboken, New Jersey.
Published simultaneously in Canada.

For general information on our other products and services please contact our Customer Care Department within the U.S. at (800) 762-2974, outside the United States at (317) 572-3993 or fax (317) 572-4002.

Wiley also publishes its books in a variety of electronic formats. Some content that appears in print may not be available in electronic books.

Library of Congress Cataloging-in-Publication Data:
Conti, Peter.
    Buying real estate without cash or credit / Peter Conti and David Finkel.
      p.   cm.
    Includes index.
    ISBN-13 978-0-471-72831-3 (pbk.)
    ISBN-10 0-471-72831-4 (pbk.)
    1. Real estate investment—United States.   2. Real property—Purchasing—United States.   3. House buying—United States.   4. House selling—United States.   I. Finkel, David. II. Title.
    HD255.C618 2005
    332.63'243'0973—dc22
    2005045233

Printed in the United States of America.

10 9 8 7 6 5 4 3 2 1

To the nearly 5,000 Mentorship Students who have come through our Mentorship Program over the past decade. Your courage and faith make every line of this book real. May you continue to make massive amounts of money with your investing so that you can give away huge amounts of it in ways that bless the world.

CONTENTS

PART ONE
At the Intensive Training

> The Paradox of Playing It Safe • The 3 Biggest Obstacles to Getting
> Started With Your Investing • The Foundation of All Winning Real
> Estate Deals • How to Call Up FSBOs and Landlords About Buying
> Their Properties

> 3 Key Coaching Points to Increase Your Effectiveness on the Phone by
> up to 300% • How the Numbers Work Out When Prospecting By
> Phone • A Simple Test to See If You Are Looking in the Wrong Place
> for a Deal

3 Steps to Any Deal • Why Using Your Own Money Can Cost You Big • The Difference Between Good and Bad Debt • 2 Rules to Build Safety into Any Terms Deal

PART TWO
The Real World

PART THREE
Your Turn!

How a Corporate Road Warrior Became a Full-Time Real Estate Investor

When Peter and David asked me to share my story as the forward to this, their fourth, book, I was blown away. Over the past four years, Peter and David have been two of the most important influences in helping me turn around my financial life. I owe them a debt that I can never repay, only pay forward to other beginning investors. That is why I want to share my story with you as you start this new book of theirs. I pray that something about my story touches you to make you realize how totally and completely possible it is for you to succeed in real estate—if you just face your fears and get started now.

Once upon a time, I was a young consultant for the health care industry. It may sound glamorous, and it was for the first few months. But after that the travel—on the road four weeks out of each month—not only got exhausting, but it literally tore my family apart. I'm married to a loving wife, Leta, and have three amazing young sons. The part I hated most about my old life on the road was saying good-bye to them each week as I spent over 90 percent of my life on the road, aching for more time with them.

After a few years of this, I knew I had to make a change. I started researching potential businesses to start or buy. I looked into franchising; I looked into home-based businesses. Then one day, one of God's little "accidents" happened—I found this real estate book at my local bookstore. I literally couldn't put it down and read it cover to cover. That one book sparked me to change my life. The title of that book was *Making Big Money Investing in Real Estate without Tenants, Banks, or Rehab Projects*. It was the second of Peter and David's books and it's what started me investing in real estate.

The book showed me revolutionary techniques to get started investing in real estate without using my own money and without taking major financial risks. I chose to get hands-on help by joining Peter and David's Mentorship Program within a week or so of finishing the book, and I am so thankful I did. In this book you'll get the chance to get the same powerful strategies, techniques, and mentoring that I did as one of their Mentorship students. In fact, by reading this book you'll even get the chance to "attend" exactly the same Intensive Training that I did as part of the program. Three months after leaving that training I had picked up five homes!

I wish I could tell you that it was easy, that you'll read this book and make millions in the next ten days, but I can't. What I will tell you is that this book will give you the concrete tools, strategies, and specific how-tos to make it as a real estate investor. I think all of Peter and David's books are incredible, but this one is even more special. There is something about getting to watch as a handful of brand new investors get trained and mentored by Peter and David and their coaching team to make it as real estate investors. It will be like having Peter and David be your own personal real estate mentors, and that will help you create true wealth.

If I had to put in one sentence what Peter and David have done with this book for you I would say: The book simplifies the complex world of real estate investing so that anyone—and I do mean anyone—can get started today making money investing in real estate.

As I said earlier, it hasn't been easy. I can remember the first time I sat waiting for a buyer to show up to give me a certified check as a nonrefundable deposit on a property of mine he was purchasing. I was terrified that he wouldn't show up. The time I spent waiting for him seemed like a million years . . . but it wasn't. Eventually he did show up and handed me a certified check for $6,000. Within the next week I had actually sold two of my other houses on rent-to-own terms, collecting another $9,000 in up-front money and generating over $96,482 of back-end profits.

Since that start almost four years ago, I have participated in every training course that Peter and David offer, from investing in single-family houses, to buying foreclosures, to owning commercial real estate. The results speak for themselves. Using their strategies and systems, my first year investing I completed over thirty deals. Since that time, I have created several real estate investment companies that own, among other things, single-family homes, several apartment buildings, a shopping center, a storage yard, and a 108-space mobile-home park. The monthly income this generates has more than replaced my corporate salary, plus it has added well over a million dollars to my net worth. However, by far the greatest gift real estate investing has given me has been time with my wife and three sons to do my best to repair these relationships and be a family again.

I urge you to read this book through at least twice. The first time through, you'll feel *compelled* to keep reading, the ideas and story are that good. But go back a second time, highlighting and underlining as you go. You'll find powerful scripts and concrete tools for you to apply right away to get started making money investing in real estate. Their techniques and strategies will work for you, just like they did for me.

I wish you success and happiness along the way.

Rob Powell
Past Mentorship Graduate
and Current Mentorship Coach

Over the years many people have had a hand in making Mentor Financial Group and our books so successful. We literally could not have done it without their help. This book is no exception. First we would like to thank our team at MFG. Your commitment to helping our clients succeed investing in real estate has directly touched the lives of our over 100,000 clients, and indirectly touched the lives of millions more. We've grown to the point where we can't list all your names individually, but please know you're contribution is clearly written in the lives and successes of our company and students. You are so special to us.

Next we would like to thank those directly involved in this book project: Larry Jellen, Mike Hamilton, Laurie Harting, and Laura Macomber. Thank you for giving this project life and impact.

Both of us want to also thank our families for their love and support. You mean so much to us and we love you.

Finally, we want to thank our 100,000 clients for not only choosing to work with us over the years, but more importantly for proving for all time what is possible when you go after your dreams with the right knowledge, coaching, and guidance. We appreciate your faith and trust.

You *Can* Succeed Investing in Real Estate

Have you ever wondered how so many ordinary people have been able to create rags-to-riches stories by investing in real estate? Have you ever met someone or seen people in the media that created financial freedom and security with real estate and wondered to yourself if it was possible for you too?

That's exactly what this book is about: taking you by the hand and showing you step-by-step, action-by-action, strategy-by-strategy the fastest way for you to start succeeding investing in real estate.

Over the past ten years, both of us have built multimillion dollar net worths and large streams of passive cash flow investing in real estate. We have taught over 100,000 investors how to profitably, intelligently, and ethically invest in real estate. And these investors have gone on to buy and sell over a *billion* dollars of real estate. Now it's your turn.

It's no accident that you chose this book. We believe that you were guided to do it, and that you are meant to be wealthy.

Maybe you're saying that you have never invested in real estate before, or that you are starting without cash and without credit. It doesn't matter. We can show you how it's possible for *you*.

How can we be so certain? Because we've already traveled the road ourselves and, more importantly, we've guided thousands of other investors down the same road, too.

People like Jeannie, an ex-pharmacist in California who began working with us two years ago. In her first eighteen months investing, Jeannie and her husband completed eight deals and earned over $325,000 in profits.

Or take Patrick, an orthopedic surgeon in Texas. Patrick did so well with his investing that he literally walked away from his medical practice to invest in real estate full time.

Or take Frank, a barber from New Jersey. Frank netted over $25,000 on his first deal!

And these are just a handful of the thousands of stories of beginning investors who used real estate as the vehicle to their financial dreams, establishing a well-marked and proven road for you to travel on to reach your financial dreams.

This book is designed for two groups of people. The first is the person with little or no experience investing in real estate. For you this book will cut through all the confusion and uncertainty and give you the definite, tangible, real world tools you need to get started *today* making money investing. For those seasoned investors who picked up this book, you'll get powerful and specific strategies and techniques to refine your investing skills to make more money with less time and effort. Whether you're just getting started or you've been investing for years our commitment to you is that you find dozens of usable strategies, scripts, and techniques that will reap you big rewards when you apply them in your investing.

WARNING! This Book May Be Dangerous to Your Employer!

You just may discover, as thousands of our other students have, that investing in real estate full time is more profitable, more fulfilling, and more fun than your current profession. Or maybe you'll just use the ideas in this book to create cash flow in addition to a career you love. Both ways are fine, just don't say we didn't warn you!

Learn from Watching Other Investors Getting Started

The structure of the book is simple. You'll follow the journey of six beginning investors as they learn how to launch their investing careers. Each of these characters is based on a composite of many of our actual Mentorship students.

You'll meet:

Tim and Nancy Tim is a laid-off sales manager and Nancy, his wife, is a burned-out corporate technology manager. Watch as they learn to confront the single biggest obstacle to making money investing in real estate.

Mark a pilot with a large commercial airline. Mark has seen the massive changes in his industry and knows that he needs to create security and freedom for himself or he'll be vulnerable to the next round of "early retirements" and forced wage cuts.

Leon and Mary Leon is retired after 33 years in the military and Mary his wife is a homemaker. They've got a head start on their investing with three rental properties they've bought the "traditional" way, but now they're stuck. Banks won't lend more money to buy more properties, and they know they need to cultivate alternative sources of funding to structure their deals.

Vicki a single mother who is a hard-working nurse with two young children. With so many demands on her time and no one to do the investing with her, Vicki is going to have to create the time and emotional courage to launch her investing on her own.

You'll join each of these struggling new investors as they start their journey toward financial freedom and security. Along the way you'll learn the key strategies and steps you'll need to take to launch your own investing career.

The Three Parts of the Book

Part One takes place at the three-day workshop all our Mentorship students attend called the "Intensive Training." This workshop is designed to help you filter out all the noise and overload of information available on how to invest in real estate, and to give you the specific tools you need at this moment to get started making money by investing. You'll learn how to find motivated sellers, what stops most beginning investors, and exactly how to meet and negotiate with sellers in the real world. You'll also learn how to structure deals without needing cash or credit. For those of you with cash, you'll learn how to maximize your returns on your cash and to intelligently invest it.

Part Two takes place during the 90 days immediately following the Intensive Training as our six Mentorship students start to apply the lessons they learned at the training in the real world. You'll get to watch exactly how these beginning investors are able to face the typical challenges that new investors face when they are getting started, and to listen in to the specific coaching we give them to meet and overcome these challenges and opportunities. As you set out on your journey as a new investor, you'll face these same challenges and obstacles. The key difference is that you'll be able to apply the lessons from Part Two of the book to accelerate your success as a new investor. You will literally save months or perhaps even years off the average learning curve.

Part Three is where it becomes *your* turn. In this section we've laid out the specific action plan you'll need to make your real estate dreams become reality.

GO ONLINE

Register for Your FREE *Quick-Start Investor Success Program*

Simply go to **www.QuickstartInvestor.com**!
(See Appendix A.) A $1,595 value!

And to make sure that you actually get the results you are committed to, we've also created a FREE Quick-Start Investor Success Program for readers like yourself. This 30-day, comprehensive online training program will help you immediately get started converting the ideas in this book into tangible results for yourself. This program starts off with a specially developed proprietary success assessment called *The Wealth Factor Test™*. In less than ten minutes after taking this test you'll know if you have what it takes to succeed as a real estate investor. What's even more important, you'll receive individualized feedback on your specific strengths that you'll be able to leverage and your specific weaknesses that you'll have to overcome to become wealthy. Next, you'll use the *Strategic Investors Business Plan Creator™* to map out a personalized real estate business plan that will take you from where you are to where you want to go. Finally, you'll tap into hours of online training and other powerful investor tools so that you can get started making money investing in real estate right away. Normally, this program would cost a new investor $1,595, but as part of the promotion of this book, for a limited time we are letting readers enroll FREE. Appendix A has all the details about this free program including exactly how to register. Consider it our gift to you. It's our way of rewarding you for reading and applying the ideas of this book. (To register just go to **www.Quickstart Investor.com**.)

This book is the first in the three-book *Creating Cash Flow* series. This series is designed to teach you everything you need to know to not just make money investing in real estate—that part is easy—but to show you how to turn your investing business onto autopilot and create passive cash flow so that you can enjoy the freedom and lifestyle of a truly wealthy investor. This progression of residualizing your real estate income is one that most investors miss. They never learn how to take themselves out of the doing, and as a consequence they are always working hard to care for and manage their real estate portfolio. Hence, they either fall into the landlord trap of tenants and toilets or they are constantly scrambling to find their next great deal so that they can sell it for a fast profit. Or they give up altogether, saying real estate takes just too much work.

What they didn't know—in fact they weren't even aware it was possible—was that there's a better way. There is a way to invest in real estate so that, over the course of several years, you build your investing business to be an independent entity that not only can look after itself, but, better still, can produce consistent cash flow and equity build-up, month after month, year after year.

To reach this goal requires you to progress through the **Three Investor Levels** (see Chapter 7). Level One is where you learn to get started investing in real estate and prove to yourself that real estate works for you. Level Two is where you not only develop your skills as an investor but you begin to build a real estate investing business instead of just being a real estate investor. Level Three is where you transition yourself out of the day-to-day operation of your real estate business so that you can truly enjoy the freedom and security you have worked so hard to earn.

That's what the *Creating Cash Flow* series will be teaching you. Just like with anything worthwhile in life, it isn't the result of a quick fix. Instead, it's a process that begins with a growing awareness of what's possible for you, and then it moves, in fits and starts, through the landscape of trial and error until it ultimately reaches its destination. You've begun your journey by picking up this first book of the *Creating Cash Flow* series.

We're honored you've chosen us to be your mentors as you get started on this exciting and important journey to financial freedom. We are going to expect a lot from you, but we also promise to give you even more in return. You see, we don't have to write any more books, or even buy any more real estate for that matter. We've already reached Level Three success. If we wanted, we could simply retire (Peter at age 45, David at age 35) and withdraw from the world. So why do we do it? Why do we push ourselves? Because it is part of our passion in life to be the catalyst for positive change in people's lives like yourself. It is our mission to inspire and empower a generation of investors to create massive wealth, and then put that wealth to worthy purposes blessing the world. That's what keeps us writing books. That's what fuels us to train and mentor thousands of investors every year for over a decade now.

Are you ready to get started on the road to financial freedom and security? Then turn the page and join a class full of other new Mentorship students on the first morning of the three-day Intensive Training workshop. There is a whole new world of riches awaiting you, but your journey begins with this one simple step: answering the Burning Why question. Once you've completed the exercise that follows, then and only then turn the page and join us at the Intensive Training.

Burning "Why?" Exercise*

One of the most important things you can do to guarantee your success investing in real estate is for you to get clear on what is driving you to succeed. And why failure is not an option.

1) What is it that you are hoping real estate investing can and will do for you?

2) What are the top five reasons you are committed to becoming successful with your investing?

3) Who is counting on you to make your investing work?

4) What will happen to them if you quit?

5) If you have a tough moment, what one thing more than anything else is going to help you get back up and on course with your investing again?

*To activate your FREE online "Real Estate Success Journal" just go to **www.QuickstartInvestor.com**. Not only will you find the exercises from this book available for you to complete online, but you'll actually be able to create your own real estate investing business plan right there online with our proprietary "Real Estate Business Plan Creator"™ software!

PART ONE

AT THE INTENSIVE TRAINING

CHAPTER ONE

Your Dreams Meet Your Fears

Vicki walked into the Intensive Training and finished the registration packet. She was a mix of so many emotions: scared, excited, anxious, hoping. As a single mom with two young kids, she had to move heaven and earth just to free up the time to be here for the next three days, not to mention the challenge she had to overcome to pay the tuition for the program out of her nurse's salary.

But she had always dreamed of providing something better for her kids. It tore her heart out when she had to drop them off at day care each morning and go off to her 10-hour shifts at the hospital. Not for the first time she thought about the child support payments that always seemed to be late. No, if something was going to be different, she thought, it's going to be up to me to make it so. That was her driving reason for stepping out on faith and committing to become a real estate investor.

She found a place to sit next to a sweet-looking woman in her late fifties wearing a red wool sweater.

"Hi, my name's Vicki."

"Hi Vicki, I'm Mary, and this is my husband Leon," the woman said pointing to the man next to her. He looked to be in his early sixties.

"It's nice to meet you both. It's a little overwhelming this morning," Vicki said.

"I know what you mean. I'm not sure what to expect myself," Mary replied.

Just then a short woman with a name badge that read Beth came by handing out a flyer. The woman smiled at Mary and Vicki as she handed them the paper and continued handing them out.

Vicki looked down and read the sheet of paper.

Pre-Training Assignment

Introduce yourself to at least three people sitting next to you and find out a little about them. Most importantly, ask them what their "burning why" for investing in real estate is. *Why* is it that they are committed to being a success in real estate no matter what?

It's been said that with a big enough WHY any HOW becomes possible.

Vicki thought for a moment about what she read. Then she turned to Mary and said, "Well I guess we're supposed to share with each other a little bit about ourselves and why we're here." Vicki shared her burning why for investing and about how she was a single mom, and then listened as Mary shared her and Leon's story.

"Leon retired from the military about a year ago. He was in for 33 years. Me, I spent that time raising our four kids. But they're all grown up and out of the house now. I have three grandkids. We moved down to Florida when Leon got out. Over the past year we've been able to buy two rental houses. Plus we had our old house in Georgia where we used to live that we've also turned into a rental. We got our start after reading a book called *Rich Dad, Poor Dad*. That book totally changed our thinking about money."

Vicki excitedly broke in, "I read that book too! About two years ago. I've been trying to figure out how to do the things the book said to do ever since."

"Yeah, we're in the same place. That book was amazing in that it opened our minds about what it meant to be financially literate, but while it shifted our context, it didn't give us enough of what we needed to actually do the things it said to do." Vicki was nodding as she listened.

"Anyways, we started talking with real estate agents in our home town and looking at properties. I'm not sure how we did it but we were able to pick up two more rental properties using conventional financing. They both cash flow about $200 a month, but now the bank says that we have too many loans in our name and they cut us off. I've talked with a few different mortgage brokers and they all say the same thing. Because we're living on a fixed income they don't want to give us any more loans. But we don't want to sell these houses because the cash flow and value are going up each year.

"That was why when we came across Peter and David's book at our local bookstore we couldn't put it down. Here—finally—were all the details we needed to make real estate work. Both Leon and I want to be able to travel and enjoy our retirement. Plus, we've always wanted to do real estate together. That's why we joined up with the Mentorship Program four weeks ago. We've just been going through the online orientation and real estate prep course and waiting for this weekend ever since."

"I'm so glad to have met you Mary. I was so scared when I walked in here this morning, but something about talking with you and sharing my dreams, and hearing about you and Leon . . . well, it's really helped to calm me down. Thank you."

Mary smiled at Vicki and reached out for her hand. "Don't you worry Vicki. I bet you're going to be great at this."

The man to Vicki's right introduced himself. "Hi I'm Tim."

"Hello Tim, I'm Vicki."

"Hi Vicki, tell me about yourself and why you're here." Vicki again shared her background and reasons for being at the training. She noticed right away that Tim was a very animated listener.

When she was done sharing, Tim said, "I've been in the corporate world for about the last twenty years, most of it in sales. I took a buy-out package from my last company when they downsized—laid off really about 600 people. It's been tough. My wife Nancy," Tim said pointing to a professional-looking woman in her midforties, "she has been great about it all. She said that this is the chance I've always been waiting for to do something on my own. You see I've always dreamed about starting my own business. I wasn't sure what that business would be, but it would be my own deal. After being in technology sales for the past ten years where things aren't too stable, I was tired of being at the mercy of decisions that other people make. As for Nancy, she's been complaining about all the corporate politics she has to play with her company. She's one of the most competent business-women I've ever met, but in her company there is still that bias against woman executives. I think it's just worn on her over the years. So when Nancy and I were at a conference Peter and David held about a month ago and they explained about the Mentorship Program, we signed up."

Vicki turned to her last neighbor, a medium-height, attractive man in his mid-forties named Mark, and again shared her story for joining the Mentorship Program and being at the training. "Now it's your turn Mark. What's your burning why?" Vicki asked.

Mark smiled and answered, "I work for one of the larger airlines as a pilot. I've been doing it for over twenty years now. As you can imagine things have really undergone some serious changes over the past few years. I find depending on an ailing industry for my future doesn't sit well with me. Besides, my passion is music, singing in particular, and I want to use my real estate to get to a place where I can quit my job working for the airlines and lead a school choir program."

Vicki felt her spirit drawn to this gentle man and had so many questions for him. But just then she looked up on the stage and noticed that someone was standing there now. He was tall and athletic looking, and in his mid-thirties or so. As soon as he started to talk Vicki immediately recognized the voice from all the CDs she had been listening to—it was David of Peter and David!

"Welcome to the Intensive Training everyone!" David said in a warm and excited voice. "Over the next three days you are going to learn everything you need to know to go out there and succeed in your real estate investing. Let's take a moment and get real here. How many of you were scared to tell a friend or family member about your coming here this weekend? Come on, after ten years of doing this I know that many of you were scared of their reactions so you kept this weekend to yourself. Raise your hands if you did that," David asked. With David's promptings over a quarter of the audience admitted they had kept the workshop secret from friends or family.

"I want you to know that I understand. I remember when I got my start investing. I guess you could call me the first Mentorship student Peter ever had. I was terrified of telling my family and friends about my new business. I was scared that they would criticize me and tell me that I wouldn't be able to do it.

"It's not just telling them that you are starting to invest in real estate that makes you feel so vulnerable. It's telling them about your dreams. Sometimes the hardest thing to do is to share with other people that you even have dreams because so many people in our past have squashed our dreams over the years. It gets even harder when your friends and family see you start to back up your dreams with decisive action because then they often get scared that maybe you won't make it and you'll get hurt. Or they get scared that maybe you *will* make it and what would that mean for *them* in their lives.

"Here's the critical piece. When they get scared by your taking positive action by joining the Mentorship Program and being here this weekend to get to work learning how to create wealth with real estate, they don't look or sound scared. In fact, they look and sound sure that you are in danger. They tell you things like, 'You're crazy to try investing; only rich people make money investing, not people like you and me.' Or, 'That's too good to be true.' Sometimes they clothe their fears in advice like, 'I tried investing in real estate one time and it didn't work for me. In fact, I lost money in the deal. Come to think of it, every person I ever knew who tried investing in real estate lost his shirt.'

"In my family, when I dropped out of college to start my first business I heard, 'David you're crazy! You're nuts! Don't be stupid! Finish your degree.' But over the years I've learned how to translate. My family was really saying, 'We love you and just want to make sure you are safe.' How many people do you know who have given up their dreams in order to play it safe?

"If there is one thing I have learned in my years teaching people to success-fully invest in real estate it's this: there is no safety in playing it safe. In fact, play-ing it safe is often the riskiest thing of all to do.

"My real point is that it took a tremendous amount of courage and commit-ment for you to be here this weekend, and I want to acknowledge you for this. You have our personal promise that we will do all we can to help you reach your finan-cial goals. This is a commitment from the *entire* coaching team.

"As most of you know the coaches you'll be working with over the next year of your Mentorship Program are all extremely successful full-time investors. They could have stayed home with their families or gone out this weekend and bought another property or two, but instead they chose to be here with you. And in case you're wondering, it's not because of the money; Peter and I are a pretty frugal pair. They're here because they get something—we all get something—that enriches our lives by helping you get your dreams through real estate. Real estate has given us all so much in our lives we feel we have a great debt to repay by working with you, and it starts here this weekend.

"None of you had it easy getting here. All of you had challenges and obstacles to overcome to earn the right to be in this room. Many of you felt like the biggest challenge for you was time—finding a way to organize your life to get three full days away.

"I was talking with several of you this morning before we got started and I was talking to Mark," David said pointing to the pilot sitting near Vicki. "He shared something that has stayed with me. He said, 'David, I have a different take on the time challenge. I felt so busy in my life that I knew I had to be here. I literally can't afford to take an extra year or two to figure this out on my own. That's why I joined the Mentorship Program to begin with—to have your coaching team and systems help me shorten my learning curve to three to six months instead of a couple of years.' In an important way I think that really could be the theme of the Mentorship Program—to help you all succeed in your investing by getting you on the fast track.

"But for us to help you onto the fast track you're going to have to be open and coachable. The students I've seen who have been most successful made the commitment to listen to and follow the expertise of our coaching team.

"For many of you, the financial commitment was the biggest obstacle to your being here this weekend. I understand that the program isn't cheap, but who would want it to be? I've always felt that if money was the biggest thing stopping a person from doing what they knew in their gut was the right thing to do, then they had to find a way to make it happen. It's been my experience that whatever reason someone uses to give up in one area of life is the same excuse that person uses to quit in another area of life. Whether it be finding the money to fund a deal or the money to invest in your education, I have a core belief that says if you are committed there is always a way.

"All these obstacles aside, what do you think the real underlying obstacle for 90 percent of new investors really is?" David asked.

Several people in the room shouted out, "Fear!"

"That's right . . . one of the ugliest four-letter words around—FEAR. Most people never come out of hiding and start doing their investing simply because they are too scared and they don't have a support structure to help guide them through the process. One of the things I respect most about you all here is that you stepped up to the challenge of fear and did what it took to get yourself here. I promise you that our coaching team will be right there with you every step of the way, to give you support and encouragement and to give you feedback and coaching.

"Now that we've got that out of the way, I want to give you the big picture of what you'll be learning at this workshop. First, this weekend is not about stuffing you full of facts, figures, techniques, or information. Most of you are already on information overload from all the books you've read on real estate.

"This weekend is about cutting through all that blizzard of data and leaving you with the essential core you need to get started right now and do your first deal in the next 60–90 days.

"Our job isn't to share everything we know about real estate with you in three days; our job is to give you exactly the right information you need at exactly the right time, and to provide a place for you to use that information in a way that you can't procrastinate or run away, so that when this weekend is done, you have proven to yourself that you have everything it takes to make it in real estate. I understand that we've laid out an aggressive standard for us all at this training, but time after time we've watched amazing results manifest from this very same workshop.

"We're going to start off here this morning getting you all on the telephone, making real calls to actual sellers of properties. We call this 'doing dials.' Our team has put together a list of hundreds of potential sellers for you to be calling. Now, to make the calls manageable and not quite so scary, we're going to match you all into groups. You'll be doing your dials with your calling groups. Our goal from the calls is for your calling group to set up a few appointments for you to meet with sellers on the final day of the training. Think of it as your graduation exercise—one of the final ways to tie this weekend together is for you to go out on actual appointments with real sellers. But rather than have you face this potentially intimidating situation of meeting with a seller on your own, you'll be going as part of a small team so that you not only can give each other moral support, but you can also give each other instant feedback when you're done.

"Now I'd like to introduce you to three of the coaches you'll be working with here this weekend. Many of you have already gotten to know them through the coaching calls or through questions you've posted on the discussion board. They are part of our very special coaching team. As I introduce them to you here today remember one thing: At one point in time they were *all* sitting exactly where you are sitting today—as beginning Mentorship students.

"All of our coaches got their start investing as Mentorship students. In fact we have always groomed our coaching team from the ranks of our successful Mentorship students. And there is a reason for this. Not only does it let you know that they can relate to what you're going through and coach you on your deals because they have done it themselves, but equally importantly is that Peter and I can trust them to teach you the way we taught them so that you get the very best we have to offer. I *know* they learned it the right way because Peter and I spent years teaching it to them.

"As an aside, I'm hoping that some of you have an interest a few years from now in being a part-time coach for the program. I'll just consider this a seed planted, and who knows what will grow out of that. It's been Peter's and my commitment from the very beginning to only grow the program at the pace that our coaching team of graduate investors could support it in an excellent fashion. We're not willing to hire some call center and hand them a manual and turn them loose as coaches. I know that some companies in the industry do it that way, but we just wouldn't feel good about that. Instead we decided ten years ago that all of our coaches would come from the ranks of our best Mentorship students and we'd structure it in such a way that our coaches were full time investors first, and coaches second. We just felt that was the right way of doing things."

David turned to the side of the stage. "John why don't you start us off? Would you share your story?"

A young man in his late twenties stepped forward. He had a quiet, gentle way about him. "When I first met Peter and David, it was at a small introductory workshop my wife Jackie and I went to. After getting a chance to watch David share how he did his investing I knew right there that I wanted to learn from him and Peter. At the time I was working doing construction—installing carpeting in commercial buildings. I had done that for four years ever since I got out of high school. I knew I wanted something better for my wife and my kids but I didn't know how. I was really intimidated with the whole idea of investing on my own. I was just a kid at 22 years old when I got started with my investing seven years ago. Honestly, I didn't think anyone would take me seriously. It took me four months to get my first deal, and I have to admit I felt like quitting several times. There were some weeks where I was working 12 to 14 hour days for a few weeks straight on a job that had a tight deadline, and I was so tired by the time I got home, I didn't want to do my dials and go meet with sellers. But I kept plugging away and came real close to three or four deals before at month four I found my first deal. It was a small, three-bedroom, two-bath house in the south part of San Diego. The owner was a retired man who was moving to Arizona and needed to sell quickly.

"You might wonder why he didn't just sell it himself. I used to wonder why a seller would ever sell to me in the beginning when I got started with my investing. The house he had was very outdated inside. He had the original carpeting and ugly, lime green wallpaper he got when he originally bought the house, close to thirty years earlier. He was convinced he didn't need to update that stuff, and, well, I guess he did since no retail buyers wanted the house. So I went in there and agreed to buy the property from him under the condition that the seller participated in the financing, letting me pick up the property with less than $1,000 down. I remember feeling so proud of myself, after all that time to finally have signed up my first deal. I ended up reselling the property for a $25,000 profit 12 months later. Looking back it was actually the smallest of the deals that I've done on houses I've bought, but for me it just may be the most important because it was my first. It gave me the confidence that I could make real estate work."

"John, I know that you now focus more on apartment buildings and such, but how many houses do you buy in an average year?" David asked.

"Over the past nine months I've picked up six more houses ranging in value from $220,000 to over half a million dollars, which, for my area in California, is the middle of the market. Actually, some of the houses are the lower part of the middle of the market. I don't need to do a large volume of houses in my area because the average profit per deal is over $100,000 per house. During that time I picked up two small apartment buildings too, and opened up a company doing loans for sellers in financial distress," John answered.

"Thanks John for sharing your story. Do you have any final thoughts that you want to share with people today?"

"Yeah, look, if I could make real estate work for me, you can do it a whole lot easier. It is so worth it. Every day I get to work out of my house and set my own schedule. I start my day by taking my two little girls to school and I get to be there in the afternoon to pick them up. I used to have to get up and go to work before they even got up, and sometimes I even had to work through the night when I was laying carpet because that was when the office building was closed. Now I get to make spending time with my family my highest priority. My wife quit her job two years ago and joined me in the business. She does the organizing part and runs the office. Real estate has opened up a whole new world of choices for me."

The room applauded as John stepped down from the stage just as a smiling, warm woman stepped up onto the stage.

"Hi everyone my name is Cheryl and many of you already know me because of Peter and David's second book, *Making Big Money Investing In Real Estate*. I'm the 'stay-at-home mom' who did 14 properties in her first 24 months of investing.

"I have a different background from what John did when he got started. I was a wife and a mom with three kids, and my husband was one of the ministers at a local church up in Oregon. I knew nothing about real estate when I got started investing. I've got to tell you when I got started I lucked out and got my first deal pretty quickly, before I even came to the Intensive training you are all attending. I met a couple who had been transferred to a new city due to a job they had and they were about two hours away from the house they left behind. When I went to talk with the seller I was so scared. I pulled up to the driveway and I had my two teenage sons with me in the car. I hate to admit it but yes, it was a minivan." Everyone in the room laughed, and several of the moms in the room jabbed their husbands in the arm.

"Those of you with teenagers will appreciate this, I left them in the car and they were just playing around with the radio. I went inside to meet with the couple about their house. The guy looked at me and said, 'So you're an investor.' And I must admit, I did say yes out loud in response, but inside I had this very loud voice that was saying, 'No you're not, you're just a housewife.'

"God must have put us in each other's paths because they needed someone to help out with the property and I needed someone to help me put together my first deal. And that's exactly what the seller did. He took all my clumsy explanations and put them into clear language and explained to his wife why this was such a good deal for them. I just smiled and said, 'Yeah, what he just said.' I walked out after I finished signing up that deal and got into my car. My sons were all eager to hear what happened and I just said with closed lips, 'Sit down and put your seat belts on. Let's get out of here first.' I was so scared that the guy would come chasing me down the drive saying wait he'd made a mistake. I pulled the van over a few blocks away and we started high fiving each other. It was so exciting. I ended up selling that house three years later for a $34,000 profit. Now my business is different from John's. I tend to focus on foreclosures that need to be fixed up and then can be resold at a profit. My target is to do three or four of these deals at a time, plus two other nonrehab deals each month. I actually like overseeing my crews who fix up the homes. My family calls me the 'Home Depot Queen.'"

David stepped forward and said, "I have to share with them all Cheryl that I'll never forget when you came to that first training about two months after you joined the Mentorship Program. You walked into the seminar room the first morning and came up to me holding a small photo album in your left hand. I thought to myself how great it would be to see your family and photos of your life in Oregon. Each page in the album was the same house from a thousand different angles! In case you're wondering," David said, turning to the room, "They were all photos of that first house Cheryl had bought!"

"Oh yeah, I was so thrilled that I had actually done it," Cheryl said.

"Thanks Cheryl so much for sharing your story. Scott, let's get you to share your story, and then later we'll get some of the other coaches to share their stories."

"Hi everybody I'm Scott," a trim man with very short hair in his mid-forties stepped up on the stage. "I guess you could say I was another of the high-tech casualties of the dot-com bust. I was on my fourth startup when I finally said enough was enough. I had started to research franchises and business opportunities after the third company I worked for went under and had decided that real estate was what I was going to do. I was in a book store and found a copy of Peter and David's second book, the one that shared the story of Cheryl the stay-at-home mom!

"Anyway, I called up and talked with one of the program consultants and decided to take the plunge and do it. I have to confess, I didn't tell my wife Cindy that I had spent the money on the program or that I had been laid off. You see I was laid off right before we had planned to take a week vacation together and I didn't want to ruin the vacation. So on the last night of the vacation I turned to Cindy and said, "Honey you know how I was planning on going back to work tomorrow morning? Well the good thing is now I don't have to. The company laid off a whole bunch of people and I was one of them. And oh, I joined that Mentorship Program I told you about a few weeks ago.

"I'll say this for the Mentorship Program, it sure took Cindy's focus away from my layoff!"

"All kidding aside, real estate has without question been the best thing that ever happened for me and my family from a financial perspective. There were times when things got really tough in the early months. I'll be honest with you, early on I even took a paper route to generate some cash flow to see us through a lean start. But sticking with it made all the difference in the world. Listening to the coaches made all the difference in the world. Listening to Peter and David made all the difference in the world.

"My first year investing I picked up 18 properties and never looked back. Now I'm still doing some single family houses in Denver, but like John I've started to make the move into more multi-unit buildings and commercial real estate.

"The other coaches tease me and say that if an ex-computer geek like me can make investing work, then any normal human being can sure do it. And they're right. I am a computer geek! And if I can make investing work for me, you can too. A few years ago I was right there sitting next to you. Just trust the coaches and do what they say. And make sure you don't quit in the early months when times can get tough." The room applauded Scott as he stepped down from the stage.

"Right now I would like to bring up the co-founder of Mentor Financial Group, and my mentor in real estate and best friend. Please help me welcome Peter Conti to the stage!" The students in the room stood and cheered as Peter ran up through the center aisle, high fiving students on his way to the stage.

Peter stepped up onto the stage and said, "Good morning everyone. Did you know that sometimes there is something much scarier than failure? It's called success! How many of you have ever been as scared or more scared of succeeding at something than you have been at failing?"

"I understand," Peter continued. "There was a time in my life that I craved the comfort of failure because with each new success I was pushed further and further away from what I knew and away from how I saw myself. It was a real key to my success to learn to expand my self-image to encompass myself as successful and wealthy.

"Remember that when I got started with my investing I was an auto mechanic scraping by at $9 per hour. Every time I told someone I was a real estate investor in the beginning, I'd hear this voice in my head say, 'No you're not! You're an auto mechanic!'

"Many of you are having the same conversation. Relax, that's perfectly normal. Just give yourself two things. First give yourself some time to get used to seeing yourself as an investor. Second, consistently take the small, little actions that investors do. This will build the foundation you need to help you expand your self image.

"This morning as we build that investing foundation together, we need to start off dispelling one of the most pervasive and costly myths that people buy into when they get started investing. All your life people have told you, 'Real estate is all about Location, Location, Location.' But they were wrong.

"Real estate is not about location first. In fact real estate is not about location second. Location only comes into play third in line."

With this, Peter clicked an image onto the screen.

Winning Deal Formula

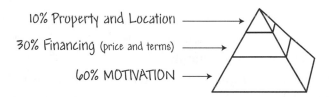

10% Property and Location ⟶

30% Financing (price and terms) ⟶

60% MOTIVATION ⟶

"This is the Winning Deal Formula. It lays out the relative importance of the three key ingredients of any winning real estate deal.

"As you can see, the foundation that great real estate deals are built on is *not* location, but motivation. The first concern when you are looking at a deal is why is the seller selling the property. This is the **first key ingredient of a great deal—finding a seller who has a strong motivation to sell**. It's the seller's compelling reason to sell, with a perceived time crunch within which to do it, more than any other factor, that helps you get a great real estate deal. Remember this and say it to yourself over and over again—the foundation of all winning real estate deals is the seller's motivation to sell. It's almost as if what the seller initially tells you is his reason for selling is the tip of an iceberg. The real reason is the hidden 90 percent that is below the surface. But it's this hidden 90 percent that is the key ingredient for a winning deal.

"**The second level of a winning deal is the financing—the price and terms.** To make money on a deal you need to either purchase the property for cash at a steep cash discount, or you need to get great terms of financing. If you buy for cash at a discount, your low cash price guarantees you a profit. If you buy on flexible terms where you are making the payments to the seller over time, then the financing lets you hold onto the property over time with positive cash flow and make even more money on the back end when you eventually resell or refinance the property to tap into your accumulated equity. For any deal to be a winner, the numbers must make sense.

"Later we'll spend a concentrated session going into the specifics of structuring deals, both cash deals and flexible terms deals. For the moment, all that's important for you to understand is that the financing details of a deal are the second most important ingredient of a winning deal.

"Now, **third in line in importance are the location and physical structure and condition of the property.** Over the long haul, the location does matter. The right location will appreciate in value significantly more than the wrong location. But, and this is a *big* but, the only way you can safely know you'll be able to hold onto the property over the long haul is for the first two ingredients—motivation and financing—to be in plentiful supply.

"Any property at the right price and terms is a great deal. But the only way you'll ever find a seller who is willing to give you the best price and terms is if that seller is a motivated seller. That's why the right motivation is so important. As I've just mentioned, the right price and terms—the financing—guarantees you a profit. The location and the physical condition of the property are important for two reasons. First, they matter because they significantly impact what the right price and terms for a property are. After all, if the property needs a huge amount of fix up then that needs to be factored into the price. Or if the property is in an area with zero appreciation, then the numbers you agree on for the price and terms need to be such that you build a profit into the deal from day one. Second, the location and physical structure impact your exit strategy on the property. If the house you are buying is in a great area, you may be much more likely to hold onto the property over the long term. This may mean that you structure the deal in such a way that you trade the seller a higher price in exchange for you getting great long-term financing to enable you to profitably hold onto the property over time. Or if the building is in a war zone, perhaps you want to negotiate a very low cash price with the plan to resell the property right away to another investor who specializes in low-income housing in that neighborhood.

"So I hope you see that location matters, but only after the first two levels of the Winning Deal Formula are factored in. This is a major shift from how most people think about investing in real estate. **This shift from real estate being about location, location, location, to real estate being about motivation first, price and terms second, and then, as a distant third, location greatly impacts how you structure your real estate business.**

"If real estate is about location, then smart investors would spend their days looking for the best areas to invest in. In fact, they would spend more time looking for the perfect location than they would in talking to and connecting with sellers. In the end, location investors would find some great areas to invest in, but, they would have no real skill in finding the best deals in those locations. They would be at great risk from not being able to buy smart enough to be able to profitably hold the properties over time so that they could get the benefit of the location. Remember, the real benefit of location typically comes over the long term through above-average appreciation of the property.

"Instead imagine investors who followed the Winning Deal Formula approach in their investing. They would know that the single most important ingredient to a great deal is finding a highly motivated seller. So they would spend the majority of their time in the beginning looking for ways to find motivated sellers. Next they would get very good at emotionally connecting with sellers so that they would be willing and comfortable sharing their real reasons for selling with them. Then they would get skilled at structuring deals so that the financing—price and terms—made sense. Then, finally, they would factor in the location and the physical condition and structure of the property to make sure the numbers really did guarantee a conservative profit.

"So what does this all mean to you?

"It means that you need to spend less time thinking about the perfect location in which to do your investing and more time in mastering the art of finding and negotiating with motivated sellers. You need to spend less time falling in love with the physical property and more time learning to structure deals with price and terms that guarantee you a profit.

"And that's the way this weekend will be structured. In a moment we'll get you on the telephones calling up sellers of for-sale and for-rent property, looking for motivated sellers. This is the first and most important step in putting together a profitable real estate deal—finding a motivated seller. Later today, we'll get into the details about other ways to find motivated sellers, but we've been talking long enough. Now it's time to get you all *doing!*

"I'll demonstrate a few calls first, but within the next 10 minutes all of you will be on the phone making dials. We'll go through more of the technique part after you get into action. Too many wannabe investors spend their entire lives avoiding actually *doing* anything that will make them money in real estate. They avoid making calls to talk with owners of properties for one reason—fear. We're going to knock that crutch out right from the start."

At this point Peter turned to a speaker phone on the front table and started to punch in numbers. As the phone dialed Peter flashed the overhead on.

Property For Sale Script

Hi, this is _____.

PASS   NO PASS

☐   ☐

I was calling about your home for sale...
Sounds like I caught you in the middle of something...

Is your property still available?

☐   ☐

Can you tell me about the property? (i.e., Where is it located? How many bedrooms? How many bathrooms?)

This sounds like a wonderful house, why would you ever consider selling it?

Check Any One to Qualify:

V ☐   **Vacant** – "Is anyone living in the home now?"

R ☐   **Rental** – "Has this been a rental property or have you lived in it?"

O ☐   **Other Home** – "Where are you moving to?" "Have you picked out your home yet?" "When do you close on it?"

"You all have this script in front of you in your manual. I need you to be very quiet here as we get started."

Just then the phone was answered. "Hello?"

"Hi, my name is Peter. I was calling about your property for sale. Is it still available?"

"Yes it is."

"Great. Sounds like I caught you in the middle of something?"

"No, what can I do for you?"

"Can you tell me about the property?"

"It's a four-bedroom, three-bath brick home. It's got a two-car garage—"

Peter interrupted here, "Great! It sounds like a wonderful property." Peter's voice slowed and got softer, with his tone getting lower, "why in the world would you ever consider selling it?"

"We're moving to Florida."

"Wow, that's exciting," Peter said, and then scrunched up his face and sounded a bit confused. "Why would you move to Florida?"

"My husband's company gave him a promotion. Actually we've been wanting to move there for a while. My family is all living there now, except for my one brother that is. We're moving down in six weeks."

"Oh, that makes sense. I'm sure it will be nice to be near your family. Have you already found your next place down in Florida?"

"Actually we have a house under contract right now. It's a new construction house and we're buying it from the builder there."

"That's wonderful. I'm sure the house is great. A question for you." Peter's face got scrunched up again. "If this house that you're selling doesn't close before you move, are you still going to close on the other house or will you need to pass on that other home until this one closes?"

"We'll still go ahead and buy that other house. We're hoping to have this one sold before we move, but if it doesn't we're still going anyway."

"That makes sense. May I ask you a question?" Peter asked with his face scrunched up. "Because I'm an investor who focuses on nice homes in nice areas can you tell me, is your home a nice home in a nice area?"

"It is. In fact our house is just four blocks away from the Greenbrier Park."

"Well it sounds like a house I'd like to see. Do you have your calendar handy so we can find a time to meet to have you show me through the inside of the property? Actually, looking at my calendar I'm pretty much tied up all weekend at this workshop I'm at. About the only time I'm free to meet is on Monday at around 1:45 or 2 P.M. Boy there's probably no way you can free yourself up to show me through the inside of the property then, huh?"

"You couldn't meet any other time, like after five?"

"No, I'm sorry but I'm totally booked up with appointments. I'd hate to never have the chance to see this house . . ."

"Well I guess I could move some things around and make that time work."

Over the next two minutes Peter got the street address of the house and directions for the appointment. As he worked with the seller, the students sat in rapt attention, in awe over how easy he made it seem.

"Now that was pretty lucky to get someone like that on the first call. Usually it takes five or six dials before I even find someone who's home! But over time, the averages say that for every twenty dials you make you'll generate on average one or two decent leads to meet with a seller.

"We call the script you'll use a Quick Check Script because in two minutes or less you want to be able to determine if you have a motivated seller or not. **The single greatest time waster in real estate is trying to do a deal with a NON-motivated seller.** If the seller isn't motivated to sell, why should they sell it at below-market prices or with attractive terms of financing? The answer is they shouldn't. As an investor, if you can't get either a discounted cash price or attractive terms of financing then you shouldn't be buying the property. We'll talk about this in detail after lunch. The key thing for you to get now is that your first step in *any* profitable real estate deal is to find a motivated seller.

"A motivated seller combines two things." With this Peter turned to the board and wrote:

Motivated **S**eller

o   i
t   t   Motivation = Compelling Reason + Time Crunch
i   u
v   a   Situation = Lots of equity or doesn't <u>need</u> cash out immediately
a   t
t   i
i   o
o   n
n

"A motivated seller has both the 'M'otivation and the 'S'ituation that will allow you to structure a win-win deal. *Motivation* is a compelling reason to sell and a definite time crunch within which to do it. *Situation* means that the seller either has enough equity that they could discount the price for a cash sale, or they don't absolutely need to have all their cash and could participate in the financing so that you could structure a terms deal.

"What one question did I ask here that really got to the heart of whether the seller has a compelling reason to sell?"

Tim raised his hand and answered, "Sounds like a wonderful property, why would you ever consider selling it?"

"Yes, that's the question. Did you notice her answer? She said she was moving in six weeks. How many of you think that is a good answer from your perspective?

"On a scale of 1 to 10 with 10 being extremely motivated to sell, what did you all think her level of motivation was?" Peter paused for a moment as the audience shouted out various answers. "Personally I'd say she is around a six or seven on the motivation scale. They want to sell, but they aren't quite strongly motivated yet.

"The second part of the script qualified for the seller's situation. This is where the 'VROM' part of the For Sale Quick Check Script comes into play. To be qualified for situation you need to be able to check off one of these four boxes. You don't need all of them. If the seller passes any one of them, the seller has enough of a situation to merit taking the next step with them.

"First, the seller can qualify if the property is vacant. This qualifies the seller for situation because it means that the seller doesn't need all the equity from this property to buy their next house to live in. How do we know this?" Peter asked.

"Because the house is vacant and the seller's got to be living somewhere else already," Nancy answered.

"Exactly right. And if the seller doesn't need their equity out from the sale then they have a situation that would work for what type of deal?"

Vicki pulled together her courage and answered hesitatingly, "A terms deal?"

"Yes. Now the second and third ways the seller can pass the qualification for situation is by either having the property be a 'R'ental property or by having an 'O'ther place to live. Both these qualifiers for situation are similar to the 'V'acant qualifier. If the property is a rental, then obviously they seller doesn't absolutely need the equity out to buy his next house to live in; similarly, if the seller already has an 'O'ther place to live, he doesn't need the equity either.

"Now, there will be times when you find a seller who passes this Quick Check qualification but still isn't willing to do a deal with you—many times. But the key to making this work is to use the script to quickly sort through potential sellers to only spend time with sellers who are *more likely* to be ready to do a deal with you. You use the Quick Check Script to get a fast first look to see if you should then slow down and spend more time with a particular seller.

"The final way the seller can pass the For Sale Quick Check Script qualification for situation is by having 'M'assive equity. A seller with a lot of equity presents you the most options when you're thinking about structuring a win-win deal. Now, rarely on a first phone call to a property advertised for sale will you be asking directly if the seller has a ton of equity. But sometimes you get that information from the seller in subtle things they tell you. If you're lucky and the seller lets this information come out, then know that the seller is qualified for situation."

Leon raised his hand and asked, "Peter, don't all sellers want their equity in cash at the closing?"

"That's a great question. Just as most of you would want, if you gave the seller the choice between all cash at closing or accepting a terms deal, most sellers would *initially* choose to get all cash. But if the seller is motivated to sell fast, and you are there with a solution that, although not perfect for them, satisfies their real needs, then many of them will be open to a terms deal. If the seller is going to participate in the financing, the key is that the seller can't need all their equity out of the property at closing. Although many sellers may *want* to get all cash at closing, many sellers don't absolutely *need* it.

"Now if you just come out and ask a seller, 'Hey do you need all your cash at the closing?' 99.9 percent of sellers will say yes. Of course they will. The key is to ask this question, but to be more subtle about it. The single biggest reason a seller would need all cash at closing is to use that cash to put down on the purchase of their next home to live in. That's why on the call I just did I asked the seller if she already had another house picked out and purchased. If the seller already owns a house to move into, they don't really need all their cash at the closing. In this case the seller had another property under contract, but I needed to find out if that contract was contingent on this house selling. The softer way of getting that same information is to ask them, 'If this house doesn't close, are you still going to close on the other house?'

"Now, I asked one more question there at the end of the script. I asked them if their house was a nice home in a nice area. This is one question that is critical to use word for word. You are going to use this question not to elicit information, but to convey information to the seller.

"The question is designed to subtly share with the seller that you are an investor. The magic word in that question is the word 'because.' It's the word *because* that shifts the focus away from the fact that you are an investor and instead puts the focus on the seller having to justify that they have a nice home in a nice area. It took us over two years to get this question just right. Once upon a time our students used to hear the objection from the seller that they didn't want to work with an investor. Now if you hear an objection over and over again, what should you do?"

"Learn to overcome it," Tim answered quickly.

"Learn to overcome it? That's a good way of handling it. But an even better way is not just to handle the objection when it comes up, but to pre-empt the question in the first place. Keep it from coming up at all. That's what this question will do for you—it will pre-empt the objection to working with an investor in over 95 percent of the situations that you use it in. Remember, the whole reason you came to David and me was because you said you wanted to learn all the powerful insider secrets to investing that would otherwise take you years to learn on your own. You said you wanted us to just teach you the right way, the first time. Well, this is one of those seemingly simple little techniques that took years to uncover and get just right.

"Now let's try some for rent dials. Turn to the For Rent Quick Check Script in your manuals."

Property For Rent Script

Hi, this is _____.

I was calling about your property for rent...
Sounds like I caught you in the middle of something...

PASS **NO PASS**
☐ ☐

Is your property still available?

Check All
Three to Qualify:

Can you tell me about the rental property?

T ☐

That's great, I am looking for a long-term lease of at least two years. Is that okay?

O ☐

Assuming all of my rental payments came in on time, would you consider selling at the end of two years?

N ☐

_____ (seller's name), because I am an investor that just focuses on nice homes in nice areas can you tell me... is this a nice home in a nice area?

Peter picked up the phone and started to dial again. The number went to an answering machine. The next three dials went to answering machines before Peter reached his first For Rent property owner.

"Hello?"

"Hi, this is Peter. I was calling about your property for rent. Sounds like I caught you in the middle of something?"

"No, I was just getting things organized for the day. How can I help you?"

"Can you tell me about the rental property?"

"Sure, it's a three-bedroom, two-bath single story house over near Palmer High School. Are you familiar with that area?"

"I am—can you tell me, I'm looking for a long-term lease of at least two years. Are you open to that?"

"Yes Peter, I would love a long-term tenant in the property."

"Great. And assuming all my rental payments came in to you on time would you consider selling it to me at the end of that time?" Peter was scrunching up his face as he said this to produce the right tonality.

"Actually Peter that's not something I'd be open to. I plan on keeping it as a rental for the long term. It's been a pretty easy property to look after and it's part of my retirement plan."

"Well I sure do understand. Actually I am looking for a place I can buy down the road. Thank you so much for your time and I wish you luck with the property."

"Thanks."

As Peter hung up he turned to the class. "Did it make sense why I got off the phone there so fast at the end of the call? She wasn't motivated to sell. With a for rent property the owner needs to pass *all* three qualifying questions: First, they must be open to a long-term lease of at least two years. This question will screen out the landlords that are in very tight control of their rental properties, who by the way, typically aren't open to selling you the property cheap or with flexible terms. Next, you qualify for the owner being willing to sell you the property at some point in the future. Finally, you make sure the owner understands that you are an investor using that powerful, 'Because I'm an investor' question we've already discussed."

"The bottom line with qualifying for rent properties is that you are looking for either a tired landlord or an accidental landlord. A tired landlord is someone who owns a rental property but is sick of looking after it. They would love to sell and often are very open to taking payments over time with some type of terms deal, which we will cover in detail later today.

"An accidental landlord is an owner who got stuck with a house that wouldn't sell and they needed to rent it out because they didn't want to leave it empty. These tend to be the very best source of for rent property leads.

"Now I know you probably have a ton of questions, and we'll get to each and every one of them. However, before we do it's time to get you doing some dials of your own. It's been my experience that far too many new investors procrastinate about the scary parts of investing like calling owners on the phone and meeting with sellers in person. That is why you will *all* be doing both things here this weekend. The coaches and I will demo how to do every step, then we'll give you chances to practice them for yourself. Finally, we'll send you out to the real world here this weekend to try them out for yourself.

"We haven't finished talking about your calls, and we haven't shared with you about how to structure deals. We'll get to all that later, it's time for you to get into action.

"Right now we are going to break you into calling teams to make dials to for-sale and for-rent properties. The goal is to get you all to realize how doable dials are and how effective they can be. If you find a seller who passes the Quick Check Script, what I want you to do is to actually set up an appointment for you to go and meet them at their property. Don't worry about what the heck you are going to say or do on that appointment, we've got three days to teach you everything you need to know to go on that appointment. The key for you right now is to get out of thinking mode and into *doing* mode."

With that, Peter divided them all into calling groups and gave them their final instructions. Off the Mentorship students went in their groups of five or six people finding a quiet spot to pull out their cell phones and get dialing.

CHAPTER TWO

Doing Dials—Two Minutes to Find Motivated Sellers

Vicki was a bit relieved to find herself in a group of five other people who sat at the same table she did and whom she had already started to get to know: Leon, Mary, Tim, Nancy, and Mark.

Once they found a good spot in one of the back corners of the room to do their calls from, they settled down and organized themselves.

"Who wants to be the first to start us off?" Mark asked, looking around at the circle of faces.

"I will," Tim said, stepping up to the challenge. He pulled out his cell phone, took the list of for-sale-by-owner (FSBO) and for rent numbers that their group had received, and punched in the first number on the list.

As he waited for his call to be answered, Tim was surprised by just how nervous he was. He was so used to making calls for his work as a sales manager that he just assumed that it would be easy for him to make these calls. But everyone was looking at him and he felt his mouth go dry. Finally, after what seemed like forever, the owner finally picked up the phone on the other end.

"Hello, this is Tim. I was calling about your house for rent . . . Sounds like I caught you in the middle of something? . . . Can you tell me about the property? . . . How big is it? . . . How many bedrooms? . . . What's the square footage? . . ."

Just then Tim noticed Scott, one of the coaches, come up to their group. *Great*, he thought, *as if I wasn't nervous enough!* Scott softly introduced himself to the other members of the group and sat down to listen in to Tim's phone call.

"And how much were you asking for rent? . . . Can you tell me about the appliances? . . ." Tim noticed Scott listening intently and jotting down something onto his notepad.

Finally, after what seemed like a long time, Tim got off the call and explained to his calling group that the owner wasn't interested in selling anytime soon and so didn't pass the Quick Check Script.

Scott smiled and shared some feedback with Tim. "Great job on the phone. You'll find that all of us coaches give our feedback as 'liked bests' and 'next times.' 'Liked bests' are the things that we observed that we think went well and want to positively reinforce. 'Next times' are things that we see that could be improved, but rather than being critical and saying that so and so did this wrong, we focus on the useful feedback that can immediately be applied the next time you are faced with that situation. My biggest liked best is that you made the dial. Believe me when I tell you that I understand how huge that is. I remember how three years ago I was at my first intensive training, not as a coach but as a Mentorship Student just like you, and how tough doing these dials were for me. My other liked best is that your pace on the phone is great. You're soft and down to earth on the phone, exactly where you need to be." Tim was relieved to be hearing this positive feedback.

"My one 'next time' for you," Scott continued, "is to cut down on the questions you are asking the seller about his property and get to the real qualifying questions faster. I know it seems strange, but you really don't need to know much of anything about the property itself until you know that you have a motivated seller. So all those questions about size of the home, what the backyard is like, just eat up your valuable time. It may seem like only a few extra minutes, but when you multiply the extra five minutes you took before you found out that the owner wasn't even open to selling by 10 other owners you talk with later in the session, you have almost a full hour of your time spent with owners who aren't motivated to sell. So the key is to get to the qualifying questions fast. You can even go to the extreme of saying something like, 'Can you tell me about the property?' Seller answers, 'Well it's a two-bedroom one-bath townhouse.' You break in with, 'Great, I'm looking for a long-term lease of two years or so, is that ok?' Do you scc how I just broke in with an exclamation like, 'Great!' or 'Wow!'? And in that pause I get on with my next qualifying questions."

"But won't the seller think that's weird that here you are saying, 'Great,' when you haven't really even found out much about the house?" Nancy asked.

"What a great question," Scott replied. "Remember, the seller has talked with so many people that they won't even remember who they've told what about the house. Plus, they just assume you've got the full details they put in their classified ad."

Tim, who was feeling a bit more relaxed by this time, thanked Scott for his coaching, and Scott went off to the next calling group.

It was now Vicki's turn, and she started to dial but stopped, looked around at her group, and said, "I am so scared to do this with all you watching me. It's really intimidating for me, especially with how comfortable you sounded on the phone Tim."

"Comfortable? I was scared out of my mind. I'm on the phone all day at work but it's never been as tough for me as that last call!"

"Really? But you looked so calm about it," Vicki replied.

"Trust me I was sweating big time on the inside."

Mary smiled warmly at Vicki and put a reassuring hand on her knee. "Just give it a go Vicki. Who knows, maybe you'll get lucky and just get an answering machine!" The whole team laughed, and Vicki realized she wasn't doing it by herself but that she had a whole group of people who were going through the same thing with her and would support her. She didn't feel so alone anymore.

With that, Vicki began to dial the next number on her calling sheet.

Doing Your First Dial Session

1) ❏ List 20 numbers of for sale by owner (FSBO) or for rent properties from your local paper. Only list those numbers that look like they will put you in direct contact with the property owner and not the agent or property manager for the owner.

2) ❏ Pick up the phone and get started with your dials. Let go of any concern for the outcome. Your real goal is to make your investing real by DOING.*

*For more online training on how to use the telephone to make your dials and find motivated sellers go to **www.QuickstartInvestor.com**.

(continued)

Doing Your First Dial Session *(continued)*

3) ❏ Once you've called all 20 numbers, give yourself a fun and uplifting reward. Maybe dinner out with your spouse. Or rent a funny movie to watch this evening. Or get an ice cream cone. Something simple but specific for having the courage to do what so many wannabe investors never will do—calling up owners of properties.

PHONE NUMBER:	FOR SALE	FOR RENT
1. _____	❏	❏
2. _____	❏	❏
3. _____	❏	❏
4. _____	❏	❏
5. _____	❏	❏
6. _____	❏	❏
7. _____	❏	❏
8. _____	❏	❏
9. _____	❏	❏
10. _____	❏	❏
11. _____	❏	❏
12. _____	❏	❏
13. _____	❏	❏
14. _____	❏	❏
15. _____	❏	❏
16. _____	❏	❏
17. _____	❏	❏
18. _____	❏	❏
19. _____	❏	❏
20. _____	❏	❏

REWARD:

CHAPTER THREE

Lessons on Screening Sellers Over the Phone

When the students all got back into the room, Scott greeted them from the stage. "So did you have fun?" Scott asked with a smile.

Many of the heads were nodding up and down, others were plainly not nodding at all.

"By a show of hands," Scott asked, "How many survived making your dials?" Just about everyone in the room started to laugh. "Good thing, because if any of you here didn't survive the telephone you would have really been intimidated by the alligator wrestling we're going to do as part of the negotiating section." Scott's humor really brightened the mood of the group.

"A little more seriously though now," Scott asked, "How many of you, by the end, actually felt pretty comfortable making calls to sellers and landlords?" Scott looked around the room and counted about half the students with their hands up.

"Good. Let's talk about what just happened there. As an aside, how many of you felt like everyone else in your group was more comfortable and better at these calls than you were?"

Scott looked around the room at the sea of raised hands and nodding heads and said, "Isn't it funny how we can just assume that everyone else is confident and comfortable. You want to know the best part of all? Most everyone in your group thought you were better at the calls and more confident then they were! If they only knew how scared you really were right?" People in the room were smiling. They recognized the message Scott was sharing.

Three Key Coaching Points to Increase Your Effectiveness on the Phone

"Let me give you some coaching as a group. As I went around and listened in to various groups making dials I noticed **three key coaching points** I want to make that will increase your effectiveness on the phone by 200–300 percent.

"The **first point** is that when you're on the phone, what's your real goal?"

"To find a motivated seller," Nancy shouted from her seat.

"That's a great answer Nancy, but it wasn't the one I was looking for. In my opinion the best answer is **you are looking to sort out all the nonqualified sellers as fast as possible to leave you with a pool of potential motivated sellers you can spend more time with later.** Now this may seem like a small difference, but the results it will get you are huge. Let me lay out the average numbers that I've seen from students over the past couple of years about converting dials into leads."

Scott turned on the overhead projector and wrote:

Typical Dial Session of 20 Dials

You get: 10 answering machines or wrong numbers
10 people answer:
2 to 3 answer and pass Quickcheck
1 to 2 answer, pass Quickcheck, and are motivated

"For every 20 dials you make, you'll probably talk with an average of 10 sellers or landlords about their properties. The rest of your calls will get you answering machines, wrong numbers, real estate agents, or property managers. Of these 10 you talk with, on average, only two or three will pass the Quick Check Script's qualification," Scott continued.

"As I observed most of you making dials, I watched you spend, on average, four or five minutes on each call before you ended up asking the really important qualifying questions. On the for sale script, that is the question, 'This sounds like a wonderful property, why in the world would you consider selling it?' And on the for rent script it's the question, 'Assuming all my rental payments came to you on time, would you consider selling me the property at the end of two years?' Here's the thing . . . since only one out of three of the people you talk with are going to pass the qualification, any extra time spent with the other two sellers is wasted time. I recommend that you get to the real qualifying questions faster, and if the seller passes them, then and only then spend more time with them. I think you should be able to get to the real qualifying questions in about 60–90 seconds, but I'll give you two minutes max. The way the Quick Check Scripts were designed was to cut out all the wasted verbiage and focus on the core qualifying questions, in a specific order, that consistently produce the result of sorting out the poor leads and leaving behind the much higher quality lead pool.

"Now before we talk about where most of you got pulled astray in your dials so that you took two to three times longer per call with nonqualified sellers than you will as you get better at your dials, let's first get clear on what this means to you. Your number one resource as an investor isn't your money, it's your time. If you can cut down your time with each nonmotivated call by 200–300 percent, as we're talking about here, you'll be able to find more deals faster with less effort.

"It all goes back to what you are trying to accomplish on the phone. If you are looking to find a motivated seller, you'll need to slow down so you don't miss a clue that says that Seller A is a motivated seller. If, however, you are looking to quickly sort out the *nonmotivated* sellers as fast as possible, you can quickly dive through your calls and anytime a seller doesn't give you the answer you need, you thank them for their time and get on with your next call.

"So if we all want to save time and get better on the phone, where do we get pulled off the centerline of the script? In my experience coaching several thousand Mentorship students who were just getting started, what leads investors off the script isn't the seller . . . it's the property. They get too involved with trying to ask the seller all about the property—its square footage, its features, its location—before they have ever really finished qualifying the seller for motivation and situation! Now here's the real test to see where you fall in this minichallenge. Look down at the information sheets you have from your dials. How many of you see more notes on the physical features of the property and its location than you do about the seller's motivation or the financial details on the property?"

Scott waited a moment for the students to look through their information sheets. Amazingly over three quarters of the students saw that they actually had *three times* the information on the property than on the seller's motivation or the seller's situation.

"Yeah, but Scott, isn't it important to know about the property?" Leon raised his hand and asked.

"That's a great question. Remember when Peter taught you about the Winning Deal Formula he shared how the seller's motivation and the financing equaled 90 percent of a good deal, with the property and its location amounting to only 10 percent? Well, just know that the purpose of your dials is to sort through and find potentially motivated sellers by eliminating those that don't qualify. The property itself *does not matter*, until you have satisfied yourself that the seller passes muster.

"Personally I recommend that you ignore the details about the property itself until you're satisfied you have a seller who passes the Quick Check Script. You can always go back and ask the seller to repeat all that information about the property later. All you would have to say to the seller is something like, 'You know what, Mr. Seller, I have talked with so many sellers about their properties this week that I think I must be mixing up your house with all the rest. Would you be willing to just remind me about what your property is like?' Not only will the seller be fine telling you all the descriptive details again, but it doesn't hurt that you've subtly let the seller know that he's got plenty of competition from other sellers you've been talking to."

"Thanks Scott," Leon said. "That makes sense now. I only wish I would have known that before I almost wore my hand out trying to get down all the details about the houses!"

Scott smiled and then continued, "So how do you avoid the mistake of focusing on the property? Train yourself to break in on the seller after they have shared one or two features about the property in a firm but kind way, and then quickly move to the next qualifying question on the script. Don't worry, they've talked with so many people on the phone that they won't remember they didn't tell you all about the property already! In all my years of making dials I've never had a seller say, 'how do you know it sounds like a beautiful house, all I told you was it was a three-bedroom, two-bath home with central air.'" Again the class started to laugh.

"The **second coaching point** I want to make is that many of you spoke very quickly on the phone. In fact you spoke so fast that the seller thought you were some smooth talking real estate agent. What I recommend you do is **slow yourself**

down. The way you do that is by leaning back in your chair, even putting your feet up if you need to, and relaxing when you make the calls. Remember you want to sound just like a potential buyer or renter for the first ten to twenty seconds; the way you do that is by being a little scared, hesitant, and unsure of yourself.

"The **third coaching point** I have for you is to **trust the numbers**. Some of you made your twenty dials and got all answering machines. Others of you made 10 dials and got four appointments. The important thing to remember is that over time the numbers even out. If you only make twenty dials, who knows if you'll find any good leads. But if you make a hundred dials each week, which will take you on average two to three hours over the week, you'll find 5 to 10 decent leads, of which two or three will be very strong leads.

"If you dropped me cold into a city and said, 'Scott find a deal in forty-eight hours or we'll publicly dunk you in melted marshmallows,' the first place I'd head would be to the local library to get copies of all the old newspapers and create my list of aged ads of for-rent and for-sale properties. After creating a long calling sheet I'd find a phone and start doing my dials. How many of you think that I or Peter or David or one of the other coaches could find a deal from these two or three hundred dials we do?

"I appreciate your confidence," Scott said, noting that just about everyone in the room had answered affirmatively. "The fact is, this is essentially what Peter and David did when they did that famous press challenge. How many of you have heard how they issued a challenge to the press to take three beginning students to any city in the United States and in three days they'd help each of these students buy or control a minimum of $250,000 of real estate? Well they didn't just meet that goal, they doubled it! And completing close to a thousand dials during the three days sure helped out a lot.

"That's how they came up with the idea to get you all on the phone so early in the training. They saw how effective it was to teach students to talk with sellers and landlords that they have been doing it at every Intensive Training for the past 10 years. The scripts have been refined over time, but the essence has remained the same. We have one of our team members put together the list of for sale and for rent properties that you've been calling from out of the local Sunday paper. My guess is, if this training works like most of our trainings do, that one or two groups will actually sign up deals on the third day. Now, I won't say *which* of the groups will be the ones to sign up a deal."

2 Most Common Objections When You're Making Your Dials

In the course of your investing in real estate, sellers will bring up specific objections to working with you. Whenever an objection comes up repeatedly, you have two choices about how to handle it. The first choice is to create a scripted response to overcome the objection. Although this works, it is not the best solution because it still hurts your chances to close a deal whenever an objection comes up, even if you smoothly handle it. Much better than overcoming an objection is to change your system and scripting to pre-empt the objection so that you keep it from ever entering the picture to begin with.

Below are the two most common objections you're likely to encounter while making calls to for sale and for rent property owners along with our response to both handle the objection and to pre-empt the objection.

Objection #1: The "Real Estate Agent" Objection

Since many owners who sell their properties for sale by owner (FSBO) are flooded with calls from agents soliciting a listing to sell the property, many FSBO sellers immediately screen any calls they get to sort out any agents fast. If your technique on the phone is off, you could get thrown out with the agents. The biggest reason a seller would think you are a real estate agent is that you sound too professional over the phone, hence you must be a real estate agent. Remember that FSBO sellers are biased against agents who call them because they have probably been inundated with calls from agents looking to get a listing. Sellers sort all incoming calls quickly to determine if you are a buyer or "everyone else." You need to make sure they categorize you as a buyer so that they will spend the time with you with an open mind long enough for you to determine if they are a motivated seller or not.

Handling the Objection

Seller: "Are you a real estate agent?"
Investor: "No [scrunching up your face], do I have to be?"*

Invariably the seller will rush right back in saying something like, *"Oh no you don't have to be! It's just that I've gotten so many calls from real estate agents trying to list my house and I'm sick of it."*

Pre-empting the Objection

To pre-empt the real estate agent objection, you need to understand that the seller is really saying that you sound so cool, calm, and collected that you couldn't be a normal buyer; therefore, you must be a real estate agent looking to

*If you ARE a real estate agent, check **www.QuickstartInvestor.com** for a modified script you can use to handle this objection.

(continued)

> ## 2 Most Common Objections When Making Your Dials *(continued)*
>
> get a listing. The solution is to learn to be less polished on the phone. Hem and haw and be nervous on the call just like most buyers who call on FSBO ads. This is essential in the first 30 seconds of the phone call when the seller is making their initial impression of you.
>
> ### Objection #2: The "You're an Investor?!" Objection
>
> Depending on how you bring it up, some sellers may object to working with an investor. They may want to only sell or rent to a person who will live in the property. Usually the cause of this objection is that the investor waits too long to share with the seller that they are an investor and the seller feels misled.
>
> Imagine you are calling a for rent property owner. The owner starts to qualify you about how many people you have in your family and what you do for a living and all the other typical landlord questions. If this happens to you it means you've lost control of the conversation. The owner is now using their "script" and you are forced to follow their lead. Remember, the owner has the goal of finding a renter, which is very different from your goal of finding a motivated landlord who is willing to sell you his rental property at a good price or terms. The person who is asking the questions is the person who is leading the conversation and ultimately the one who gets to choose the intended outcome of the call. Let's turn to dealing with this objection.
>
> ### Handling the Objection
>
> *Seller:* "So how many people are going to be moving into the house with you?"
>
> *Investor:* (assuming you do in fact have kids) "I have two kids. But actually I already have a nice home for myself and my family and I'm really looking for another investment property. Boy, you probably wouldn't even consider selling this property to an investor, even if we found a real healthy offer, huh?" [Negative phrasing]
>
> ### Pre-Empting This Objection
>
> The best long-term solution for pre-empting this objection is to make sure you get to the, *"Because I'm an investor who focuses in homes in nice areas, can you tell me is your home a nice home in a nice area?"* question faster. Also, it probably means you are waiting too long between the questions on your script. Any pregnant pauses are going to cause the seller to fill the void with questions of their own, and these questions are almost guaranteed to take you off your script and put you on their script. Ideally you will get to the *"Because I'm an investor..."* question within two minutes or less.

"Learning to do dials is critical to your success as an investor because it quickly helps you blow through any fears you might have of rolling up your sleeves and talking with property owners about buying their properties.

"Now, if you were to ask me, 'Scott, do you still do dials?' I'd share with you that now I don't. When I got started, for the first five or six months I made a ton of dials. But then as my other marketing efforts to find motivated sellers started to pay dividends I found that I really didn't need to do dials any more. The same thing will happen to you. Dials are so important at the start of your investing because they teach you exactly how to talk with property owners over the phone—which is a core skill of any successful investor. Dials are also so important because they are a quick way to stir up leads of sellers for you to meet with. The downside to dials is that they are quite time consuming to sort and sift through all those leads. Many of us coaches actually hire other people to do our dials for us or use other marketing sources to find deals—but *all* of us in the beginning relied heavily on dials to get our start in real estate."

"We're going to take a quick break. When we come back we're going to talk about the five fastest ways for you to find your first or next deal."

CHAPTER FOUR

The Five Fastest Ways to Find Your First (or Next) Deal

When everyone had come back into the room from their break Stephen and David were at the front ready to teach the next section.

"Welcome back everyone. In a moment Stephen and I are going to talk about the five fastest ways to find your first few deals. But first," David said, turning to Stephen, "perhaps you could share with the class your story of how you got started investing?"

Stephen looked out at all the expectant faces, took a deep breath, and shared his story. "My wife and I lived and breathed corporate America for years. We were making a healthy living with me in technology sales and my wife Susan as a CPA. But when we started our family, our plan was always to build something so that I would not be gone all the time away from home and that Susan could be a full-time mom. These were things that were always important to us. We had done a few conventional purchases of rental properties before we met Peter and David but were really struggling with how to take the business to the next level.

"Then Susan and I went to one of the two-day Real Estate Success Conferences that they hold throughout the country, and after learning how they approached their real estate and seeing the systems they had developed to make the investing work faster and simpler, we signed up for the Mentorship Program. It was only three years ago that I was sitting exactly where you are sitting now. I have to say that for me it wasn't the well-organized systems or the way they made real estate investing so simple that drew me to work with Peter and David. What made me want to work with them and sign up for their Mentorship Program was the integrity with which the whole company conducted their business. It was so obvious that it was about so much more than just making money. Don't get me wrong, money is the reason we all invest, but it just can't be the only reason. And it can't be the standard by which you judge your success.

Stephen continued. "We did it backwards. I quit my job and jumped full time into the investing from the start. It was tough for the first year or so. Although we quickly generated a lot of equity with our investing, cash flow was tight. Now things are much easier. I get to spend time with my two little girls now and Susan gets to be a mom again. And to think of how fast this has all happened, it literally bowls me over sometimes. All I can say is that it was so worth it."

David interrupted and asked, "I know when you first got started with your investing, you started off with just buying houses from motivated sellers and then worked up to some larger deals. Tell us about that transition for you."

"Our first year we picked up 18 properties. We made so many mistakes along the way, but I wouldn't trade any of them away. We made a lot of money from those deals, but it was the learning experiences that I see as our real payoff from the first 12 months. Then, in the second year, we started to develop more relationships with people in our area. We started doing a lot more foreclosures, negotiating with banks to sell us properties cheaply or to short sale houses."

"In case you didn't know," David shared with the class, "A short sale is when a lender agrees to take less than what's owed on a loan on a house that is in foreclosure. It's a way to buy a house that doesn't have enough equity to make it a good cash purchase, and build a conservative profit in by getting the bank to take less money in exchange for a fast solution.* Stephen and Susan have gotten to be experts at working with lenders. In fact, I know that you are now buying blocks of homes from lenders at steep discounts, but I'll let you tell everyone about that.

"As we got better with our investing we started buying blocks of properties from

---

*To download a FREE e-book, *Shortsales—Making Money On Deals With Little or No Equity—Six Simple Steps to Make a Short Sale Happen*, go to **www.QuickstartInvestor.com**.

investors who wanted out of the rental business or from lenders like those David mentioned. We also made the shift to do a lot more investing in apartment buildings, establishing many relationships with private investors to fund deals for us. But it all started with this same training that you are all going through right here."

"Thanks Stephen for sharing your story," David said. "Now it's time to talk over other ways to find motivated sellers. How many of you recognize that there are literally over a hundred ways to find motivated sellers?" David asked.

"In fact, you all have the complete list of those hundred ways along with scripts, step-by-step instructions, and detailed, sample marketing materials. It's included in your Mentorship Starter System™ that you all got as part of your participation in the Mentorship Program. But one of the themes of this training is to cut out all the excess information and leave you with only the most critical and essential ideas you need right now to get started in your investing over the next 90 days. Therefore, as valuable as that comprehensive material is, Stephen and I want to give you a prioritized summary of the five fastest ways for you, or any beginning investor for that matter, to find your first few deals."

Stephen added, "The goal we have here is to not just to give you information, but to give you the bottom line, processed information that will shorten your learning curve. Down the road you'll each find what works best in the markets that you invest in, but **for the first 90 days we are going to choreograph your marketing campaigns and activities so that you start off with the greatest chance of success**.

"The first technique is the one we've had you doing this morning—your dials," Stephen said. "Dials to for sale and for rent ads are not long-term marketing solutions for your investing business because they are too time intensive, but they are one of the best ways for you to get started. Not only do they get you skilled at talking with sellers and landlords on the phone, but it's a fast way to get you enough of a volume of appointments with sellers that you can learn to negotiate with sellers in person."

"Do you realize," David said to the class, "That the average investor calls up less than 100 property owners each year. You'll be making 100 calls to for sale owners and for rent owners each *week* for the next 90 days. You'll literally get 10 years of experience talking with property owners in the next 90 days. Think for a moment what that will mean for your pace of success. The best part is that when you use the scripts and techniques you've already learned, it will only take you about three hours per week to make those dials."

4-Step Dials Action Plan

1) ☐ Gather up an aged list of the local Sunday paper as follows:
- Past three months of for sale properties
- Past three weeks of for rent properties

(If you haven't been stockpiling your local Sunday paper, go to your local library and photocopy these sections or try your local paper's website to see if they have an online archive of classified advertising that you can access.)

2) ☐ Quickly take the numbers from the paper for qualifying properties and transfer them to a separate calling list.

3) ☐ Break out the list into chunks of twenty numbers to call. This is the perfect amount for a "Dial Session."

4) ☐ Schedule in and complete a minimum of three dial sessions per week with your goal to generate an average of one appointment with a seller per dial session.

"David, I have to say that when I got started I hated doing dials because it intimidated me. Looking back, I see dials were crucial to helping me develop my investing skills and succeeding so fast." Stephen continued, "But the other reason why I am so thankful I did dials is that when I started spending money to get sellers to call me about selling me their homes, I was already fluent on the phone so I didn't waste money with my advertising budget."

"That's a great point, Stephen. If someone is spending $500 on classified ads to generate five calls from potential sellers, that means that every call is worth $100. If you aren't able to comfortably talk with and process these leads on the phones, that's money that's wasted," David replied.

"The second way to find motivated sellers," Stephen said, holding up a bright yellow sign, "Are these tacky, ugly, obnoxious, but oh so profitable I BUY HOUSES signs that many of you have seen before."

I Buy Houses!
1-888-555-1212 ext. 34
24-hour recorded message

"I know what you're thinking. You're thinking, 'Stephen, you want me to put up those ugly signs? What if someone sees me putting them up, what will they be thinking?' The answer is, *yes*, I do want you to seriously consider using these signs, and as for what people think, who cares! My best sense from all the students I've talked with on the coaching calls is that, for every 100 signs you put up, you should be able to get one deal. How's that for a little motivation to get those signs out there!"

4-Step "I BUY HOUSES" Signs Action Plan

1) ☐ Order your I BUY HOUSES sign.*

2) ☐ Get wooden stakes and staple gun, along with zip ties, from your local building supply store in preparation for your sign-posting adventure.

3) ☐ When your signs arrive, put out 50 signs per week. (Make sure you have investigated local ordinances controlling use of signs in your area and that you are comfortable using this deal-finding technique.)

4) ☐ If you like the results of the first few batches of signs you put out, get more systematic about it. Divide your sign area into eight chunks and put up signs in a different chunk each week, rotating through the eight areas, so that every eight weeks you are back at the same area again.

*As part of the Quick-Start Real Estate Success Program, we have prenegotiated inexpensive rates for signs for you. For details and to order conveniently online, just log onto **www.QuickstartInvestor.com**.

David added, "Dollar for dollar, signs are the most effective advertising you can use. Of course, there are probably local ordinances that control signs in your area, so make sure you check with your local city government, attorney, CPA, or psychic before you make your own adult, autonomous decision whether to use signs. We are not telling you to do this; we're only saying that we and other investors have used them to great effect. How's that for a disclaimer?" David and the audience laughed, understanding his point though.

"The third way to find deals fast," David continued, "Is to place an "I BUY HOUSES" classified ad in your local paper. Here are a few sample ads you could use," David said, flashing another slide up on the screen.

Classified Ads to Get Motivated Sellers to Call You

I'll Buy Your House Fast!
Stop Foreclosure / Double Payments!
No commissions or fees.
Call 800-555-1212 ext 23 Rec. Msg.

I'll Buy or Lease Your House In 7 Days or Less!
No Equity / No Problem!
Call 877-555-1212 ext. 33
24-Hr. Rec. Msg.

Soccer Mom Looking to Buy Investment Property
Any Area or Condition
Call 877-555-1212 ext. 15
24-Hr. Rec. Msg.

"The key to your classified advertising," Stephen said, "Is to make sure you put it in the right paper and in the best section of that paper. Because it's expensive, it's critical to maximize your responses. We recommend you use your local Pennysaver or ThriftyNickel type of paper. These are the free want-ad circulars that usually are sent out via direct mail to people's homes. The reason why these tend to work so well is that more people tend to read the classified ads in them."

"That's a good point Stephen. I've often coached students to ask themselves which paper would they advertise a moving sale in and to use that publication as the first place to test out their I BUY HOUSES ad," David said.

"You can also try out your local daily paper, but just know that in many areas that is a very expensive option, although it can be more than worth it in many cities," Stephen said.

ACTION STEP

4-Step Classified Advertising Action Plan

1) ☐ Create a list of potential papers in which to run your classified ad.

Potential Choices:
– Daily paper (large circulation)
– Small, local daily or weekly paper
– Local Penny Saver / Thrifty Nickel type of paper
– Specialty papers (e.g., military papers if you live near a base, etc.)

2) ☐ Order and set up your voice mail box for use in your classified ad.*

3) ☐ Choose one paper to run your 60-day test in. Call this paper and place your ad for 60 days. If it is a weekly paper, run your ad once a week. If it is a daily paper, run your ad in the Saturday and Sunday papers. Your ad should run in the "Real Estate Wanted" section or in the "Real Estate For Sale" section.

4) ☐ Track your responses over the 60-day test. Evaluate the results and tweak your ad copy itself or the placement or the paper you run it in if needed. Re-evaluate your ad results every 60 days.

*For information on the toll-free voice mail system our Mentorship students use, go to **www.QuickstartInvestor.com**.

"After you choose the publication you are going to place your ad in, you need to determine what section of the classifieds to run the ad," David continued. "If you are running your ad in a small weekly paper, or in the Pennysaver or ThriftyNickel type of paper, I recommend that you run the ad in the Real Estate For Sale section, ideally as close to the front of that section as possible."

"David, if I may also add, when you place your ad it is a great time to practice your rapport building and negotiating skills to not only get premium placement, but also to get the best rate for running your ad. You're planning on running your ad for months or even years, as long as it generates solid leads, and you might very well get a discount for putting the ad onto an automatic running schedule where they just charge your credit card every week or month for your ad."

"That's a great point Stephen. When I lived in San Diego, which is where I got my start investing in real estate, for years I had my ad running with the local Pennysaver, with the publication just charging my credit card every two weeks," David responded. "Now what do you do if the paper doesn't have a generic 'For Sale' section, or if they won't run your ad in that section? Typically, in the larger daily papers, they will try to push you to run your ad in one of two places. One of these two places is a total waste of your money. It's called the 'Real Estate Services' section, and you need to insist that your ad *not* be placed there. Instead, if the paper won't let you run in the generic 'For Sale' section, ask to have your ad placed in the 'Real Estate Wanted' section of the classifieds. The only downside to running an ad here is that, in many larger city dailies, this section can be crowded with other investors. Don't let this stop you, but also do your best to get your ad to the top of the list!"

BRIGHT IDEA

3 Biggest Marketing Mistakes Most Beginning Investors Make

Mistake #1: Waiting to Start Marketing Until They "Know It All"

So many beginning investors think they need to understand all the details and intricacies involved with structuring deals and managing properties before they actually pull the trigger on their marketing activities. This is a hugely expensive mistake because the final cost is that these timid investors never actually get started with their investing. They end up living in the land of "Someday Maybe." *Someday* they'll get started. *Maybe* after they take one more class or read one more book.

Information and training can save you years of trial and error effort—if you are able to get yourself into action while you are learning.

So learn all you can, but start your marketing activities, especially your dials, right away. Get yourself on appointments with potential sellers and practice your negotiating. You can refine and hone your marketing strategies and tactics as you go. In the end this will be the fastest path to get you what you want— profitable real estate deals.

(continued)

---

3 Biggest Marketing Mistakes Most Beginning Investors Make *(continued)*

Mistake #2: Getting "Bored" with Winning Marketing Campaigns

When you find a marketing campaign that consistently produces quality leads, don't change it—use it consistently. In fact, when you are fortunate enough to find a winning campaign, look for ways to expand and supersize the campaign to get it to produce even more results.

Although it is important to regularly test out new marketing ideas, it's a mistake to let new marketing ideas totally replace proven winners. Instead put 5–10 percent of your marketing budget of time, talent, and money into testing new campaigns to see if they can outperform your proven control campaigns. Sometimes you can find a new winner to replace your old winner with, and other times you can have the best of both worlds by both keeping the old campaign and adding in the new winner to your existing marketing mix.

Mistake #3: Not Systematically Tracking Your Marketing

Never spend money on your marketing unless you can track every marketing campaign you run. You need to track what goes into the campaign in terms of time and money, and what you get out of the campaign in terms of leads, lead quality, and the ultimate results. This way you will be able to refine and optimize all your marketing activities.

"The fourth technique for you to find your first few deals fast is direct mail," Stephen said. "There are two specific mailing campaigns that we recommend you test out first. In your Mentorship Starter System™ you have over a dozen campaigns to use, along with sample mailing pieces, but here are the two that are simplest for you to use at the start of your investing. The first is to test out a postcard campaign to out-of-town owners. These are people who own property in a specific zip code, but the mailing address on file for the property tax statements go to a zip code that is at least an hour away."

"The reason we want you to start with postcards instead of the letter campaigns you have in your Mentorship Starter System™ is that postcards are less expensive to mail, take less time to stamp and label, and typically generate a good response. Later, as you develop your investing business, you'll test our letter sequences to your out-of-town-owner lists and choose the method or methods that prove to be the most effective. But in the beginning of your investing, it's more important for you to get started using a marketing technique than it is to master it. Mastery comes with time. The key we'll be stressing here all weekend is for you to get into action and start using these ideas right away."

"The second mailing campaign for you to try out over the next few months," Stephen shared, "Is a postcard campaign to landlords in a specific area." Stephen put a sample of a mailing piece for an out-of-town-owner campaign onto the screen for everyone to look at.

I'll Buy Your Property — *FAST!!*

Here's your quick and easy solution:
✓ *FAST* Closing!
✓ *INSTANT* Debt Relief!
✓ *FREEDOM* From Maintenance Hassles!
✓ *GUARANTEED* Written Offer Within 72 Hours!
✓ *HARD-TO-SELL HOME?* No Problem!
✓ *NO* Commissions Or Fees!

1-888-555-1212 ext. 34
24-hour, **FREE** recorded message

"Again, this list is created by comparing the mailing address of the property tax statement to the physical address of the property. For this campaign, simply choose an area of town you like and mail to the owners of any likely rental property in that area."

7-Step Direct Mail Action Plan

1) ❏ Get a list of out-of-town owners or landlords for you to use in your mailing campaign.*

2) ❏ Pick one mailing campaign, either out-of-town owners or landlord list, to begin with, and get enough postcards to mail to that list printed up. Although you will be mailing to the list a total of three times over the next 120 days, you might want to only print enough postcards for one time through the list, just in case you discover a problem with the mailing you can inexpensively make whatever corrections need to be made. Also, purchase postage and mailing labels to mail the postcards out.

*To download the FREE special report, *Three Ways To Get Out Of Town Owner and Landlord Mailing Lists*, go to online to **www.QuickstartInvestor.com**.

(continued)

7-Step Direct Mail Action Plan *(continued)*

3) ❑ Do a "mail merge" on your computer to print your mailing labels and get your postcards ready to mail.

4) ❑ Send out mailing one.

5) ❑ 60 days later, repeat with same postcard to this list for mailing two.

6) ❑ 60 days after mailing two, send out mailing three.

7) ❑ 30 days after the third mailing, evaluate the results of your mailing campaign and tweak your efforts to increase your response rate.

"One key point to notice," David added, "is that for all your mailing campaigns, and for your ads and signs for that matter, the phone number you list is going to send the seller to a voice mail box. We'll go into more detail about tracking your marketing efforts and the use of a toll-free phone number in your marketing pieces, but for now just make a note that you won't be giving out your home or cell phone number in these ads."

Using a Toll-free Voice Mail System in All Your Marketing

BRIGHT IDEA

It's essential to be able to track the specific, demonstrable results of all your marketing campaigns. We recommend that you use a toll-free voice mail system to point all your marketing efforts toward because of the ability these systems have to help you track your marketing results.

The system we have our Mentorship students on lets you track up to 90 marketing campaigns concurrently by the use of specific extensions placed in the advertising. The system has all the outgoing messages pre-scripted and ready to use right from day one to save our students time and effort.*

*For more information on how to sign up for the powerful toll-free investor voice mail system that our Mentorship students use, go to **www.QuickstartInvestor.com**.

(continued)

Using a Toll-free Voice Mail System in All Your Marketing *(continued)*

We've found that for every 10 messages from sellers your marketing generates, on average 5–20 sellers have called into your voice mail in response to your marketing, but they hung up before they left you a message. Most investors think that particular marketing effort only produced 10 calls, but in reality it produced 15–30 calls.

The power in a toll free voice mail system, like the one our Mentorship students use, is that it lets you generate a "Call Detail Report" that lists out all the phone numbers of every caller—including the ones who didn't leave a message. With these extra non-message captured numbers, you can actually **increase your marketing results by 50–300 percent!**

You now are able to call back the people who hung up without leaving you a message.

"Hi, this is _____. It sounds like I caught you in the middle of something?

"This is a little awkward for me, but I have a message here that someone from this number gave me a call earlier today. I'm not even sure what it was about. I think it might have been about a house they had to sell or something like that. But boy, you probably don't even have a house you want to sell, huh?" [Negative phrasing]

If they answer yes, flow right into the For Sale Quick Check Script.

Stephen continued, "The fifth and final way to find motivated sellers is probably the scariest one for new investors, I know it was for me. It's to cultivate a referral network to bring deals to you."

"Me too Stephen!" David laughed. "I was afraid if I asked my friends or family to help refer me a lead they'd say, 'David, you're broke, just out of college, no job, how could you ever invest in real estate?' How many of you in the room today find the idea of asking friends and family to pass you leads a scary one?" Over three-quarters of the students in the room raised their hands. "That's totally normal. However, it's a very expensive fear to hold onto. Every person in this room either knows someone or knows someone who knows someone who could give them a winning lead on a deal in the next 30 days if only you do one specific thing. I bet you want to know what that one specific thing you need to do to find a deal in 30 days or less don't you? Here's the secret answer." Turning to the board David wrote:

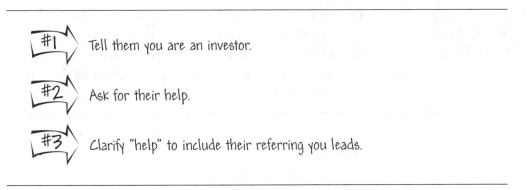

#1   Tell them you are an investor.

#2   Ask for their help.

#3   Clarify "help" to include their referring you leads.

"It really is that simple," David said. "The only reason you wouldn't get a lead from friends and family is because you haven't asked them. There are deals in your network of contacts if you are willing to just bring up the subject and let people know what you are looking for."

Script for Asking People You Know to Refer You Leads

Hi _____. How have you been?

[catch up and build rapport]

I'm not sure if I ever told you since the last time we talked but I am just getting started investing in real estate. To be honest, it's pretty tough. I'm trying to do all the right things. I'm taking the classes, reading the books, meeting with sellers, but it's still a bit intimidating for me right now. Can I ask you for a favor?

Your opinion and support mean a lot to me. If you ever see me struggling or having a rough day with my investing, would you be willing to give me some encouragement?

Thanks _____. As I said, your support means a lot to me. And if you ever come across someone who needs to sell their property fast, or maybe someone who had a really bad renter experience, or who has an empty house, if you could let me know that would really help me out. Is that something you'd be willing to do?

Oh, that's great _____. Look I know that you'd do it because you're my friend, but I'd still like you to know that if any of the leads you pass my way ever turn out to be a deal, I'd like to send you and _____ (their spouse or significant other) out to dinner. You pick any restaurant in the city and I'll pick up the tab. Fair enough? And I'll even pop for the sitter.

"Let me share with you the fastest way I know to get over the fear of letting people know you're an investor," Stephen said. "Go out and buy two I BUY HOUSES magnetic car signs for your car and put them on. I guarantee you'll get over the 'I can't tell the world I'm an investor' fear fast. The root of this fear is that our self-image isn't big enough at the start of our investing for us to see ourselves as an investor. The reason the car signs work so well is that you are making a public statement that you are an investor, and it forces you to shift your way of thinking about yourself. Every time you pull up next to another car on the road and the driver of that car looks over at you, you'll be thinking of that person seeing you as an investor. Our self-image is directly impacted by how other people see us."

"Stephen's right about the signs," David added. "When I first put my signs on my car, it scared me to death. It took about six weeks for me to start to get comfortable with the signs. After three or four months I actually started to enjoy how it felt to have the signs up on my car."

"What I've noticed has worked for me was that, as I grew more comfortable talking about my investing to people, the more referral business Susan and I generated. Now we find a healthy percentage of our deals through the relationships we've established with lenders and real estate professionals in our community." Stephen paused for a moment and added, "But just remember that it takes a little time to develop these contacts in your area. Just keep talking with people and following up with the leads they give you and doing your best to source and serve them, and you'll find that in six to twelve months you have established a stable core of referral relationships."

"Stephen's exactly right with how over time, you'll be able to build your referral relationships. With your investing, you'll find that you'll have to spend one of two things to find deals in the beginning. Either you'll invest the time to hustle up leads for yourself—as you do with your dials or by inviting a real estate agent out to lunch to network—or you'll invest your money in marketing to generate leads for yourself. This could mean placing your ads and mailing out postcards. You will need to spend one or the other to find deals. Personally, I will always spend money to save time. I feel time is infinitely more valuable than money. Whatever you decide, just be sure to consistently follow through in your marketing activities. Your investing business will thrive or die based on your ability to consistently find great deals."

4-Step Referral Action Plan

1) ❏ Go to your local office supply store (or online) and get 500 business cards printed for your real estate investing business.

2) ❏ Ask two people each day, five days a week, to refer leads to you.

3) ❏ Twice a month, add a real estate professional to your referral network by calling up a different real estate agent, broker, mortgage broker, etc. and introducing yourself.

4) ❏ Every time someone sends you a referral:
   – Let them know the result of that lead.
   – Reward them no matter the outcome. If you sign up a deal that you close on, pay them a referral fee. If the lead doesn't work out, send them a small thank you gift such as a note or $5–$10 gift card.

David took a step back and looked at the room. "I think it's time for us to take a quick break. When you come back we'll start talking about how to structure win-win real estate deals."

BRIGHT IDEA

5 Fastest Ways to Find Your First (or Next) Deal

1) Doing your dials.

Outbound calls you make to for sale and for rent classified ads in your local paper are the first and most important early techniques for finding motivated sellers. Not only is this the fastest way to get lots of practice talking with owners of properties, but it is also one of the cheapest ways! Bottom-line is that it works.

Your Next Step: With your appointment book in front of you, turn to the Dial Action Plan on page 42 and schedule in the specific days and time you will make your first three dial sessions.

Reward: For completing three sessions of 20 dials each REGARDLESS of outcome of those dials, select one Reward Card from your Monthly Reward Card Deck.*

*To learn more about your "Monthly Reward Card Deck" and to download a FREE deck of rewards for your investing, go to **www.QuickstartInvestor.com**.

(continued)

5 Fastest Ways to Find Your First (or Next) Deal *(continued)*

2) Place your "I Buy Houses" classified ad.

Getting sellers to call you who are more strongly motivated is one of the keys to a sustainable, successful real estate investing business. This is a way to leverage the money for the ad to save you time finding deals. With one phone call you can have your ad out there 24/7 finding you deals. Test your ad over 60 days. If you choose to test out a daily newspaper, start out with running the ad on Saturday and Sunday only. If after 60 days you aren't generating any qualified leads, test out a new paper to run your ad or a new ad to put in the paper.

Your Next Step: Review the Classified Ad Action Plan on page 45 and take steps 1–4 within the next 7 days.

Reward: For successfully following through and completing your 60-day test select three Reward Cards from your Monthly Reward Card Deck.

3) Put out your "I Buy Houses" signs.

Dollar for dollar, your tacky, ugly "I Buy Houses" signs are one of the best lead sources. Make sure you check with local ordinances in your area regulating their use, but seriously consider adding them to your marketing mix. We suggest a minimum of 50 signs per week on a regular and consistent basis.

Next Step: Register for your Quickstart Investor Success Program and click on the Order Signs button. There you'll see links for the best deals we've prenegotiated on signs for your business. Order your first set of signs.

Reward: For putting out 50 signs within 10 days of receiving them from the sign company select two Reward Cards from your Monthly Reward Card Deck.

4) Test out direct mail.

Once you've had some practice talking with sellers on the phone and have met with at least 10 sellers, test out two simple direct mail campaigns to generate leads. The first is a postcard campaign to out-of-town owners. The second is a postcard campaign to landlords. (See "Direct Mail Action Plan" on page 48 for details.)

Next Step: With your calendar in front of you, schedule in the exact day and time you will take steps 1–3 of the Direct Mail Action Plan. (We suggest you set this appointment 60–90 days after you launch your investing business.)

Reward: For testing out one direct mail campaign of at least 1,000 postcards with accurate tracking of the results select three Reward Cards from your Monthly Reward Card Deck.

(continued)

5 Fastest Ways to Find Your First (or Next) Deal *(continued)*

5) Spread the word that you have started to invest in real estate and generate referral business.
The easiest form of leverage to find great deals is to get other people who you know or meet to help you find deals. Your referral network is a critical piece of your long-term investment success. Both of us have found our best deals from referrals. The only question is whether you will have the courage and discipline to consistently build your referral network.

Next Step: Get 500 business cards for your real estate investing business from your local office supply store or online. (Step 1 of the Referral Action Plan listed on page 53.)

Reward: For stepping up in the next 30 days and asking five people for referrals to potential motivated sellers, select two Reward Cards from your Monthly Reward Card Deck.

CHAPTER FIVE

Structuring Deals Without Cash or Credit

"**I**t's time to focus on what just may be the single most important session of the weekend—how to structure profitable win-win deals," David began the next session.

"At the most basic level, there are **three steps to any deal. Step one is to find a motivated seller who has the right motivation and situation.** Remember that you bring value to the deal by helping a seller solve a pressing real estate problem. If they're not motivated, then there is no way for you to bring enough value to the table to make it a win-win deal. This is why it's essential that the seller you work with have a compelling reason to sell.

"**Step two is to meet with this seller and find a way to structure a deal that meets the seller's most important needs and has a conservative profit in there for you.** Once you have created this win-win solution with the seller, you need to make sure that the agreement is in writing and signed by both you and the seller. We call this "putting the property under contract."

"**Step three is to execute your exit strategy for the property.** This almost always means you must find your end user for the property. This end user might be a retail buyer who is purchasing the property from you if you've decided that your exit strategy is to immediately resell the property. Or your end user could be a renter if your exit strategy is to lease out the property for a period of time. Or your end user could be a tenant buyer if your exit strategy is to sell the property on a rent-to-own basis.

"As you can imagine, the seller's needs and situation are going to determine to a large degree how you structure the deal, as is your plan for dealing with the property once you've acquired it. The key to structuring a winning deal is to plan both your way into and out of any deal. Your way into a deal is called your '**acquisition strategy**.' This is how you structure your *purchase* of the property. Intelligent investors know that they make their money when they buy, not when they sell. This requires them to make sure that any deal they do has a built in profit at the time of *acquisition*. Your way out of the deal is called your '**exit strategy**' and this is when you harvest the profit you've created from the deal. Notice you don't make a profit when you sell; you make your profit when you buy. You merely *harvest* your profit when you sell. The key lesson here is that you will never enter into any deal that you don't have a clearly laid out strategy for gracefully exiting.

"Today you are going to learn about the four basic acquisition strategies, along with the five main exit strategies, so that when we're done you will have a clear, big picture understanding of what your options are going into and coming out of a deal. Remember this weekend is about getting you the right information you need to launch your investing success. This means that rather than dazzle you with dozens of sophisticated techniques for structuring deals, we're going to focus on the fundamentals that will provide you with a strong foundation upon which to build your future investing success. During our time working together in the Mentorship Program, we will layer in more acquisition and exit strategies as we go.

"There are two main ways to buy a property and make a conservative profit. Either you buy the property for "cash" at a deeply discounted price or you buy the property with attractive terms of financing that allow you to make your profit because of the great financing with which you acquired the property. Think about this as though it was a decision tree. At the first juncture you have your first real decision to make as you structure the deal—will it be a cash deal or a terms deal?"

David drew a diagram on the board:

Winning Deal Decision Tree

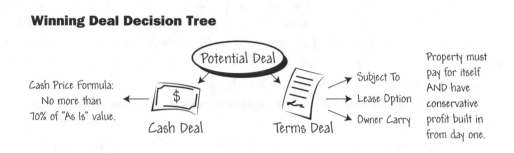

"Depending which way you go, there are specific formulas and critical lessons for you as you structure the front end of the deal. We'll start off with the details of buying for cash. Then I'll move into the three acquisition strategies for term deals. Then I walk you through the five major exit strategies.

"When you are buying for cash, one key distinction is that the cash you are using can be yours or it can be money you borrowed from some third party like a bank. The key distinction in a cash sale is that the *seller* is getting all of her money up front from you and not waiting for payments over time. Once you've purchased a property for cash, you can either hold onto the property over time or move to sell it right away for more than you paid.

"When you are buying for cash, the reason for the big discount is that as an investor your cash is a valuable commodity—one that most sellers want. It is also a limited commodity. Once it's committed to being invested into a specific piece of real estate, you lose out on the ability to quickly access it to purchase your next screaming good deal. Because of this, you need to always highly value your cash and use it to maximum effect. This means that if a seller requires an all-cash purchase, you require a deep cash discount to move ahead with the deal. We'll cover more about this later. For the moment, the point to understand is that any time you give cash to a seller, you need to get something of equal value in return—like a deep cash discount. When you buy for cash you typically take on more risk than if you enter into a terms deal—having more money in the deal means you potentially have more to lose—and risk always needs to be rewarded. If your risk isn't being adequately rewarded in a deal, then why take it? In a cash deal the way you get rewarded is by getting a deep cash discount.

"Buying for cash is one of the most misunderstood areas for investors. Over the past ten years I've observed many investors get caught in bad deals simply because they didn't understand the fundamental formula for profitably buying for cash. Now I know that sure sounds like a fancy way of saying something, but hang in there for a moment while I walk you through an example.

"I was taking my dog Blue for a walk several months ago and saw this car with its lights on parked in front of a house. I know I've done that myself and found the battery dead later, so I went to the house to tell the owner about it.

"The name of the owner of the car was James, and it turns out that he was just getting started investing in real estate. In fact, James told me he had purchased that very house 'for nothing down.'

"It turns out that he had worked with an aggressive mortgage broker to get 100 percent financing for the house. As I listened to him, one thing became obvious—James didn't understand what it really meant to buy a house for cash. He had made the fatal mistake that I watch so many other investors make. He mistakenly thought that since he bought the house with 100 percent financing that it wasn't a cash deal. Instead he thought it was a 'nothing-down' terms deal. James was 180 degrees wrong.

"The determination of whether you are buying for cash is not dependent on whether you are using your cash or someone else's cash. The determination is really the seller's point of view. If the seller is receiving all of his or her money at the closing, then you are buying for cash. This means that even if you borrowed all the money, as James did to make the purchase, but the seller is getting totally paid off at closing (as was the case in James's deal), then you are buying for cash. And anytime you are buying for cash you need to get a cash price.

"Why does this even matter? Remember how we already talked about the only two ways to consistently make money investing in real estate—buying for cash at a deep discount or buying on terms where the great financing builds in a profit for you? If you buy for cash but don't get a cash discount you are not investing . . . you are speculating. You're speculating that the property will go up fast enough in value and that you won't need to sell for a while until this happens. This is a bet, and you may win and you may lose. As for me, I don't believe in gambling with real estate. When I buy I do so because *I know* I will make a profit. Isn't that a smarter way to do your investing, to only buy when you *know* you'll make a profit?

"The most important way that I know I'll make a profit on my deals is that I've already built in my profit on the deal from the moment I purchased the house by getting a deep cash discount *or* by getting excellent terms of financing.

"Not only didn't James get a deep cash discount (in fact he paid close to full value for the property) but since the financing was from a conventional lender James had to personally guarantee the loan! That meant he not only overpaid for the property because he bought the house with cash and didn't get any deep discount, but he also took on a great deal of risk by personally signing on the note. The combination of these two things is deadly to your long-term wealth.

"But maybe you're saying that his seller wouldn't sell it to him for less. Well, lets look at this closer, because there are a lot of lessons in this simple example that I am hoping will keep you out of trouble in your own investing.

"Let's start by looking at the part about the seller not being willing to give him a deep cash discount. First of all, let's go over the Cash Price Formula." With this David wrote the following on the board:

Cash Price Formula

Highest "All Cash" Price You Can Pay = 70% of the "As Is" value of the property
$\qquad$ (Go for less!)

"It's really this simple. When you are buying for cash, never pay more than 70 percent of the as-is value, and you'll be taking one of the most important steps to never lose money with your investing, which as we all know is an important part of the game, isn't it?

"First of all though, what do I mean by the 'as-is value'? Let's look at that concept for the moment." Again David wrote on the board:

"As Is" Value = The after-repair value of the property less the CONSERVATIVE cost of getting the house in the condition so that it will SELL in 90 days or less.

"So if you have a house that would sell for $450,000 if it were in great showing condition but conservatively needs about $50,000 of repairs to get it in that condition, then the as-is value of that house is how much?"

"$400,000," several attendees shouted.

"That's right. So using our Cash Price Formula, the most any of you in the room today would ever pay for that property would be $280,000. $280,000 is 70 percent of $400,000."

"But David," Nancy interrupted, "What if the seller wouldn't have accepted an offer from James for that low a price?"

"Good question. Before I answer it though, I have a question for you Nancy. If the seller is set on a cash deal, and won't accept a price that's low enough to make you as an investor a conservative profit, what does this let you know about the seller?

"That the seller wasn't motivated," Nancy responded.

"Exactly Nancy. And if the seller isn't really motivated, what is James doing buying their house? He's speculating. Smart investors never speculate; they buy intelligently so that they make money no matter what happens. Besides, why should I use my precious cash, or tie up my precious credit, to buy a house when I'm not getting a great deal on it? The answer is obvious—I shouldn't. And neither should James and neither should you."

Leon sheepishly raised his hand, "David, I just realized that on my three rental houses that I bought before I got started in the Mentorship Program, I overpaid for two of them. They were worth about $250,000 and I paid $220,000 for both using conventional financing."

David's voice was softer now. "I understand Leon. I've been guilty of overpaying for a property before. That's why I'm spending so much time and energy on showing you the right way to buy. I'm curious. How many of you after learning about the Cash Price Formula realize that you overpaid for a property or two in your past before you got started in the Mentorship Program?" David looked around the room and counted roughly twenty-five people with their hands up.

"While we can't rewrite history," David continued, "if you got nothing else from the Mentorship Program except this formula, and you applied it to save you from making any more mistakes on future deals, do you realize that you would have recouped tens of thousands of dollars on your tuition to be part of the program? The bottom line is this: when you are buying for cash you need to be using the Cash Price Formula.

"One last part to the Cash Price Formula that I need to point out. Notice how it says the 'highest' price you can pay is 70 percent. Most times you'll get even a deeper discount from a motivated seller. Ideally you'd be paying 60 percent or less of value. But as long as you don't pay more than 70 percent you should conservatively be making a profit in all your cash deals."

"But David," Tim interrupted, "I still don't get why I couldn't buy the house for more than 70 percent and still make a profit."

"Can you give me an example of a deal where you think you could pay more and be sure you'd make a profit Tim?"

"About three weeks ago I met with a seller who had a four-bedroom house in my home town. The house needed about $10,000 of simple cosmetic work—paint and carpet—and had an after-repair value of $210,000. The seller said he'd take an all-cash offer of $170,000 just to be done with it. The way I figured it, after I put the $10,000 into it, I'd still have a total price of just $180,000, which would leave me a $30,000 profit when I resold it. What's wrong with that?"

"You know Tim there is nothing wrong with making $30,000. The problem is that you really wouldn't have made $30,000. Let's look at it closer." David took out a marker and began to put the numbers down on the board.

After-Repair Value of Property: $210,000
Conservative Estimate of Repairs Needed   -$10,000
"As Is" Value = $200,000

Tim's Price with Seller   -$170,000

Amount of Potential Profit =   ($30,000)

"Now Tim, I understand that you're thinking you buy it for $170,000, put $10,000 of work into, and just sell it right away for $210,000, is that right?" David asked.

"Yes," Tim replied.

"Okay, but what about the other costs involved? For example, you have the closing costs when you buy the property to cover things like escrow fees, title insurance, transfer tax, and things like that. Plus, if you are borrowing the money from a conventional lender, you're going to have other costs like origination fees and points on the loan, appraisal and inspection fees, a lender's title insurance policy, and things like that. Plus, once you buy the property and start to fix it up, what's the lender going to want 30 days after you close on the house?"

"Their monthly payment," Tim answered.

"That's right. You also need to factor in the holding costs of property for things like the monthly loan payments to the utilities that you have to pay until you resell it. Then there are the selling costs when you resell the property. You'll have closing costs a second time, plus, if you're going after top dollar for the house, you may very well have a real estate agent commission to pay. Do you see how all of this is adding up? What's happening to your profit Tim?"

"It's getting eaten up!" Tim responded.

"It sure is. Let's go back to the numbers and go through this a second time. **One simple shortcut you can use to quickly calculate the closing costs when you buy, the holding costs, and the selling costs when you resell the property is to use 10 percent of the selling price.** This assumes you are buying a property with the intention of fixing it up and reselling it within three to six months. Of course this 10 percent does *not* include any fix-up costs. That would have to be factored in separately. What this 10 percent shortcut gives you is a simple way you can make a quick and fast estimate knowing you'll go back over the numbers more carefully if the deal is one you plan to move forward on.

After-Repair Value of Property:	$210,000
Conservative Estimate of Repairs Needed	−$10,000
"As Is" Value =	$200,000
Tim's Price with Seller	−$170,000
Amount of Potential Profit =	$30,000
Expenses: Closing Costs / Holding Costs / Selling Costs (shortcut: take after-repair value x 10%)	−$21,000
Profit <u>IF</u> Property Sells for Full Price =	$9,000

"Tim, how is this deal looking to you now after you factor in the costs involved for you as an investor? Remember, you don't just get handed a $9,000 check at closing. You still have to spend three to six months of work to make the deal happen, not to mention the risk you take by signing personally on the loan to buy the property, assuming you could do it with 100 percent conventional financing, which is questionable."

"I understand now why my Mentorship Coach John said on the conference call that the deal wasn't at a good enough price. I'm sure glad I listened to him, although I must admit, it didn't make this much sense until I saw you lay it out like that," Tim said.

"I have a question David," Leon asked. "What if Tim just used money he had in his savings account to do this deal instead of borrowing the money. That way he'd save a lot on the holding costs since he wouldn't have any payments due. Plus he'd save on the loan costs."

"While there are times when it does make sense to use your own money, I personally don't think this deal warrants it. Also, it's bad business to think of using your own money as 'free.' Although you may not have to send a payment in to yourself, **using your own money still costs you in three big ways. First, you take on magnitudes more risk.** Remember, the more money you personally have in a deal, the more you have to potentially lose. That's the biggest reason why I don't use my money for anything less than great deals.

"Second, using your money isn't free. I'm going to assume that Tim had his money working for him somewhere else; if he didn't that's another conversation we'd need to have. So by taking his money out of that other investment, he'd lose out on the money he would have made had he not touched that. In effect, that's just like the cost of borrowing the money to begin with. Now, depending on where he kept his idle cash, that may or may not be a smart thing.

"The third reason to be careful about using your own money is the opportunity cost of tying up your cash. What happens if the day after Tim buys this house using his own money Tim finds a $300,000 house that he could buy for $155,000, but the seller insisted on getting cashed out within 48 hours? He may be forced to pass up on this better deal and be stuck in a marginal deal instead. Can you see now why I say be very picky about deals you put your own cash into, Leon?"

"Yes that makes sense now," Leon responded.

"Good. Let's go back to our example deal and go through the right way to buy it using our Cash Price Formula." David started to write the numbers out on the board.

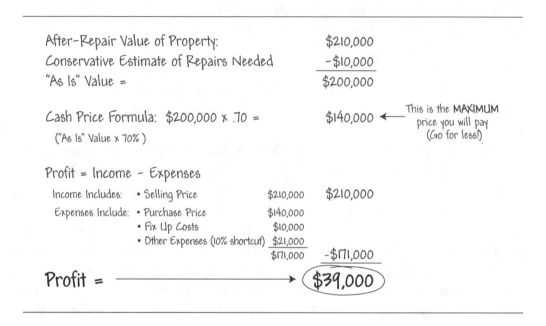

After-Repair Value of Property: $210,000
Conservative Estimate of Repairs Needed   –$10,000
"As Is" Value = $200,000

Cash Price Formula: $200,000 x .70 = $140,000 ← This is the **MAXIMUM** price you will pay (Go for less!)
("As Is" Value x 70%)

Profit = Income – Expenses

Income Includes: • Selling Price $210,000 $210,000
Expenses Include: • Purchase Price $140,000
                   • Fix Up Costs $10,000
                   • Other Expenses (10% shortcut) $21,000
                                $171,000   –$171,000

Profit = ⟶ $39,000

"Using the Cash Price Formula you'd net $39,000 on this deal—more if you negotiated the price lower than the maximum our formula will let you pay! Now, this type of profit makes the deal much more attractive for you as the investor," David said.

"Imagine you find a seller who owns a property valued at $250,000 who is highly motivated. It seems he and his two sisters inherited this house from their mother who had just passed away. The house is dated inside and none of the adult children want the hassle of remodeling it before they sell. Instead, they sell the house to you in it's current condition for $165,000. You spend about $6,000 doing the cosmetic upgrades and then resell the house for a $70,000 profit. That would be an example of a cash deal. You buy the house with your money or money you borrow and give to the seller. And then in this case you immediately fix up and re-sell the house for a healthy profit.

Why Every Investor Is a Cash Buyer

Money Is NOT An Issue

Many investors think that money (or lack of money) is what stops them from closing a deal. This myth is one of the most limiting things that holds investors back. Understand that money is NEVER an issue—if the deal is right. Later in this chapter we'll cover the six best sources to fund your deals. The key for you to understand right now is that only one of these six sources to fund a deal is your own money! The other five sources are forms of using other people's money.

Say the following words to yourself over and over,

"If the deal is right, I will find the money!"

If you negotiate the right price and the right deal, you can and will find the funding. The key is that the deal MUST be right. For a cash deal, this means a price at MOST 70 percent of the conservative as-is value. This means you are going to have to begin your cash negotiations at 50–60 percent to leave yourself room to negotiate up if you need to. This will kill many deals. That's okay, the ones that do work out will be easy to find the funding for because there is plenty of potential profit to warrant an outside party funding your deal.

Profitable Deals Only

It's critical that the deal be conservatively very profitable (i.e., will make you money even if you made a few mistakes estimating repairs, etc.). This will allow enough profit in the deal to split with an outside investor who funds the deal or to make an outside lender feel secure in lending you the money you need to proceed with the deal on your own. We'll cover both of these options in detail later in this chapter. For the moment the most important point is to understand that if the deal is right, *you will find the money.* Never lose sight of that.

Funding Hangups

The only two reasons why you wouldn't be able to find the funding for a great deal are fear and ignorance. Fear stops you from locking up the deal and actively searching for someone to help fund it. Ignorance prevents you from knowing what a great deal is and how to negotiate and put the deal under contract. With a willingness to actively move forward in a deal and the knowledge of how to find outside funding, any investor can be a cash buyer.

"Cash deals are what most people think about when they think about what it means to invest in real estate. It's a great way to make a profit, but you have the most competition with cash offers. Why? Because this is the only way that 90 percent of investors know how to invest. It's the old, "Buy Low, Sell High" or "Buy Low, Hold, Then Sell Very High" strategies. They definitely work, but if they are all you know, you are missing out on some of the most profitable niches in real estate.

"The second main way for you to buy properties is on terms. This means you structure the deal so that the seller is not getting all her money up front but instead is going to get paid at some future date. With a terms deal, you use the excellent financing that the seller participates in to make your profit. Usually, on a terms deal you make sure that the property can afford to pay for itself long enough for it to go up in value enough to resell at a profit. Or you make sure the property is one in which the financing is so valuable that you are able to use it to make your money regardless of whether or not the property goes up in value.

"Now, many of you who are here this weekend have read some of our earlier books about some of the creative financing strategies we teach, such as lease options, buying subject to the existing financing, and using owner-carry financing.* What I would like to do now is to give you a general look at what most terms deals have in common, and then go through the three main Terms Deal Acquisition Strategies so that the big picture of a terms deal and how it is different from a cash deal comes into sharp focus.

"There are two kinds of debt in the world of real estate: good debt and bad debt. **Good debt is debt that the property itself can afford to pay and debt that is nonrecourse.** Bad debt is debt that you have to personally feed, and it's debt that you have to personally guarantee. Think of debt like adult children; they should be old enough to look after themselves! The problem is some investors let those 30-year-olds move back into the house and freeload off mom and dad! The reason most traditional investors make this mistake is quite simply

---

*For more detailed explanation on terms deals see, Making Big Money Investing In Real Estate Without Tenants, Banks or Rehab Projects, pp. 29–90 and, Making Big Money Investing In Foreclosures Without Cash or Credit, pp. 27–89.

Six Things Most Terms Deals Have In Common

1) The seller isn't getting all his money up front. A terms deal usually means a seller isn't getting all of his money up front but is waiting to get his money over time. This might mean monthly payments, or a lump sum payment down the road, or some combination of the two.) While with some terms deals where the seller has very little equity, it may be possible to structure a deal in which the seller gets all the money due him at closing, in most terms deals the seller is going to be waiting for his money to be paid to him over time.

2) Your exit strategy will generally call for you to hold onto the property over time. Most of the properties you buy on terms you will hang onto for a while before you resell them for your biggest chunk of profits. This is because, when you structure a terms deal, you end up being more generous to the seller on price, but you negotiate the financing details to allow you to make a large chunk of your profit when you resell the property down the road.

3) The property comfortably cash flows. The reason you are willing to hold properties you bought on terms over a period of time is because the monthly income that property generates is greater than the total cost you must pay each month to hold the property. The cash flow the property generates is one of the key profit centers in most terms deals.

4) The purchase required little or nothing down. Since the motivated seller is financing a significant part of any terms deal, a skilled investor can negotiate to do the deal with little or no money down. If a small amount of money is required, a trained investor can often offset this with money collected from the end user of the property. This could be in the form of a nonrefundable option payment from a tenant buyer if you resell the property on a rent-to-own basis, or it could be first and last month's rent if you merely lease out the property to a renter.

5) Your credit is NOT an issue. Again, since the motivated seller is the one who is financing you in a terms deal, negotiated properly, the motivated seller will never ask about, let alone check, your credit scores. This means you are able to buy using terms acquisition strategies even if you have the world's worst credit.

6) You won't have to personally guarantee the debt. Money that you borrow and personally guarantee repayment on is called recourse financing. Money you borrow that you do NOT personally guarantee is called NONrecourse financing. With terms deals, because you aren't borrowing from conventional lenders but rather from the motivated seller, you won't need to personally guarantee the financing. This massively reduces your risk when investing.

because they don't know better. They can only do what they have been taught to do.

"Please write down the **first rule of safely structuring a terms deal**," David said turning to the board.

Rule #1 – The property must be able to pay for itself.

"This means that the income a property can generate must be equal to or greater than the total costs to maintain that property. These costs include the cost of financing, property taxes, property insurance, vacancy allowances, and other operating expenses for a property. Ideally you want all your terms deals to cash flow—to have income in excess of the expenses producing a net profit—by a minimum of 10 percent. This not only produces one of your profit centers from a deal, but it also builds in a margin of safety in your deal."

"David, does that mean you'll only do a deal that has a cash flow right from the start?" Mark asked.

"Normally yes. But that is going to depend on several factors. If the property is in a great area that is strongly appreciating and that has a good long-term outlook, I am much more willing to take a break-even deal or maybe even a small negative cash flow. However, I will make sure that if I do this that I am getting my initial price low enough so that I already have some equity from day one so that, if need be, I can immediately sell a property for a small profit should my personal circumstances change.

"Also, if there is some other sweetener in the deal that I am able to negotiate that makes the deal good enough, I am more than willing to take on a small negative cash flow. For example, one house we bought with a Mentorship Student included an attached vacant lot with the owner carry purchase. We sold the lot for a quick $22,000 profit. I'm sure you can see how the lot was a sweetener that made the small negative cash flow in the purchase of the house palatable.

"Let's go to the second rule for terms deals," David again turned to the board.

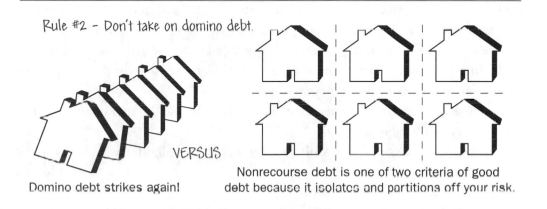

Rule #2 – Don't take on domino debt.

VERSUS

Domino debt strikes again!

Nonrecourse debt is one of two criteria of good debt because it isolates and partitions off your risk.

"I don't personally guarantee debt on terms deals. In fact, if I have to personally guarantee the debt, then it's almost always not a terms deal—it's a cash deal. The safest way to do your investing is to buy on terms in such a way that each property is an isolated and distinct deal. What happens in one deal is compartmentalized from what happens in your other deals, just like the water-tight compartments of an ocean liner are separated from each other with strong bulkheads.*

---

*For the exact language of the "non recourse clause" we use in our contracts, along with other key contract clauses for buying properties download the FREE ebook, *The Nine Essential Contract Clauses When Buying Real Estate*. Go to **www.QuickstartInvestor.com**. While there you'll also be able to download a free report, *The Three Ways to Get Powerful Investor Friendly Contracts*.

"Let's be clear here. If you are using conventional bank financing to buy a house, the lender is always going to make sure you personally guarantee the loan. However, if you are using conventional bank financing to fund a purchase, what type of deal is that?" David asked.

"A cash deal?" Vicki answered.

"Exactly! It would be a cash deal. And you build safety into a cash deal by buying at a deep cash discount. Let's keep pushing forward in our development of how to structure deals. When you buy on terms, the seller is the one who is financing the purchase for you. In just about every terms deal the seller is participating in the financing in some way or other. That's what makes a term deal work—the seller's participation in the financing.

"The key to making a terms deal work is the same key to making a cash deal work; it's a motivated seller.

"One thing I mentioned a while ago, but I didn't highlight was about building in a margin of safety. Who remembers how you minimize your risk and build in a margin of safety into a terms deal?"

"By making sure the property cash flows well," Mark answered.

"Exactly, you build a margin of safety into a terms deal by making sure the property not only can afford to cover all it's expenses, but that it creates at least a 10 percent surplus. The reason this usually works as a minimum safety factor is that market rents tend to be buffered from the volatile fluctuations of the real estate market. This means that while property values may go up or down in a wildly moving market by 15 percent or more, market rents rarely move so dramatically. Remember that many renters in an area are already leasing on a long-term lease of a year, so their rent will remain stable. This buffer means that even if an area's rental market suffers a down market, usually the market rents will take significantly less of a hit than the resale market will. Hence the 10 percent minimum safety factor. Of course, if you are buying in a down market, you know better than to pay too much for the property, but this safety margin will give you a guideline to use as a minimum cash flow to work into your deal structuring to create your cushion of comfort.

The Three Most Important Terms Deal Acquisition Strategies

Terms Deal Acquisition Strategy #1: Lease Option
Long-term lease + agreed upon option price.

The first and perhaps the most common way to structure a terms deal is for you to negotiate a long-term lease on the property along with an option to purchase the property. This means the seller agrees to let you take possession of the property (i.e., lease) and the seller has agreed to give you a fixed price at which you can buy the property at any point over your lease period (i.e., option).

- **The lease portion of the deal** lets you control possession of the property including allowing you to sublease the property to a tenant.
- **The option portion of the deal** gives you control over the sale of the property and any future appreciation by locking in a price at which you have the exclusive right to buy for the specific period of the lease term.

Case Study #1: We found this motivated seller who owned a three-bedroom, two-bath townhouse. The seller was a burned-out landlord who was tired of managing the property and just wanted out. The property was valued at roughly $130,000 and had been rented in prior years for $1,000 per month.

We agreed to lease out the property for five years for a monthly rent of $915 per month. We also agreed to pay for all the day-to-day maintenance for any repair less than $200 in any one month. What this gave the seller was a great long-term tenant who was responsible for all the minor maintenance. These guaranteed monthly payments with no day-to-day maintenance responsibilities was very appealing to the owner.

Why would we agree to do this? Because we negotiated one more thing up front. We agreed on a purchase price for which we could buy the property at any point during the five-year lease period. This is called a "lease with an option to purchase." In this deal, our option price was $115,000 (notice we did negotiate a small discount off of the $130,000 value).

What did we do with the property? We sold the property on a rent-to-own basis. This meant we found a future buyer, called a "tenant buyer," who subleased the property from us, and we gave our tenant an option to purchase the property from us at an amount higher than our option price with the original seller. We made our tenant buyer responsible for all the maintenance and to make sure they treated the property much better than any renter ever would, we charged them a nonrefundable payment up front of 3–5 percent of the purchase price to lock in their price over their lease period. In fancy

(continued)

The Three Most Important Terms Deal Acquisition Strategies *(continued)*

language this is called an "option payment" and it applies toward the purchase price if they choose to exercise their option to purchase. On this deal we collected a nonrefundable option payment of $7,000. Here are what the complete numbers looked like.

MOTIVATED SELLER	YOU/INVESTOR	TENANT BUYER
$915	Rent	$1,025
$115,000	Price	$140,000
5 years	Term	2 years
1	Payment	$7,000

As you can see, we put our tenant buyer into the property for a higher rent amount, which created $110 per month in positive cash flow. Also, we had a spread between our option price with the seller and the tenant buyer's price with us. This spread generated an additional $25,000 in profits, of which we collected $7,000 up front from their option payment, with the balance of $18,000 due at closing when our tenant buyer gets a new loan to cash both us and the original seller out of the property.

Case Study #2: We found a seller who was making double payments on two properties after a recent move who wanted to just get out from under the second payment. We agreed to step in and do a 3-year lease option on the property for a price of $235,000. We sold the property on a 2-year lease option for $295,000 and netted over a $65,000 profit for our efforts.*

Terms Deal Acquisition Strategy #2: Buying Subject To the Existing Financing
Seller deeds you the house and you make payment every month on the existing loan in the seller's name.

On most properties you buy, the seller doesn't own the property free and clear. She has a loan against the property for some amount. How did the seller get that loan in place? She applied with a mortgage lender who required her to show three things to qualify for the loan: credit scores, financial resources to pay for the loan, and a cash down payment, The lender doesn't do all this for free, it charged the borrower application, appraisal, and origination fees, plus points on the loan. And the lender required the borrower to personally guarantee the loan.

*For more details on all three terms deals acquisition strategies, see *Making Big Money Investing in Real Estate Without Tenants, Banks, or Rehab Projects*, pp. 29–106 and pp. 181–230, or download a **FREE e-book** titled *5 Fun, Easy Ways to Structure Terms Deals to Generate Over $100,000 in Profits This Year*. To download this e-book go to **www.QuickstartInvestor.com**.

(continued)

The Three Most Important Terms Deal Acquisition Strategies *(continued)*

- **With subject to financing, you get all the benefits of the loan that's already in place with none of the risk, none of the cost, in fact, with virtually none of the downsides of conventional financing.** What you do is simply buy the property and leave the existing financing in place. You own the property, the seller owns the debt. Of course you agree to pay the payment each month on the existing loan because if the loan isn't paid each month the lender's claim to the property comes before your claim to it. In fancy terms, you own the property "subject to the existing financing that exists against the property."

Case Study #3: We got a referral to meet with a couple who were four months behind on their mortgage payment and about to lose their home to foreclosure. After meeting with them, we agreed that we would make up the back payments, buy the property, and take over making payments on the underlying loan in their place. Here are what the numbers looked like on the front half of the deal:

Value: $180,000

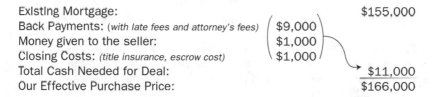

Existing Mortgage: $155,000
Back Payments: *(with late fees and attorney's fees)* $9,000
Money given to the seller: $1,000
Closing Costs: *(title insurance, escrow cost)* $1,000
Total Cash Needed for Deal: $11,000
Our Effective Purchase Price: $166,000

To make this deal work for us we immediately found a tenant buyer for the property who gave us $6,000 of option money plus first months rent of $1,600. In essence we recouped $7,600 of the $11,000 we needed to do this deal within three weeks of buying it. Over the next five years we had two different tenant buyers go through the property and choose not to exercise their option to purchase (remember, our tenant buyers have the option to purchase, not the obligation). During that time, these tenant buyers paid us rent every month, took care of maintaining the property, and both gave us sizable nonrefundable option payments. Five years later, the property had increased in value to $300,000. We ended up selling the property to our third tenant buyer for $280,000. After paying our share of the closing costs, **we ended up netting $110,000 from this sale**.

Terms Deal Acquisition Strategy #3: Owner-carry Financing
Seller accepts a promissory note for some or all of the money owed to them.

When you are doing your investing, you will at times run across sellers who have a very large chunk of equity in their properties, or perhaps even own the

(continued)

The Three Most Important Terms Deal Acquisition Strategies *(continued)*

property free and clear. In situations like this, it is often possible to structure the deal with the seller agreeing to finance your purchase of the property by "carrying back" some or all of the purchase price as a loan that you will pay back over time.

Case Study #4: We called up a FSBO ad in the newspaper. The seller owned a large 5-bedroom house in an up-scale section of San Diego. He not only owned this property free and clear, but he had already purchased another home near Palm Springs that he wanted to retire to.

After negotiating for three days, we agreed on a purchase price of $595,000 with a down payment of 10 percent and the owner to carry back the balance as a first mortgage at an interest rate that was about two percent lower than the best rates conventional lenders would offer at that time. Why did the seller agree to give us such attractive financing? Because he wanted a fast and easy sale. We gave him a price that was fair and we told him not to worry about repainting the interior of the house. We held onto the house for four years, put a little money into sprucing it up cosmetically, and resold the property for $925,000.

Case Study #5: One of our Mentorship students in Virginia found an elderly couple who were selling their home. Since the couple owned the property free and clear, our student, an attorney in the area, talked with them to see if they would participate in the financing.

After going back and forth, they agreed on a purchase price of $380,000, with our student to bring in a new conventional first mortgage of $180,000 and the sellers to carry back a second mortgage for the other $200,000. The sellers got the $180,000 from the new conventional loan up front at the closing, and our student was able to finance the deal 100 percent (roughly half from a conventional first mortgage and half from the owner carry second mortgage). Why wasn't this a "cash" deal since the owner got so much money up front? Because the seller carried back a second mortgage for $200,000 with an interest rate of just two percent! This allowed the property to have incredibly low mortgage payments. Our student decided to move into the property and live there for a few years before reselling it for a healthy profit down the road.

4 Biggest Benefits of Owner Carry Financing:
1) No loan costs
2) No intrusive or overwhelming paperwork to "qualify"
3) Below-market interest rates
4) No recourse on the loan

Why Cash Investors Benefit by Structuring Term Deals

BRIGHT IDEA

Surprise #1: We recommend beginning investors get started investing *without using their own cash.* It is hard to believe, but sometimes having money can be detrimental to learning to be the best investor you can be. It's just that we've seen money used as a crutch to make a marginal deal go through. Sometimes access to cash tempts you to throw money into a deal when a little more patience and skilled negotiation would have been more effective. With an open mind and the right investor training, investing without cash or credit can spark you to grow to be a faster, more creative, and more skilled investor.

Surprise #2: Liquid cash gets used up fast. We've watched traditional investors literally pour over half a million dollars into one or two deals and then have to wait until they sold those properties before they could free up enough of their money to go out and buy more properties. You'll never regret learning to buy without money. It will make you a much more savvy investor for those times you do decide to use your own money or conventional financing.

Combining Acquisition Strategies for Maximum Profits and Minimum Risk

"Let's go back to an earlier deal we discussed and go through what I think is the best way you could structure the deal by combining the best part of the subject to acquisition strategy with the best part of negotiating a low cash price."

David started to write the numbers on the board.

After-Repair Value of Property:	$210,000
Conservative Estimate of Repairs Needed	−$10,000
"As Is" Value =	$200,000
Cash Price Formula: $200,000 x .70 =	$140,000 ← This is the MAXIMUM price you will pay (Go for less!)
("As Is" Value x 70%)	

(continued)

Profit = Income − Expenses

Income Includes:	• Selling Price	$210,000	$210,000
Expenses Include:	• Purchase Price	$140,000	
	• Fix Up Costs	$10,000	
	• Other Expenses (10% shortcut)	$21,000	
		$171,000	−$171,000

Profit = ⟶ $39,000

"If you called in on a coaching call and presented this deal and said, 'David, how can I turn it from a good deal into a great deal?' here's what I'd coach you to do. One of the most profitable yet overlooked techniques for funding a rehab deal is to do a "short term subject to rehab." Let's go through how it works using the case study of this deal. Imagine that the owner still owes $100,000 against the property secured as a first mortgage. Rather than spend $140,000 of your cash to pay for the house plus another $10,000 to do the fix up work, why not use the existing financing as a short-term loan to fund most of your purchase? You buy the property subject to the existing $100,000 mortgage. You agree to pay the seller $40,000 for his equity at closing. You buy the house and fix it up. This means rather than the $150,000 (plus holding costs) of your cash you would have invested had you done it the old fashioned way, you now only have one third that amount tied up or $50,000 ($40,000 to the seller and $10,000 of fix-up) plus holding costs. Then after you resell the property you use your new buyer's money to cash the old seller's loan out and make your $39,000 profit."

David wrote the following numbers on the board.

	Old Fashioned Way	New Hybrid Technique
"As Is" Value:	$200,000	$200,000
Purchase Price:	$140,000	$140,000
Your Cash to the Seller:	$40,000	$40,000
Amount of existing loan paid off at closing:	$100,000	0
Amount of existing loan left in place:	0	$100,000
Fix up costs:	$10,000	$10,000
Your total cash in deal:	**$150,000**	**$50,000**

Your Selling Price:	$210,000	$210,000
10% "short cut" of misc. costs:	$21,000	$21,000
Net Profit:	$39,000	$39,000

Return on your cash ⟶
Invested in the deal: 26%   78%
(net profit/cash invested)   ($39,000÷$150,000)   ($39,000÷$50,000)

"Do you see now why the best places to look to fund a deal is at the existing financing? I always ask if there is some way I can use the loans that the seller already paid for and applied for to fund part or all of my purchase of the property. I do this whether it's a one-bedroom condo or a 100-unit apartment building. Subject to financing is one of the best ways to structure a deal in my opinion."

"David," Mark asked, "couldn't we just get the seller to wait a few months for their $40,000 and do this with even less of our money in the deal?"

"Exactly! Now you're thinking. Always ask if there's any way you could fund part or all of your purchase with an owner carry. In this case, because the seller is so motivated, maybe he would be willing to take a note (an IOU) for his $40,000 if you agreed to pay for all the closing costs. This would save him a few thousand dollars. In exchange for this, he agrees to wait up to six months for you to fix up and resell the property. He's protected just like any lender because he records a mortgage against the property to make sure that you pay him off when you resell.

"If you do it this way, you need $40,000 less cash up front! This boosts your rate of return on the cash you have in the deal to 390 percent!

"Actually this deal also demonstrates my second favorite source of funding to make a deal work. Anybody pick up on the source I'm talking about?" David asked.

"The buyer?" Vicki tentatively offered.

"Yes, that's right, the buyer. In this deal, the buyer's new loan and down payment brought in $210,000 of cash, which you used to pay off the existing lender, the old seller's $40,000, and to make a $39,000 profit for yourself. Pretty nice of the buyer, huh?"

6 Best Sources to Fund Your Deals

(BEST) #1: The Seller

The first and best place to look to fund your deals is the seller. Remember, any terms deal that you negotiate with the seller, whether it be a lease option, or a subject to deal, or an owner carry deal, is, in essence, the seller funding part or all of the deal. The seller can lend you some or all of his equity or the seller can let you tap into the existing financing against the property by accepting monthly payments from you. Either way it is still really the seller funding your deal.

(SECOND BEST) #2: The Buyer

There are two main types of buyers to turn to to help fund your deal. The first is a retail buyer—someone who wants to buy the property so that he or she can move in and live there. A retail buyer can fund the deal using their cash in the form of a down payment or option payment, their credit in the form of a new bank loan, or a combination of the two. The second type of buyer who can help fund your deal is another investor—also known as a wholesale buyer. You can quickly "flip," that is, sell, your deal to another investor for a fast cash profit, and let this other investor use his or her money to fund the deal.

Example: One of our Mentorship students in Washington, D.C. found a motivated seller through the Internet. He negotiated over the phone and put the property under contract to purchase at a discounted cash price. He aggressively advertised and marketed the property and found a buyer who fell in love with the home. Our student was able to sell the property for a $45,000 profit to this new buyer. He structured the sale to be what's called a "simultaneous closing," which meant that he did a double closing in which he took his new buyer's money from the loan his new buyer secured, and gave most of it to the original seller to pay this original seller the discounted cash price, and, in the process, the $45,000 spread in prices became our student's profit. The buyer "funded" this deal by getting a conventional loan to pay for the property, with our student using a large chunk of this cash to pay off the original seller.

Example: A Mentorship student in Phoenix found the owner of a beat-up, ugly house and put the property under contract for a discounted cash price of $14,500. Then, a short while later, our student found another investor who gutted and rehabbed homes in this area who paid our student $10,000 to buy the contract to purchase the house. Our student made $10,000 cash for assigning his contract to this new investor. The new investor used his money to rehab the house and later resold it for an even larger profit. The buyer, who in this case was this rehab investor, "funded" this deal by paying our student cash for the

(continued)

6 Best Sources to Fund Your Deals *(continued)*

right to buy this house at a deep discount, and this rehab investor also "funded" this deal by using his own money to pay the original seller the $14,500 owed to him.*

(GOOD) #3: Private Money

After you have gotten a bit more experienced with your deals you'll start to meet people who are willing to lend you money for your deals as long as they can have the loan secured by a first mortgage on the property. Often times these private lenders are average people who prefer to earn market interest rates for a first mortgage versus the poor earnings of a CD at their local bank. The key for a private lender is that the loan be safe. Security is their key concern. To that end, don't overpromise too high a rate of return or you will scare them away.

Example: You find a motivated seller who agrees to a discounted cash price of $300,000 on a house that is valued at $430,000. You find a retired executive who has a retirement account with $750,000 in it earning three percent interest. After spending time getting to know him, he agrees to lend you $300,000 as long as he is secured by a first mortgage on the property. You agree on an interest rate of eight percent, which makes him happy (he is getting five percent more than the money market fund paid) and you get great long-term financing in place that "funded" the purchase of this property.

(OKAY) #4: Your Cash or Credit

Although we don't recommend you use your money to buy a property unless the first three sources of funds don't work for you, if the deal is a good one and you have the money, or if you have the credit to get easy access to conventional financing, then funding a deal yourself makes good sense. Simple sources of this money:

1) Your liquid assets (e.g., saving or checking accounts)
2) Borrowing from a conventional lender
3) Borrowing from your 401k or pension
4) Equity lines of credit (secured by real estate)
5) Cash advances on credit cards or other unsecured lines of credit
6) Selling some of your stocks/bonds/collectibles or borrowing against them

Although this is an exception to the "without-cash-or-credit" theme of our style of investing, both of us strongly believe that if you have the money or access to it, then you should consider using it to make more deals happen. All we ask is that you use it intelligently. We have both used our own cash and credit on plenty of

*Download a FREE copy of the e-book, *3 Simple Steps to Flip a Deal For Quick Cash Profits*, by going to **www.QuickstartInvestor.com**.

(continued)

6 Best Sources to Fund Your Deals *(continued)*

deals, and we'll continue to do this again and again provided the profit and deal warrants the extra risk. As an interesting point, our favorite use of our money is not by buying a property for all cash. Rather, our favorite use of our money is to cash out a seller and make up back payments when we buy a preforeclosure or a foreclosure property subject to the existing financing, or as the down payment on an owner-carry deal.

Example: You find a four-plex owned by an extremely motivated seller. It's valued at $750,000 and you lock it up under contract for just $475,000. You use $95,000 of your savings for a 20 percent down payment and get a conventional mortgage to purchase the property. You decide to keep the four-plex as a rental property, and after you pay the monthly management fee and other costs of the property, you have $800 per month positive cash flow. You "funded" the deal both by using your savings for the down payment and by using your personal credit to secure a conventional loan for the other 80 percent of the purchase price.

(SO-SO) #5: Hard Money

Hard money comes from a third-party lender, but whereas a private money lender only wants market rates, a hard money lender is an experienced investor who is willing to lend to you not based on your creditworthiness or character, but based on the security of the loan. The main difference between a hard money lender and a private money lender is in the rate of interest and fees charged.

Hard money lenders typically require five to ten percentage points higher in the loan interest rate than private money lenders (or conventional lenders for that matter) charge. Plus, hard money lenders will charge you "points" on the loan. A point is prepaid interest, with each point equal to prepaid interest of one percent of the value of the loan. Although this sounds like and is a lot to pay for your money, if the deal is a good one, and you only need the money short term, a hard money loan may very well be the way to go.

Two easy places to find a hard money lender:
   1) The "money to lend" section of your local paper.
   2) Through your local real estate investors association.*

Example: One of our Mentorship Students put a 4-bedroom house under contract for a discounted cash price of $130,000. The property was conservatively valued at $220,000. Our student borrowed $150,000 from a local hard money lender. The money was used as follows:

*For a complete state-by-state listing of the 200 local real estate investor associations go to **www.QuickstartInvestor.com**.

(continued)

6 Best Sources to Fund Your Deals *(continued)*

Purchase Price:	$130,000
5 "Points" (hard money lender charged):	$6,500
Closing Costs:	$2,000
Fix up costs:	$11,500
Total Loan:	$150,000

It took our student four months to fix up and resell the property. During that time she had to pay the hard money lender interest payments on the loan (loan rate was 12 percent). But because she only needed the money for a short time, when she resold the property for $220,000 she ended up netting $40,000.

(LAST) #6: Equity Money Partner

Sometimes you turn to a private party to provide the funding to make a deal work. When this person requires a share of the deal rather than a rate of return, you have an equity partner. An equity partner can put her own money into the deal, or she can agree to get a conventional loan in her name to fund the deal. Either way, we listed equity money partners as sixth on the list because they generally will want to have a large chunk of the deal to be willing to partner up with you, sometimes as much as half of the profits. In most cases, if the deal is good enough, you are much better off using any of the five prior sources to fund your deals and should hold this final option in reserve as your last choice. That said, if you're faced with the choice to either equity partner and get half of a $80,000 deal or not be able to do the deal and make nothing, we suggest you partner up, take your half of the profits, and cheerfully give your equity partner her half of the deal.

Example: You find a motivated seller with a $500,000 four-bedroom house who is four months behind in his payments. You agree to make up the back payments and buy the house subject to the seller's existing loan. The only problem is you need $10,000 to make up the seller's back payments, plus you have agreed to give the seller another $30,000 for his equity. You figure you'll need another $2,000 for closing costs. Here's what the numbers look like:

Value of Home:	$500,000
Existing First Mortgage:	$350,000
Back Payments:	$10,000
Amount You Agreed to Pay Seller for His Equity:	$30,000
Closing Costs:	$2,000
Equity You Get When You Buy:	$108,000

(continued)

6 Best Sources to Fund Your Deals *(continued)*

You know the deal is great, after all there is over $100,000 of equity waiting for you from day one, but you don't have the $42,000 cash you need to close the deal. So you partner up with another investor who "funds" the deal and you agree to split the profit 50–50. In this deal you funded part of the purchase with a money partner ($42,000) and you funded part of this deal from the seller's existing mortgage ($350,000).

The Five Most Important Exit Strategies

Exit Strategy #1: "Retail" the Property

This means that you will sell the property for the highest price you can on the retail market. This is how most homes are sold, whether they are listed with a real estate agent or sold for sale by owner. Your buyer, when you retail a property, borrows from a conventional lender and almost always moves into the property to live there.

There are two main ways to implement this exit strategy:

Plan A – List the property with a great real estate agent in the area and let them sell it for you. If you choose this option make sure you ask around for referrals for the best agent in the area of town and for the specific type of property you are selling. We recommend that you interview at least three agents prior to listing your property and get a written commitment from them of the specific action steps they will take and by when to get your property sold fast. When we want to retail a property, we will often choose this option. Top agents are worth every penny of commission they earn because they will simplify the process and do almost all the work for you.

Plan B – Sell the house for sale by owner. This is a viable option for many investors. The biggest downside to this option, aside from the time factor, is that most homes are sold to buyers who found out about the property through the "Multiple Listing Service" or MLS for short. The MLS is the proprietary database of properties for sale that real estate agents have access to. If you choose to sell a property yourself, then you'll have to aggressively market the property with for-sale signs throughout the area and with classified advertising in the local paper.

(continued)

The Five Most Important Exit Strategies *(continued)*

One useful middle ground is to list the property with a flat-fee real estate broker. These real estate companies will put your property into the MLS and do some of the marketing in exchange for a flat fee sales commission, usually less than a few thousand dollars. If you choose this option, you will have to be willing to pay a sales commission to the real estate agent representing the buyer of the property (typically 3 percent of the selling price.)

Exit Strategy #2: "Flip" the Deal
This is a fast-cash exit strategy where you lock up a property under contract and then sell your contract to another buyer, typically another investor, who will pay you a cash fee to assign your contract over to them. The biggest benefit of flipping a deal is that it generates instant cash. For many new investors it's more important to them to get a quick cash payday than it is to hold onto a property over a period of time to make the maximum amount of profit. The most important lesson for your long-term success, if you choose to flip deals early on in your investing, is for you to remember that it's critical that you choose the best properties to hold onto over time. If you don't, no matter how much money you are making flipping deals, you are still caught on the treadmill of needing to find and flip your next deal… and the next one.*

Exit Strategy #3: Lease Out the Property to a Traditional Renter
This is perhaps one of the most common exit strategies of average investors. They buy a house and put a traditional renter in it. This renter leases the property either on a month-by-month rental agreement or a longer-term lease (typically for one year).

The four benefits of renting and holding onto a property over time are:

1) Cash flow
2) Appreciation
3) Amortization (the loan paying down)
4) Tax Savings

The three significant downsides to this exit strategy are:

1) Paying for the maintenance
2) Time to manage the rental property (Dealing with tenants and toilets can be very time consuming.)
3) Expense of "renter turnover" (The most expensive thing for most landlords is the cost to rerent out an empty property. Not only do you have the cost of the lost rental income while the property is vacant, but you also have the cleaning and painting and "prep" costs to get the property ready to show to prospective renters.)

*Log onto **www.QuickstartInvestor.com** to create your personalized investor business plan with our online software and find the right mix of flipping versus holding properties for your investing goals.

(continued)

The Five Most Important Exit Strategies *(continued)*

Exit Strategy #4: Offer the Property on a "Rent-to-Own" Basis

Wouldn't it be great if there was a way you could get the four main benefits of owning a rental property—the cash flow, the appreciation of the property, the amortization of the underlying loan, and the tax savings from owning a rental property—without the three main downsides of owning a traditional rental property? Good news! The rent-to-own exit strategy comes extremely close to doing the impossible—it gives you all the benefits of a traditional rental property, while minimizing the three major downsides.

The way this strategy works is that you find a tenant buyer who wants to rent to own your property. This tenant buyer will lease out your property on a two- or a three-year lease with a separate option agreement which gives them a locked in price at which they can buy the home at any point over that two- or three-year term. As part of agreeing to give them this fixed "option-to-purchase" price, your tenant buyer will pay you a nonrefundable option payment of three to five percent of the price of the property. In many cases your tenant buyer will also be paying slightly higher than the market rent because they aren't just renting the property, they are renting to own. This increased rent, when added to the option payment you collect up front, boosts your cash flow on the property. The best part of a tenant buyer isn't this increased cash flow, it's that because you have an occupant with an "owners" instead of a "renters" mentality, they will treat the property with much more care and attention. We even get our tenant buyers to take care of all the day to day maintenance and upkeep of the property!*

Because rent to own has all these advantages over traditional rental properties, you can understand our bias in real estate toward the rent-to-own exit strategy.

Exit Strategy #5: Sell with "Owner Financing"

This means that as a seller you take back some or all of the purchase price as a loan that your buyer will pay you over time.

Example: You sell a house for $400,000 where your buyer puts up a $20,000 cash down payment, gets a conventional first mortgage for $340,000, and you, the seller, carry back the other $40,000 as a second mortgage. Because of your willingness to participate in the financing, your buyer is able to much more easily get a conventional loan to fund her purchase of the house.

*For more detailed step-by-step instruction on how to implement this exit strategy see our second book, *Making Big Money Investing In Real Estate Without Tenants, Banks, or Rehab Projects* (pp. 181–230), or log onto **www.QuickstartInvestor.com** and download a FREE copy of the e-book, *7 Simple Steps to Sell Your Property On A Rent to Own Basis.*

(continued)

The Five Most Important Exit Strategies *(continued)*

Example: You bought a house six years ago subject to the existing financing. You bought it for $200,000. The current loan balance on the underlying financing is $150,000 and the loan has an interest rate of six percent. You agree to sell the property to your buyer, leaving the underlying financing in place for them for a total price of $400,000. Your buyer, who has lousy credit but great income, gives you a cash down payment of $60,000 and you agree to "carry back" the other $340,000 of the purchase price at an interest rate of eight percent. Now, not only do you make a healthy profit from the high selling price you got by agreeing to finance the whole purchase price, but you are making a great monthly income from the spread in the underlying financing (you pay the old loan at six percent but you collect at eight percent from your buyer). Your buyer is thrilled because with his lousy credit scores there was no other way for him to buy such a nice home.*

Just as offering a property on a rent-to-own basis gave you many of the best parts of a traditional renter while limiting the downsides, used intelligently, owner carry financing can be an exit strategy that gives you the best parts of selling a property, while minimizing the downsides.

Four Downsides to Exit Strategy #1—Retailing a House:

1) **Competition** – When you sell most properties retail, you are competing with other sellers who are selling their properties in the same area. This can mean more time before your house sells or a lower selling price through the negative influence of competing properties.

2) **Expense** – Often when you are selling a property retail, you have the added expense of paying real estate sales commissions—from three to six percent of the selling price. Although you can sell without an agent involved, this lowers your chances for a fast, full price sale.

3) **Time** – One function of greater competition from other homes for sale is that your property may take longer to sell. This means you have to wait longer to sell, which lowers your ultimate profit and delays your big payday.

4) **Conventional Lenders** – When you retail a house, your buyer will almost always be relying on a conventional lender to finance the bulk of the purchase. Our experiences have been that many times this lender gets picky part way through the sales process, and this can cause an otherwise willing buyer to have to back out of purchasing your property.

When you sell with owner financing you can avoid or minimize each of these four major downsides of the retail exit strategy.

*This technique is called selling on a "wrap-around mortgage" and it is discussed in more detail in, *Making Big Money Investing In Foreclosures Without Cash or Credit* (pp. 214-236).

(continued)

The Five Most Important Exit Strategies *(continued)*

Four Benefits of Selling With Terms:

1) **Eliminates Competition** – Look at your local paper and see the properties advertised for sale. Out of a hundred properties advertised for sale, only two to five will be advertised with owner financing. This means that by offering owner carry terms you are differentiating your property from over 95 percent of the competition! Not only is there a very limited supply for owner financed properties, but there is actually a much larger demand for owner carry properties because more people can qualify for the financing you are providing for them.* This means you can charge top dollar for the property (and many times a little over top dollar) and get it since anytime you limit supply and increase demand value increases—simply economics!

2) **Lowers Your Expenses** – Again since your property stands out from the competition you usually won't need any agent involved in the sale which saves you up to 6 percent of a sales commission. Plus, since your buyer has such limited options available, they are more than willing to pay all the closing costs. This saves you a few more thousand dollars on the sale!

3) **Faster Sale** – With such a valuable and scarce thing as an owner carry property you will usually be able to sell the property 30 to 50 percent faster than a traditionally retailed home.

4) **Fewer Lender Hassles** – Even if you have your buyer use conventional financing to fund a portion of the sale, since you are carrying back a chunk of the financing yourself, this makes it much easier for your buyer to secure their conventional financing. This means a much higher certainty of your buyer's loan sailing through without any snags or hassles.

*To download a FREE copy of the e-book, *"The Hidden Secrets of Seller Financing"* go to **www.QuickstartInvestor.com**.

How Your Local Market Affects Your Investing

"Now that I've walked you through the technical details of structuring your deals, I want to talk about the environment within which you are doing your investing. We call this environment your 'real estate market.' One critical distinction is that real estate markets are primarily local phenomena. Although regional and national events and trends influence your local real estate market, it is dominated by local trends and circumstances.

"There are **three main real estate markets** you'll face as a real estate investor. Because real estate markets cycle, and your local market will experience all three types of markets, you will need to master the art of successfully investing in each of these three types of markets. **Hot markets** are markets in which real estate is going up, up, up. These markets are characterized by strong appreciation rates, often in double digits, and a supply-and-demand imbalance where there just aren't enough homes to keep pace with the current demand. **Medium markets** are slow and steady areas of consistent growth. Appreciation in these areas tends to be between 4 and 7 percent per year, and there tends to be a healthy balance between the demand for housing and the available supply. **Mild markets** are often called 'buyer's markets.' These are markets where there is an oversupply of housing available and sellers face long wait times to unload their properties. In mild markets, housing values tend to remain flat or may even be declining.

"Let's get one thing straight: You can make money in *any* type of market. Many other investors have before you. The key is to know what type of market you are investing in and adjust your buying and selling strategies accordingly.*

"In a hot market you are going to have fewer deals to buy. However, with the strong appreciation and high demand for property, the properties you already own and the new property you are acquiring will make you a lot more per deal.

"In a hot market you typically are buying for time. This means any way you can acquire a property at or below value in a hot market that requires very little of your own money and in which the payments are low enough that you can make it cash flow while you hold onto it for a few years, you are going to come out of it way ahead.

"The key thing in a hot market is to realize that this is the riskiest market of all to buy for cash or with a bank loan.

"The reason that this is so is because you never can tell how long a hot market will stay hot. The market could be tipped by rising interest rates, by a major em-

---

*If you are not sure what kind of market you are investing in, use our powerful online diagnostic tool, The Quickview Market Evaluator,™ to quickly determine your local market type and how to most effectively adjust your investing strategies to consistently profit in your specific market. It's available free to readers at **www.QuickstartInvestor.com**.

ployer in the area going bust, or any one of a number of factors. And if you are buying for cash or with a conventional bank loan, you might not be able to wait out any downturn in the market.

"I want all of you to learn to do your investing the right way, with sound fundamentals. If you do it the way we are teaching you, rarely will you get caught in a spot from which you can't step back. I've personally bought a lot of houses from investors who got caught up in the excitement of a market and didn't remember that you make your profit in a deal, not when you sell, but when you buy.

"So the bottom line for a hot market is that if you are buying for all cash to the seller then you need a cash price—at least 25–30 percent under the current market value. If you are buying on terms, then don't worry so much about price. Instead go after a monthly payment that will give you a cushion of cash flow, and go after a long term.

"My favorite two buying strategies in a hot market is to buy either subject to the seller's existing loan or to buy on a long-term lease option. Both of these strategies can be utilized in a hot market to reap huge profits with very little cash or risk.

"Now, if you are investing in a medium market, then you have a stable, steady growth to rely on. However, if you are buying on terms and the property is only appreciating at 3 to 5 percent per year, you are going to need to find one more strong sweetener to make the deal a keeper. This could be negotiating 12 to 20 percent off the purchase price you are paying so you build some equity in from day one. This could be negotiating a lower monthly payment to the seller so that the property cash flows well over the years. The key is to find a way to build a more substantial profit cushion in the deal to be safe. The biggest mistake I watch investors make in a medium market is giving too much to the seller when negotiating and not have the deal be a win-win.

"As for a slow market, the key here is to remember to pick and choose carefully because you'll have a ton of sellers willing to practically give you their houses when you use the strategies and techniques we're teaching you. The biggest mistake I watch investors make in a mild market is getting excited by all the sellers who are willing to do a deal and taking too many deals all at once when some aren't really smart deals.

"Remember that in a cold market you don't just need a motivated seller who is desperate to sell; you need a seller with a situation that will also allow you to make a conservative profit on the deal you are structuring. Usually this means one of two things. Either the seller has some equity in the property and you can negotiate a winning price, or the seller's financing is attractive, so taking over the property will still allow you to make a healthy cash flow.

"Again I want to make sure that you understand that investors make a lot of money in all three of these markets. For example, many of you know that John, one of the coaches in our Mentorship Program, does most of his investing in a very hot market. In the last six months he's purchased three apartment buildings and five houses using exactly these ideas. Another example is Jeannie, in southern California. At the height of the market, she averaged more than six deals a year with an average profit of well over $60,000 per deal.

"Of course, in those same cities there were many other wannabe investors crying about how the market was too hot to find any good deals. As you can imagine, they were right. The market, when combined with their limiting beliefs about the market, was too tough for them to remain true to their dreams, and they quit. Remember, right now in your home town, some other investor is making a lot of money investing. Why not you?

"So which market is the best one to invest in? The answer is *all* of them. Personally I prefer investing right before a market takes off into a hot phase, but there is really no reliable way to accurately predict this. Also, it's not something you control. I don't want you to look at real estate as a function of being in the right market at the right time. Instead, I want to empower you with the skills and knowledge base to capitalize on the advantages of any market while mitigating the risks in those types of markets. The key is to understand that you can make a consistent profit in any market because you are intelligently *investing* not indiscriminately speculating.

"So just what is the difference between investing and speculating? Well speculating means buying a property with no profit margin built in from day one, and hoping that the property goes up in value so that you can sell it for a profit down the road. Most speculators end up losing. They're like the gambler who walks into Vegas and lays down a big bet on Red Seven. Now, the gambler may come out a big winner, but someone is paying for all those fancy lights on the Vegas strip!

"Instead, I want you to be like the casinos because no matter what time of year, they are making money. When you learn the basics of investing you can make them work in any market. Obviously this will take some effort on your part to master the fundamentals, but the reward is a lifetime of profit from your investing.

"When you are an investor you build a profit into the deal from the day you put it under contract. I don't want you guessing or wondering if you'll make a profit. I want you to *know* you will. For example, in a medium market you may pick up a property with $35,000 of equity the day you buy it and have a tenant already lined up for the property who will be paying you $275 more per month than the monthly payments. Or in a hot market you could be buying for full price, but doing it with very little money down and the owner financing the purchase for five years with payments that cash flow. Or in a cold market you may find a seller who just wants you to stop the foreclosure he is struggling with so that he can walk away from the property with his credit intact. In exchange for you making up $6,000 of back payments the seller deeds you the home, and you now have a solid investment property with 20 percent equity and a great loan already in place.

"The common thread for all investors is that they understand that they make their profit when they buy; they harvest their equity when they sell; they grow their net worth when they reinvest."

CHAPTER SIX

Negotiating Win-Win Deals with Sellers

P eter began. "Cheryl and I are going to be sharing with you the core negotiating system that we've developed over the past decade to help you get sellers to say yes to your offers. **It's called the Instant Offer System and it's without question the most powerful and simple format to enable you to successfully negotiate any real estate deal.** The best part of all this will be that once you get these five simple steps down, you will be able to use them over and over again. I've used them for every deal I've ever negotiated for the past ten years whether it was a single-family house, a foreclosure deal, or even a 200-unit apartment building."

"Rather than try to teach you hundreds of negotiating techniques, we're going to focus on these five key steps that you'll take, in the order that you'll take them, every time you meet with a seller of a property," Cheryl said. "And to further simplify things for you, all we are going to ask is for you to memorize five bridge questions that lead you into each of the five steps in the correct order."

"But if you think it's time for you to settle back into a passive mode, guess again," Peter said. "We're going to explain each of the five steps, demo them, and then get you actually role playing each step—chunk by chunk. Just in case you need it, your motivation is that two days from now you'll *all* be teamed up with one or two other students from this training and you'll be meeting with one or two sellers at their properties. These are the exact same steps that you'll take them through when you are out in the field negotiating with these sellers. Let's start at the beginning with step number one." With that Peter turned and wrote on the board:

The Instant Offer System

Step 1 Building Rapport with the Seller

"The heart of any negotiation is the affinity and trust you build with the other party. We call this **building rapport**," Peter said.

"This step," Cheryl said, "is critical. When I look back at many of the deals I've put together, I think rapport really was the key. For example, on one of the houses I bought early on in my investing career, the sellers, an elderly couple, not only sold me a house with them carrying back 50 percent of the financing as a second mortgage, but they also gave me an extra lot of land as part of the sale for free. Why did they want to make sure the deal was a win for me too? Because we built a strong relationship in which they knew I was going to take care of their most important needs, which in this case was to give them a simple sale and to actually be the scapegoat for them needing to ask their adult son to move out of the property he had been living in without paying rent for a long time."

Peter added, "That's such a key point, Cheryl, that I want to reinforce it. **The way you build deep affinity and trust in any relationship is to really listen for what the other party's needs are and honor them by doing your best to help them get those needs met in a way that wins for you too.** I like to think that you're a *consultant* who asks enough questions to help the seller figure out a fair and advantageous solution to a real estate problem they are facing. What makes this type of consultative approach work is the relationship you build with the seller. And this is why building rapport is so critical."

"Now, imagine you are in your car, pulling up to the front drive of a seller's house. You get out of the car and walk to the front door. You reach out and ring the bell. Time seems to slow. As you wait, your heart is racing. Just when you thought you couldn't wait any longer, the door opens, and there you are, face to face with the seller." Students in the room could imagine the tension and anxiety of standing there on their first appointment. "Don't worry though," Cheryl continued, "because you have a winning game plan for meeting with the seller—the Instant Offer System or IOS for short. It's at this point that you use the first 'Bridge Question' to start step one of the IOS—building rapport with the seller. Here's that first Bridge Question," Cheryl said, writing on the board:

Bridge Question

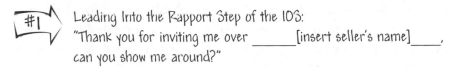

#1 Leading Into the Rapport Step of the IOS:
"Thank you for inviting me over _____[insert seller's name]____,
can you show me around?"

Peter and Cheryl went on to explain and demo the first step of the Instant Offer System, then split everyone up in pairs to role play through this step themselves. Vicki found herself paired up with Mark again. Before she began, she mentally gave herself a pep talk. *"Just use the first bridge question and then as he shows me around the house find things we have in common and allow him the chance to open up and share about his life. Look for places where I can genuinely admire and esteem him. Keep the conversation focused on him personally and off real estate. Remember, the Rapport Step is about building a relationship and not about discussing the defects or merits of the property."*

As they began the role play Vicki had to admit to herself that she didn't mind partnering with Mark again. There was something about him that she found appealing. Maybe it was his easy manner and soft humor.

"Mark, thank you for inviting me over, can you show me around your house?" Vicki and Mark laughed as he began to show her around the imaginary house there at the workshop.

"This is the living room," Mark said waving his hand through the air hamming it up a bit.

"How long have you lived in the house, Mark?"

"About six years. My ex and I bought the place when my second daughter was born. We really loved the neighborhood."

"How old are your kids now?" Vicki asked.

"My oldest daughter is nine and my youngest is turning six in a few weeks."

"That's great Mark. I have two kids myself, seven and nine. What do you like doing for fun with your kids?"

Mark answered immediately, "Just about anything. I just love being around them. With the divorce, though, it's been tough not being able to spend as much time with them as I've wanted over the past year and a half. I really miss them."

Vicki could see that Mark wasn't just making this part up, he was really sharing about his life, just as she was. She felt a compassion and connection with Mark thinking how much they had in common. "It can really be hard, I know. I finished my divorce about three years ago, and things are very different now. I have to share with you that I admire how obvious it is that you really care about and love your daughters. My ex only finds time to see them every other month or so and I know how important a father is to his children."

"Thank you for noticing that. They do mean the world to me. I'm sorry your ex-husband doesn't see it that way," Mark replied.

"What is it you do for work Mark?" Vicki asked.

"I'm a pilot for one of the major airlines; been doing that for about eighteen years now. I also just started to do some investing in real estate myself a few weeks ago." They both started to laugh when he said this.

After a short while, Cheryl stopped them and brought them all back together to discuss the role play.

"Good work on building rapport. How many of you who were the sellers in this role play found yourself liking and trusting the person you were partnered with?" Vicki was relieved to see that Mark was one of the many people with his hand up.

Cheryl continued, "That's what step 1 is all about—quickly building a bond of trust and friendship with the seller."

"In a moment we're going to go through step 2 of the IOS, but first I need to emphasize that building rapport is not just a step you take care of up front and then tick it off your mental checklist and never think about it again," Peter said. "You're going to have to monitor the interaction with every seller and remember that it's your job to maintain that feeling of rapport throughout the entire negotiation. One of the reasons our students tend to do so well in their negotiating is that they do it in such a friendly and soft way. This really stands out when you com-

IOS Step 1 Summary—Rapport

Bridge Question:
"Thank you for inviting me over, can you show me around?"

Key Goals:
1) Make a friend
2) Create an affinity for and connection with the seller
3) Develop trust and rapport with the seller

Key Learning Points:
1) Focus on the seller, not the house
2) Build bridges of commonality with the seller
3) Sincerely compliment and esteem the seller (if appropriate)
4) Spend from five to ten minutes on this step before moving on to Step 2

pare it to the way most other investors go in there and negotiate in a heavy handed and adversarial manner. If you were a seller who was feeling a little intimidated or scared selling your house, who do you think you would want to work with? The hard charging, aggressive investor, or the nice, friendly one who really listened to your needs and cared about you? Obviously you'd want to work with the latter person."

"Where's Donna?" Cheryl asked. A woman in her late forties raised her hand in the back left of the room. "For those of you who didn't know, Donna is one of our graduate Mentorship students who came back for a refresher course. At the break Donna shared with me how on her third deal the seller literally sold her two houses in Los Angeles for 60 percent of their value even though the seller had a slightly higher offer from another investor. The seller told her that she liked Donna better and felt the other investor not only didn't care about her but was also rude and aggressive in his tone with her. The approach we're sharing with you works miracles. I've seen it in my own investing. I can't begin to tell you the number of houses I've bought where the seller and I came to really just love being with each other."

"So now you've built rapport and are ready to move to the second step of the IOS—setting an up-front agreement with the seller," Peter said. "**An up-front agreement is where you get the seller to agree that at the end of your time**

together they will let you know clearly where they stand, either yes, this is a fit for them to move forward in the deal, or no, it's not a fit for them. The key is to get this agreement up front before you spend all that time with the seller. Here's the trade-off you are making: you are willing to spend all the time necessary with the seller, asking questions and listening to the seller's needs, but only if the seller agrees that at the end he will give you a clear, unambiguous decision about whether he wants to move forward in the deal or not. This is being respectful to both your needs. You won't pressure the seller for a yes, but you will hold the seller accountable to give you a yes or no. Let's role play this for everyone Cheryl. You be the investor and I'll be the seller."

"Okay. Now, to move into step 2 of the IOS I'm going to need a bridge question" Cheryl said. "And here is my bridge question to get from step one, Rapport, into step two, the *Up-Front Agreement* . . ." Cheryl wrote for a moment on the board.

Bridge Question

 "Where's a good place for us to sit and talk this through?"

"Ready Peter?" Cheryl asked.

"Yep!"

"Okay. So Peter, where's a good place we can go and sit and talk this through?" Cheryl asked using the bridge question into step 2 of the IOS.

"How about right here at the kitchen table?"

"Great," Cheryl answered sitting on the stool up at the front of the room. "Now Peter, I don't know if any of the things we'll talk about will end up working for you or not. If the things we talk through are clearly *not* a fit for you, would you be willing to let me know?"

"Yes. I'll be very willing to tell you no."

"That's good Peter. On the other hand, if what we talk through *is* a fit for you, are you okay telling me that?"

"Yes."

"Great. I'll be doing the same thing. If things aren't going to work for me where I feel I can meet your needs and make a conservative profit I'll let you know that I don't want to buy your house. On the other hand, if I see that I can meet your needs and make a conservative profit then at the end of our time together I'll tell you that, yes, I do want to buy your house. The one thing I am going to ask Peter is this: I promise to let you know when we're done either, yes, I want to move forward with this deal or, no, I don't, and I am asking you for the same courtesy in return. Is that fair?" Cheryl asked.

"That sure seems fair to me."

"Good, I'm glad you feel the same as me. So what we've agreed to do is let each other know at the end either yes it's a fit or no it's not a fit."

Cheryl stopped and looked at the room of students. "And that my friends is the up-front agreement. The bottom line is that it just means getting the seller to agree to give you a decision at the end of your time together so you don't end up with the infamous, 'I'll think it over.'"

Cheryl and Peter went on to explain their exact choice of words and several of the subtleties about how to make the up-front agreement most effective. Then they had each of the students pair up and try doing this step themselves. Vicki again found herself paired up with Mark and managed to limp her way through the language by referring back to her notes a lot. But she realized that, with some practice, she would be able to do this herself when she was meeting with a seller.

SUMMARY

> ## IOS Step 2 Summary—Up Front Agreement
>
> **Bridge Question:**
> *"Where's a good place to sit and talk this through?"*
>
> **Key Goals:**
> **1)** Get a strong commitment from the seller that he will give you a clear, unambiguous answer—yes or no—by the end of your time together.
>
> **Key Learning Points:**
> **1)** Always refer to your time with the seller as a "visit" or "conversation" and not a "negotiation."
> **2)** Always start with asking if the seller would be comfortable telling you "no" first, then and only then ask if they would be wiling to tell you "yes."
> **3)** Reinforce the up-front agreement by restating what you have both just agreed to.

"Time to move on to step 3 of the Instant Offer System," Cheryl announced from the front of the room. The role playing took a moment to die down as everyone went back to their seats. "The third step is the **Motivation Step. This is where you help the seller emotionally connect with his reasons for needing to sell and his limited time in which to do it.**"

Peter smiled and said, "So what do you all think we need to get us from the up-front agreement step into the Motivation Step? Another bridge question! And here is your bridge question to lead you into the Motivation Step." Peter turned and wrote on the board.

Bridge Question

"So what were you hoping I could do for you here today?"

"Now, this question is deceptively simple. And when you ask it, 9 times out of 10 the seller will simply respond with, 'Buy my house.' But it is a simple and effective transition to ease into the Motivation Step. You have three goals with the Motivation Step. **First**, to help the seller emotionally connect with why he needs to sell. **Second**, to help eliminate the seller's other options so that he is left recognizing that you are his best option. And **third**, to flush out the seller's real time line to sell in such a way that the seller recognizes a sense of urgency with handling his property. That's a pretty tall order, but with time you'll be able to learn to do this consistently during the Motivation Step."

Cheryl added, "One of the biggest mistakes I see students make is rushing through the Motivation Step. When you do it right you will spend up to half an hour or more with the seller slowly building the seller's motivation.

"Peter and I are going to role play the Motivation Step. I'll be the investor and Peter will be the seller."

Cheryl started into the role play. "So Peter, what were you hoping I could do for you today?"

"Well, buy my house."

Two Fundamental Negotiating Skills All Investors Must Master

There are two fundamental negotiating techniques you'll need to learn to become successful with your investing. In fact, these two techniques will often make the difference between success or failure in your negotiations with sellers.

Technique One: Reluctant Buyer

In any negotiation with a seller, one party wants the deal more than the other party. You want to always position yourself as the reluctant buyer so that the seller is naturally put into the role of selling you on any prospective deal. You do this by using the reluctant-buyer technique.

Being a reluctant buyer puts you in the strongest negotiating position of all. It works so well because it taps into the seller's fear of loss, which is one of the strongest drives in all of us.

Reluctant buyers use specific language patterns over and over again. Of these language patterns, the most common call for you to qualify any of the statements you make to a seller about your interest in moving forward in a deal.

Examples of reluctant-buyer language patterns:

'I don't know if I will be able to do this or not but...'

'My partner may hate this idea, but what if...'

'With all that's going on in the world today I'm not even sure now is the time to buy another investment property, may I ask you a couple of questions first to see if this is even a property that I would want to buy?'

Being a reluctant buyer means you are structuring your negotiation so that the seller is constantly being put in the role of selling you on the idea of making a deal happen.

Technique Two: Negative Phrasing

The second technique that is so powerful for you to tap into is called "negative phrasing." Remember that most sellers are scared when they are selling their house. For most of them it's the single biggest asset they own. So in order to protect themselves, sellers will look for what's wrong with any prospective offer. In fact, it's been our experience, and the collective experience of over 100,000 of our best investor clients, that sellers are more motivated by the fear of loss and being taken advantage of than they are by the desire to make a profit when they are selling their houses.

When sellers are motivated by the fear of making a mistake and looking for what's wrong they do something called "mismatching." Mismatching means the

(continued)

Two Fundamental Negotiating Skills (continued)

seller will say or think the opposite of many of the things you assert. For example, if you say the price is too high, they'll say it's too low. If you tell them that the property management company they are using is mismanaging the property, they will argue with you that the property management company is doing a fine job.

This brings us to one of the most powerful negotiating techniques available to you. It's called "negative phrasing." Negative phrasing is a way to tap into this tendency of the seller to mismatch what you say and give the perceived power in the situation back over to the seller in a way that increases the seller's comfort level in the negotiation.

Example One of negative phrasing used with a seller:

Investor: What have you already tried to sell the property?
Seller: I've been selling it for sale by owner now for the past several months.
Investor: Oh, and that's been working real well? [Negative phrasing]
Seller: No, not really. I've only got one serious buyer so far.
Investor: May I ask you, when are you planning on closing on the sale of the house with them?   [Negative phrasing]
Seller: Well I'm not actually sure if they are really going to buy it or not.
Investor: Oh, well when does the written agreement you have with them say they will close by? [Negative phrasing]
Seller: Actually we haven't put anything in writing yet.
Investor: Oh, then they'll be coming back sometime this week with their written offer? [Negative phrasing]
Seller: No, I don't think they are even interested in buying it from me anymore.

Example Two:

Investor: You probably hated that idea, huh? [Negative phrasing]
Seller: No I didn't hate it.
Investor: Yeah but it's probably not something you want to even bother talking through, right? [Negative phrasing]
Seller: Actually I think we should talk that idea through and explore the possibility.

The real key with negative phrasing is to soften both your voice and body language when you use it so that you come across as naïve or optimistic rather than sarcastic or condescending.

"Would you mind sharing with me what you have already tried so far to sell the house?" Cheryl asked.

"I had it listed with a real estate agent for a bit. And then for the last two months I've been selling it for sale by owner."

Cheryl stepped out of the role play and turned to the students in the room. "Peter has shared two openings for me to explore about what he's tried to do in the past to sell. My job is to flesh out each of these openings and any others that come up so that I can help him emotionally connect with the fact that nothing is working very well. Now if I come right out and say to him, 'Peter, nothing you're doing is working very well' he's going to get very defensive. That's why I'll be using negative phrasing to allow him to voice how poorly these options are working and to eliminate them *himself* as viable options. See if you can see how I let him reinforce certain of his answers by selectively not hearing them and asking him to repeat them. Also, pay attention to how I'll be proceeding slowly in my pace of speech and in the questions I ask so that, at any point along the way, the seller feels confident that he's smarter than me and that he's the one in control. Remember that sellers are more motivated by the fear of loss and making a mistake than they ever are by the desire to make a profit, so if you come into the negotiation and try to dazzle them with your intellect and sophistication, they will be very cautious and guarded. And a cautious, guarded seller simply won't allow themselves to emotionally connect with their reasons for selling the property. Instead, we want you to put the seller at ease by playing dumb. Remember dumb gets paid!" Everyone laughed at Cheryl's joke, but they had to admit it made sense.

Turning back to Peter and sitting down Cheryl said, "So you tried listing with an agent for a while . . . and that worked out well?"

"It worked okay I guess, but the house just didn't sell."

"May I ask you a question? Why didn't you accept any of the written offers the agent brought you on the house?" Cheryl scrunched up her face in a confused look as she asked this question.

"Actually we didn't have any written offers from the agent."

"I'm sorry," Cheryl said leaning forward and cocking her head, "I didn't catch that."

"I said we didn't get any offers from the agent."

"Oh . . . But what happened out of all the advertising and showings the agent did each weekend? You must have had a ton of people out here for those open houses?"

"Not really. The agent did an open house a few times, but truthfully, she didn't really get too many people out to any of them."

Scrunching up her face in confusion and allowing her voice to get softer at the end Cheryl asked, "Why do you think that was?"

"I don't know. As you can see the house looks great. I've worked pretty hard getting it all cleaned up and ready to show. I don't really think the agent did everything she should have to advertise the property."

"Really? Why do you think the ads the agent placed in the paper and the signs they put out around the neighborhood didn't work too well?"

"I don't think she did any of that. I mean, she had it advertised in the paper a few weekends that I could see, but I think all she did by way of advertising was to put the sign out front and put it in the MLS. She really didn't do enough to get the house exposed."

"Oh, okay, and how long did you have the property listed with this agent?" Cheryl asked.

"We had it listed with her for three months."

Cheryl thought for a moment before asking, "Well, since this agent knows the property now, have you thought about relisting the property with her for another three months or six months? I'm sure she would do a better job this second time."

"No we're not going to relist it with her."

"How about relisting it with another agent, maybe one of the other agents in her office?"

"No, we're not going to list it with another agent. I've had my fill of agents."

Cheryl leaned forward and shook her head for a moment, "I'm sorry, I must have spaced for a moment, what was that you said?"

Peter said louder this time, "I'm not going to list the property with another agent. I'm tired of all these agents as it is."

"Oh, okay, that makes sense."

Peter turned to the audience and said, "Did you all see how Cheryl used negative phrasing and selective hearing to help me very firmly declare that I wasn't going to list the property again? Notice how she didn't tell me how poorly listing the property had worked out. She used negative phrasing to let me come back and mismatch her by telling her all the things that didn't work about it. And then she let me repeat myself at two critical spots so that I could reinforce the conclusions that she had help lead me to."

Cheryl and Peter finished off role playing through the Motivation Step for another ten minutes, at which point they again paired up each of the students and got them role playing through the step themselves.

Vicki and Mark were in their second time through the role play when they noticed that Cheryl had come around to listen in and give feedback to them.

Mark, who was playing the part of the seller said, "At this point I've been driving back down each weekend to show the property."

Vicki found herself getting nervous with Cheryl watching, but she recognized how valuable any coaching would be for her so she kept going as best she could, "How long of a drive is it?"

"About an hour, hour and a half." Mark replied.

"That's a long way to drive each weekend. That must really get tiring doing it each week."

At this point Cheryl paused their role play to give Vicki some feedback. "Vicki, great job in your body language. You're doing it just like we showed you. One piece of coaching I have for you is on negative phrasing. It was obvious that you spotted the motivation Mark felt over driving down each weekend so far. And I could see that you wanted to emphasize that with Mark by pointing out how much of a pain that must be. What you may find is that a real seller would get defensive over that and say that it wasn't a big deal for them, and then you'd lose the value of that as a spur to the seller's motivation. Instead, I want you to go back into your role play to your response to Mark saying he drives down to show it each weekend, and that his drive is about ninety minutes, only this time I want you to try it a different way and see what happens."

Cheryl leaned over and whispered into Vicki's ear. Vicki listened and nodded. "I've got it Cheryl."

Vicki took a deep breath and turned to Mark, "Well I guess the good thing is Mark that you're lucky that you're close enough to come back each weekend to show the property. I mean, a lot of people aren't so lucky as that. At least for you it's no big deal to keep coming back each weekend even if it takes a while to find the right buyer."

"Well I'm hoping it won't take too many more trips down. They do get to be a bit disruptive on any plans I had."

"Disruptive?" Vicki said, mirroring the scrunchy expression that Cheryl had used earlier, "Tell me about that."

"Perfect Vicki!" Cheryl congratulated her. "Do you see how you were able to make your point but do it in a way that Mark was the one who actually voiced it? Keep up the great work."

As Cheryl went off to listen in to the next pair, Vicki felt so encouraged. She had been struggling with getting the language right but now she realized that with some practice she would be able to master all this. It was big relief to her. She and Mark got right back into their role playing.

IOS Step 3 Summary—Motivation

Bridge Question:
"So what were you hoping I could do for you?"

Key Goals:
1) To help the seller emotionally connect with his reasons for selling and the time pressure he feels.
2) To eliminate in the seller's mind competing options.

Key Learning Points:
1) Be a reluctant buyer.
2) Use negative phrasing.
3) Reinforce key points with selective hearing.

"It's time to move into step 4 of the Instant Offer System—the *Money Step*," Peter said. "All too often new investors, and a lot of old ones for that matter, want to talk about the money right away. They knock on the seller's door and it's like, 'Hi, I'm the investor you talked with on the phone. How much did you want for you house?' No time building rapport. No time listening to the seller's needs and situation. That's a self-centered and ineffective way of negotiating with a seller. Remember this expression, it's the one of the most important keys to putting together a fair and profitable deal." Peter turned and wrote on the board—

MOTIVATION before MONEY

"If you picked up just this one negotiating insight as a result of being here, you would have paid for your time and effort to be here a hundred-fold. It took me years to really learn how to apply this idea of building a seller's motivation before I went on to talk about the money, and the result has literally meant tens of millions of dollars of profits for me and for our students." Peter paused for a moment, and then continued, "Okay, now that we've made it clear how important the motivation step is, and that it has to come before you talk about any of the financial aspects of a potential deal, let's move on and talk about the money."

"The Money Step is the fourth step of the Instant Offer System," Cheryl said. "And we need something to take us from the Motivation Step into the Money Step. I bet you all can tell me what we need, can't you? A bridge question!" Cheryl smiled.

"Your bridge question to lead you into the Money Step is . . ." Cheryl turned and wrote on the board—

Bridge Question

 "So what was it you were asking for the property again?"

Your goal with the Money Step is to gather up all the financial details on the property that you'll need to craft a win-win fit with the seller of the property, and to gather this information in a way that *lowers* the seller's expectations. I know that's a pretty tall order, but as you'll see when Cheryl and I role play this step for you, we've scripted out the most effective language for you to use."

"I'll be playing the role of you, the investor," Cheryl said. "I want you to pay attention to the '3 R's' that I'll be using to lower Peter's expectations about price."

Using the 3 R's to Dramatically Lower the Price

1) Range Technique: Anytime the seller mentions a number in the negotiation, turn that number into a range that stretches the seller in your favor. It's a powerful way to test out the seller's real limits. After all, if the seller objects to the range you use, you can always shrink the range.

Example One
Investor: How much were you asking for the property again?
Seller: $350,000.
Investor: Oh, okay…you were asking $340 to $350,000, got it…

Example Two
Investor: What's the longest length of time you would be willing to wait to get completely cashed out of the property?
Seller: Three years.
Investor: Really? Three to four years is the longest you'd be willing to wait?

2) "Realistic" Technique: Ask the seller what she "realistically" expects to get. This question presupposes that both you and the seller know that the seller would accept less than the asking price. The key is to have your voice pitch drop lower when you say the word "realistically," just like you want the price to drop.

Example
Seller: I was asking $350,000.
Investor: What did you realistically expect to get?
Seller: I was thinking I'd get at least $340,000 maybe $345,000.

3) Real Estate Agent Technique: This third technique has you using an imaginary real estate agent to save you six percent on the purchase price. It works by you asking the seller if they would allow a hypothetical real estate agent to sell the house for them at the price you've been discussing if they knew the agent could get the deal done in thirty days or less. If the seller says yes to this question, she is tacitly agreeing that she would accept six percent less than the sales price, since this is the cost of the sales commission for an agent to sell the property on her behalf.*

*For more detailed training on negotiating profitable win-win deals go to **www.QuickstartInvestor.com**.

Cheryl and Peter then went into their role play of the Money Step.

"Well Peter, how much was it that you were asking for the property?" Cheryl asked.

"$350,000."

Cheryl nodded her head up and down and said, "$340, $350,000, Okay—and what did you *realistically* expect to get for the property?" When Cheryl said the word *realistically* her voice pitch dropped lower.

"Well I realistically expected to get around $340,000, maybe even $345,000."

Cheryl responded using the scrunchy face expression, "Really? So you *did* expect to get $330 to $340,000—"

Peter interrupted her, "Not $330,000, I'd say $340,000 to $345,000."

"Pardon," Cheryl responded. "You realistically expected to get $335,000 to $345,000."

"Yeah, I guess I could take as little as $335,000." Peter said, playing the role of a motivated seller.

Again Cheryl paused, thinking for a moment. "You know Peter . . . a thought just occurred to me. If a real estate agent came to you and said they could get the house sold for you in the next 30 days, and you knew they could do it, I mean, in your heart of hearts you knew they could get it sold in the next 30 days, maybe even for that full $335,000, you'd probably turn them down, huh? Or maybe not?"

Peter thought about what Cheryl said and said, "No, I guess I'd probably take that just to be done with it."

"You'd *probably* take it?" Cheryl obviously wanted a firmer answer from the seller.

"Yeah I'd take it."

Cocking her head and leaning forward as if she didn't hear, "I'm sorry?"

"Yes! I'd take it." Peter said louder and firmer this time.

"Oh, okay, that makes sense. Let's see 6 percent of $335,000 . . . 6 percent of $100,000 is $6,000, and we have three of those . . ." Cheryl mumbled to herself as she figured out the math.

"The commission would be around $20,000." Peter supplied the answer for her.

"Okay. Thanks. So let's see . . . $335,000 minus $20,000 . . . that would be . . . I'm getting $315,000, is that what you're coming up with?" Cheryl asked.

"Yeah, that's right."

Stepping out of the role play, Peter said, "Did you all see how quickly and easily Cheryl got me to come down by $35,000 in my price? She didn't beat me up over price or get too aggressive. She merely used three powerful language patterns in quick succession to radically lower my expectations on price. This lower number has become the new starting point for any further negotiation over price. Let's get back into our role play."

"You mind if I take some notes here? I'm having a hard time keeping all this stuff straight," Cheryl asked.

"Sure, go ahead. Here's a pad of paper for you." Peter slid a tablet over to Cheryl.

"So let's see, the full amount is $315,000." Cheryl said writing that number and just that number on the tablet where Peter could see her doing it. "The full amount is $315,000. Got it . . . and what was it you owed against the property?"

"I have a first mortgage of $290,000."

"And the payments on that are . . . ?" Cheryl left the question hanging.

"$2,100 per month."

"And does that include the property taxes and insurance?" Cheryl asked.

"Yes, it includes everything."

Cheryl stopped and looked at the audience. "And that's the Money Step. You work through the financial details all the way down to this lowered 'full amount' price, the amount owed, and the payment information on the loan or loans."

SUMMARY

IOS Step 4 Summary—Money

Bridge Question:
"What was it you were asking for the property again?"

Key Goals:
1) Draw out the financial details of the property.
2) Lower the seller's expectations of price and terms.

Key Learning Points:
1) Use the 3 R's to lower the price.
2) Only write down the price after you've got it lowered by the 3 R's.
3) Verbally label this lowered price as the "full amount."

Peter went on to explain exactly how they were supposed to use the language patterns of the Money Step and why these specific techniques were so powerful. After that he and Cheryl got the group role playing through the step themselves.*

Nancy was role playing through the Money Step with Mary when Peter walked by and started to listen in.

Nancy, who was playing the investor role, was saying, "So let's see, when we take the 6 percent commission off the $300,000 that leaves us with . . . uhm . . . I'm coming up with $282,000." Nancy paused and wrote on her notepad. "So the full price was $282,000."

Peter stepped in to give Nancy some coaching. "Nancy, great job on doing the math slowly so that your seller would feel comfortable with it. One tweak I'm going to ask you to make is on the label for the $282,000. I notice that you called it the 'full price.' What do you think the seller originally thought of when you said 'full price'?"

"I guess she thought of the $320,000 that she started with when I asked her the asking price," Nancy replied.

"Exactly!" Peter said. "The label of 'full price' already has something it's attached to, in this case $320,000. Instead of 'full price' use the label 'full amount'. Now it may seem a picky point, but the difference is important. 'Full amount' is a label that doesn't have anything attached to it until you link it to the $282,000. You might be thinking what's the difference. Well, in this case the difference is $38,000."

"Peter," Mary interrupted. "My first reaction when Nancy said full price as she wrote the $282,000 was, 'hey, wait a minute, the full price was much higher.' Now it makes sense to me why I was thinking that. When I hear you say 'full amount' and I imagine myself back in the role play, I don't think I would have flinched at her calling the $282,000 the full amount."

"Thanks for the feedback Peter. I don't think I ever would have noticed the difference if you hadn't pointed it out to me like that. May I ask you a question?"

"Sure, what is it?"

---

*Learning to negotiate is like learning a new language. To really become fluent, you've got to hear it spoken. That is why we have included some powerful online training on negotiation as part of the Quick-Start Real Estate Success Program. To access this training, just go to **www.QuickstartInvestor.com**.

"I'm having a hard time with the Motivation Step and all that negative phrasing and playing dumb stuff. I keep thinking to myself, 'Come on, get real.' The seller's going to get upset with me for being ingenious," Nancy said.

"I can understand your concern. You don't want to have the seller feeling you're being fake or condescending with them or using some technique. I will say that over the past fifteen plus years I've been using these techniques, I've never had a seller say to me, 'Come on Peter, stop using that negative phrasing stuff with me.' But you probably find that impossible to believe, huh?"

"No I don't find that impossible to believe—wait! You just used negative right there didn't you?"

"Actually I guess I did. I've been doing it so long it's a pretty hard habit to break at this point." The three of them were laughing now. "Here's the thing Nancy—if you're tone is sarcastic, then negative phrasing won't work. Instead, if you practice letting your tone be soft and confused or naïve as needed, then the techniques will work wonders for your investing, and they'll do it in a way that leaves the seller feeling whole and respected. It's going to take some time for you to get used to these techniques. Of course they'll feel like play acting at first. All I'm asking is that you struggle through them for the next 90 days. After that they'll become so normal and habitual for you that you won't even think about them again. They'll become part of your way of being when you're interacting with a seller. The result will be you'll become an incredibly effective and respectful negotiator. How does that sound to you?"

"It sounds pretty good. Thanks for your help on this."

Peter left Nancy and Mary to continue their role playing and went on to give other pairs input and coaching. After everyone finished their role playing, he brought everyone together.

"Time to get started on the last step of the Instant Offer System—the *What If Step*," Peter said. "This fifth and final step is **where you work to combine everything the seller has told you so far into an offer that meets the seller's biggest need and allows you to make a healthy profit too**. The key to this step is that when you put out ideas and potential solutions to the seller, you will never be committing to any of them until the seller has told you that, yes, that offer will work for them. When you master this step you'll learn that you'll never make an offer . . . you simply guide the conversation through potential ideas until you find one that the seller likes. At which point, you'll turn the solution into the seller's idea and then choose to accept their offer. How does this sound to all of you?" Peter smiled as he saw the disbelief in many of the students eyes.

"I know it may be hard to believe that it's actually possible to do all the things Peter is saying," Cheryl added. "Or that even if it were possible for Peter to do it, or one of us coaches to do it, it would never be possible for little old you to do it, just know that it is possible and you can do it. I remember five years ago when I first got started as a Mentorship student myself. This Instant Offer System was really a tough thing for me to follow. I was fine with the building rapport part. In fact, I used to build rapport for hours with the seller because I was scared to move to step two and beyond! But with time I swallowed my fears and ploughed through the language and scripting. At first it felt so fake and awkward. One day I went on an appointment and I said to myself, 'To heck with it! I'm going to toss the IOS out the window and just be myself.' I went in there and met with the seller and listened to her story. It went phenomenally well, I was in shock. When it was all over I realized that what I had actually done was just follow the Instant Offer System without even thinking about it. That's what will happen for you all. If you can just persevere in using the scripting and techniques for a few months of awkwardness, you'll soon reach a day when you've internalized it all and it flows out in *your* voice in a natural way.

"The bridge question that leads into this final step of the IOS is all contained in those two magic words—What If. These words just may be the most powerful words in any negotiation. They commit you to nothing, but they commit the other side to everything." Cheryl turned on the board and wrote . . .

Bridge Question

 Terms Deal:
"I don't know if I could do this or not, but what if I were to make you payments for a period of time, and at some point down the road I completely cashed you out of the property. Is that something we should even talk about, or probably not?"

"Peter and I are going to demonstrate step 5, then we'll go back through it chunk by chunk, and finally we'll give you the chance to try it out for yourselves."

Turning to Peter, who was playing the part of the seller, Cheryl said, "Peter, I don't know if this will work for you or not, you might hate this idea, and to be frank, I'm not sure if it would even work for me, but what if I were to cover your payments for a period of time, taking care of the property and day-to-day maintenance, and then at some point down the road I completely cashed you out of the property. Is that something we should even spend any time talking about, or probably not?"

"Yeah, we should definitely talk about it. How long of a period of time do you mean?" Peter responded.

"Well that depends on you. But before we even talk about that, can you help me with something? . . . Why would my covering your payments for a period of time and cashing you out of the property down the road even be a fit for you?" Cheryl said with a scrunched up face.

"Because it would allow me to relax about the double payments I have right now. Like I mentioned to you before, I've been able to cover both the payments on this place which is empty and my house in Orlando, but it's getting harder and harder to keep covering both of them."

"Oh, that makes sense. So if I'm hearing you right what you're telling me is that you want me to cover your payments and then cash you out down the road because that covers the double payments your dealing with?"

"Yes, but how long of a period of time are you saying?" Peter asked.

"Well I guess that would depend on you. My partner typically likes to go for a medium length of time like five to seven years, but you tell me. . . . What's the longest you'd be willing to go knowing that it has to work for you but it also has to work for me as an investor, and also understanding that the longer you're willing to go, the closer and closer I'm willing to come to that full $315,000 we talked about?" Cheryl took her time as she said all this and then quietly waited for Peter to answer.

"Five years."

"Really?" Cheryl said scrunching up her face. "Five or six years is the longest you'd be willing to go?"

"Well, I guess I could go six years, but no longer than that."

"Really? So going seven or eight years is out?" Cheryl asked.

"No way. The longest is six years."

Cheryl paused and thought about what Peter said, visibly struggling with his firmness on six years as the longest term. The audience could see her brow furrowed and her lips pressed tightly together. During this time Peter looked like he was willing her to accept his offer of six years, and the longer Cheryl struggled, the more it was obvious Peter wanted her to say yes. After what seemed like an eternity, but in reality was only 10–20 seconds, Cheryl looked up at Peter, slowly nodded, and slowly extended her hand and said, "Okay, you win, we'll do it for the six years." They shook hands, Cheryl looking a bit despondent and Peter looking very happy.

With that Peter stopped the role play and turned to the audience. "Did you all notice how Cheryl never jumped in and tried to sell me on the deal? Instead she laid back and played the reluctant buyer. She gave me credit for the idea of making payments over time, and in the end she gave all the nonverbal cues of having lost and my having won. Now all we have left is to pin down the details of how close she'll pay me to the full $315,000. By the way, how much of a discount in the price had Cheryl already negotiated off the original asking price of $350,000? $35,000 right? So even if she has to give in and give me my 'full amount' of $315,000 she's still got a terms deal of six years with payments of $2,100 per month and a locked in price that's about 90 percent of the asking price. Now, depending on the local market conditions, this could be an awesome deal or it may need some tweaking later to make it worth doing. If the market is a hot or medium market, then it's probably a killer deal. If it's a mild market, then we'll probably need a lower price and a lower rent potentially. The key is that Cheryl didn't have to beat me over the head to negotiate the deal. She just talked me through it step by step, giving me credit and letting me feel as though I was in control of the process. This is why the IOS works so well. It gives the feeling of control and power to the seller, while leaving you with an effective means to still get a great deal."

"So what happens if the seller rejects this what-if idea for a terms deal?" Peter asked. "So what, it isn't like you handed them a formal offer so they are rejecting you. They are simply saying the idea isn't a fit. Try another idea. Maybe an all-cash offer would be a better fit for them. In that case you use the all-cash offer bridge question."

"That's the beauty of the what-if phrasing. It lets you test out different ideas in a way that isn't perceived that you're making an actual offer."

IOS Step 5 Summary—What If

Bridge Question:

Terms Deals: *"I don't know if I could do this or not, but what if I were to cover your monthly payments for a period of time, taking care of the day-to-day maintenance, and at some point down the road I completely cashed you out of the property. Is that something we should even talk about, or probably not?"*

Cash Deals: *"Mr. Seller, I'm not sure if I could even get my partner to go along with this or not, but what if I could talk him into paying you an all-cash price for the property? Obviously we'd need to get a pretty steep discount off the full $__[insert full amount number]__ to make this work for us, but is this even something we should talk through? I mean you probably hate the idea, huh?"*

Key Goals:
1) To get a commitment from the seller that they like your what-if idea without you formally presenting an "offer" that they could accept or reject.
2) To reinforce why your what-if offer is so appealing to the seller by getting the *seller* to give you their reasons.
3) Pinning down the price and terms by the end of the step.

Key Learning Points:
1) Start with a broad, generic what-if and get the seller's initial approval.
2) Incrementally make your what-if more and more definite until you pin down the exact price and terms.
3) Give the seller credit for coming up with the idea on how to structure the deal.
4) Visibly struggle with the "seller's idea" of how they want to structure the deal… and then reluctantly accept it.

Peter and Cheryl went on to finish the role play and then went back through it piece by piece. Afterwards, they got the entire class paired up to role play through the step twice each. When the students had finished these two practice trials, Peter and Cheryl went back through and reviewed the entire Instant Offer System.*

---

*To download a 3″ × 5″ review card of the entire Instant Offer System that you can take with you to any appointments you have with sellers to help guide you along the process just go to **www.QuickstartInvestor.com**.

CHAPTER SEVEN

The Three Investor Levels— Your Proven Pathway to Real Estate Success

"When I first got started investing I really struggled to see past my desire to get my first few deals done," David said. "At rare moments I was able to dream of a steady flow of deals, but those dreams were vague and hazy in the beginning. But it's so powerful to have a clear picture of the destination you have in mind before you start any journey. Concise and precise goals are a great tool to help you reach your dreams.

"Right now I'd like to give you a detailed road map of where your investing business is going so that you know exactly what to shoot for from the beginning and as you grow. When we're done, you'll have a clear and accurate picture of where you want your investing business to go and the milestones and markers along the way. Peter and I call this model for your investing business the "Three Investor Levels."* Many of you are already aware that we've built our company on

---

*Because we felt this information is so important to help you truly succeed investing over the long term, we've made a live video recording of the key information of this chapter available for you to watch online. Just go to **www.QuickstartInvestor.com**.

this model so that we now provide you with investor support, training, and services as you progress through each level.

"First let's go through an overview of what the Three Investor Levels are and then we'll go back into each level in detail. When we're done, we will talk about how to accelerate your way through these levels so that you can begin to enjoy the rewards of each level right away.

"**Level One investing** is where we all start off. This is **where we have to prove to ourselves that real estate works**. And even more importantly, we have to prove that it doesn't just work for other people, but that real estate works for us.

"**Level Two investing is about mastering the five core investor skills, and learning to build a real estate investing business as distinct from just being a real estate investor.** Why is this so important? Because ultimately a real estate investor who doesn't learn how to leverage herself through building business systems and key team members is limited in two critical ways. First, she is limited in terms of the scale of projects and profits she can earn. Second, she is also limited in her potential to create time and lifestyle freedom for herself and her family. That's why it's so important to learn to build an investing business. In the end it's this investing business that will help you step into Level Three investing and enjoy a Level Three lifestyle. Now, while Level Two investors create healthy cash flows for themselves and increase their net worth significantly every year, Level Two investors are still actively tied to their investing business. They are the heart and engine that drives that investing business forward.

"Contrast this to Level Three investing. Level Three investors have mastered the art of building an investing business that works so they don't have to. If Level Two investors are the heart pumping their business forward, Level Three investors are the brain directing the big picture of the business and enjoying the consistent profits from that business, without getting caught up in any of the day-to-day activities for the business. The bottom line is that **Level Three investors have learned to put their investing on autopilot so they don't just make money, but they create *passive* cash flow.**

"Every investor starts out as a Level One investor with their biggest challenge being the need to prove to themselves that not only does real estate work, but that it really will work for them. Many of you, if you are being honest with yourselves,

Blueprint of the Three Investor Levels

Level One Investors: They've proven that real estate doesn't just work for other people, but that it works for them. And they have done this the most simple way—by making a profit on their first few real estate deals. Level One investors have the certainty that real estate will be their proven path to financial success. They know they still have a lot to learn, but they've seen that they can do it.

Level Two Investors: Level Two is all about mastering the five core skills of real estate investing and building an investing business to support their real estate portfolio.

Core Skills:*
  1) Creating a Deal-finding Machine
  2) Deal Analysis—How to Know You've Got the Right Deal
  3) Structuring Deals That Work for All Parties
  4) Negotiation—Getting the Other Side to Say YES!
  5) Contracts and Agreements—Understanding the "Language" of Real Estate

Level Two investors have created a positive cash flow of $5,000 to $50,000 per month, and an increase in their net worth $250,000 or more per year.

Level Three Investors: Imagine having built your real estate mini-empire in such a way that you earn massive income without having to be involved in the day to day direction of the business. Level Three investors earn at least as much as Level Two investors, but they do it passively. This means Level Three investors work less than ten hours per month. Their property portfolio and real estate business works without them needing to be there to run things.

Level Three investors know how to do BIG real estate deals on commercial real estate, how to convert excess cash into passive streams of income through joint venturing and lending, and how to build a stand alone business to support their real estate empire in a way that creates time freedom.**

*Book two of this *Creating Cash Flow* series will focus on how to master all five of these essential skills and successfully build your investing business. For information on the release of book two, go to **www.QuickstartInvestor.com**.

Book three of the *Creating Cash Flow* series will focus on how to create massive cash flow through commercial real estate and bigger deals. For more information on book three, go to **www.QuickstartInvestor.com.

would have to say that somewhere in the back of your mind you are still wondering whether you can really make your investing work.

"I remember back to when I went out on my first few appointments and I thought to myself that there was just no way I could do this thing. Sure, I told myself, other people could make money in real estate, but not little old me. I told myself I was too young. I wonder how many people say, 'If only I was older then I could do my real estate.' Or they say, 'If only I was younger, then I could do this.' Or 'if only I was more educated,' or 'if I wasn't just a housewife,' or 'if I had more time to devote to it,' or. . . . You get the picture. Let me make one thing clear: there is no better place than right here, and there is no better time than right now.

"We all have doubts when we get started. The only difference between someone who reaches Level Two investing and someone who doesn't is that the one who makes it actually got themselves to take action. You see, taking action is the key. Intelligent action, as I'll discuss in a minute, but action none the less.

"Maybe you're asking how many deals it's going to take for you to know, not just intellectually but deep in your gut, that real estate works for you. That answer is going to depend on you. Some of you will become a believer after your first or second deal. Others of you are pretty thick skulled and will need four or five deals before you prove to yourself that the first few deals weren't flukes. And some special individuals know from the very start, after a few weeks of doing the behaviors of successful investors, before they ever get the results, that real estate can and will work for them.

"To successfully move into Level Two with your investing you've got to get yourself started with Level One and that means getting yourself out of thinking mode and into action.

"Getting your first few deals is easy *if* you can keep your focus on the process and on your learning rather than becoming obsessed about the result. Over the past decade I've literally worked with over a hundred thousand beginning investors. During that time I've learned that in the beginning stages, the key is to focus on useful behaviors performed with a great attitude and learning along the way. Let go of the urgency to get your first deal and focus on the process. You do this and you will get your results, I guarantee it.

"There is one last tip to maximizing your Level One experience that deals with the other part of the key for Level One investing—the part about learning from the best.

Five Steps to Blast Through Level One as Quickly as Possible

Step 1.

Test out three different lead streams to find motivated sellers. The reason for you to test out these three lead sources fast is so that you can accomplish step two as quickly as possible.

Step 2.

Meet with three sellers about buying their houses. The point of meeting with these sellers isn't so you can buy their houses. The real point is so that you can do the scary thing—meeting with a motivated seller to negotiate to buy their property—and live to talk about it! Remember that old expression 'that which does not kill us makes us stronger'? We need you to get yourself on three appointments in the next 30 days. The reason going on these appointments is so critical is that the single biggest block for most would-be investors is simply the fear of talking with sellers on the phone and the fear of meeting with sellers in person. That is exactly why we have all new Mentorship students do BOTH these things at the Intensive Training. (That's why our Mentorship Students have such a high success rate.)

Step 3.

Find a mentor and learn the right way to do your investing.* We urge you do everything you can to learn from the best. Now that you have some experiences with which to make sense of the "book" learning, you will really profit from soaking up the best coaching you can get on your investing.

Step 4.

Take what your mentor has taught you and apply it in the real world. Learning becomes real at the point of action. It's up to you to consistently act on what you have been learning. As you use your new learnings in the world, pay attention to the outcomes your efforts produce.

Step 5.

Evaluate your actions and results and adjust your efforts to consistently produce better and better results. Then, over time, as you learn more, apply that learning to get even better, taking care to evaluate the effectiveness of all your actions. Over time this becomes a success cycle—learn, apply, evaluate—that you will repeat over and over until you've achieved the success you desire.

*For more information on finding the right mentor for you, log onto **www.QuickstartInvestor.com**. You'll find detailed information on how to make the right choice for you and your situation, plus you'll also get to listen in to over 20 success interviews with investors where you'll learn how they successfully launched their investing career and where they found the right mentor for themselves.

"There was a very famous business leader and consultant called W. Edwards Deming who is often referred to as the father of the quality movement. He was instrumental in the 1950s and 1960s in helping Japan totally revamp it's industrial model to help it top the world in quality.

"I remember reading one of his books called *Out of Crisis* in which he talked about how companies have a unique opportunity to take advantage of when they bring on new staff. I'll paraphrase what he said and apply it to beginning investors like yourself.

"He said that there is a very narrow window of opportunity that exists only when you learn something the first time, when you have it in your power to maximize that experience by learning right the first time. Remember, once you learn it, you can never again be a blank slate. Once you learn something from an inferior teacher, you'll never be able to relearn it without having to go to the extra effort to *unlearn* what you already learned that is inferior, and then learn it the right way.

"In today's world of networked communication, you don't have to settle for working with anyone on your investing unless they are the absolute best in their field. With the Internet and digitized knowledge, you can literally learn every component of your real estate from the very best of the best. Once upon a time, your only real resources to learn were either books or finding a local investor to take you under his or her wing. But just because someone has been successful themselves doesn't mean they are good at explaining to you the best approaches and steps you need to take. Also, sometimes they found a way of doing something that worked for them but their ideas are difficult for you to implement. I know that it took Peter and me over five years to translate what we do in our personal investing into the right language, systems, and coaching modules for our Mentorship students to follow to get predictably profitable results.

"I tell you what; you guys are spoiled now! Ten years ago our Mentorship students had it much tougher. Back then Peter or I could do the investing, but it was much tougher to share how. By this point, we've been able to refine and fine tune the investing and coaching systems so that it's a paint-by-numbers kind of thing for you.

"The real key is for you to choose carefully who you ask to teach you, because the clearest picture of the type of person you will become are the teachers you choose to work with and the results their students consistently get.

"My guess is that some of you are saying to yourself, 'David, that Level One and two stuff sounds nice and all, but why can't you just help me jump straight to Level Three? That's where I want to be!'

"The answer is simple. If we were to take you straight to Level Three in your investing you wouldn't be ready to handle it anyway. You see, just as it's working through Level One that prepares you to succeed in Level Two, it's the process of succeeding at Level Two that tempers you to be ready and capable of enjoying Level Three success.

"I'm sure you've heard the old expression 'you've got to learn to crawl before you can walk'? Well Level One investing is about your learning how to crawl. In it you learn how to get started investing. You deal with the fear that has held you back in the past. You learn a tremendous volume of new information, just like an infant does. And when you reach the finish line leading into Level Two you are now able to walk through a real estate deal and profitably create a win-win solution. You've still got a lot to learn, but you're firmly established on the right road to riches.

"It is in Level Two that you refine your investor skills so that you learn to run. And the rewards go up. You now get steady cash flow; you get big paydays; you get to enjoy the confidence that you can handle any type of real estate deal that gets thrown your way. But remember, it's still you who is doing the running, and eventually you'll get winded and tired.

"How many of you have ever met a burned-out landlord? Most Level Two investors get stuck in Level Two because that's all they know. To be fair, they are getting stuck earning $5,000 to $50,000 per month in positive cash flow and being able to take four to eight weeks of vacation every year, which is a fairly nice life. But you don't have to settle for that. There is so much more possible for you. This is where Level Three comes in," David continued.

"If Level Two investors have learned to run, Level Three investors have learned to *drive*. Or more accurately, Level Three investors have learned how to build a real estate business that's chauffeur driven by key people, well oiled systems, and outside vendors. They have learned how to build their real estate business to the point where they are not needed to run it.

"What I have to tell you next may blow you away, but it's absolutely accurate. Hard as it is to believe, there will come a time when having too much money rather than not enough money will be your challenge. I know it seems crazy, but there really are two kinds of money challenges—not having enough, and having too much.

"Level Three investors are Level Three because they have mastered the skill of converting the large chunks of cash they get when they refinance their debt or when they sell a property into passive cash flow. This is what frees them up to enjoy whatever lifestyle they desire. In fact, being able to turn chunks of cash into passive cash flow is one of seven critical wealth skills."

The 7 Critical Wealth Skills of the Super Successful*

1) Learning to generate massive paydays of cash and equity

2) Converting cash and equity into passive streams of cash flow

3) Recruiting and directing a core team of business and money professionals to aid you in your wealth management

4) Learning to feel worthy of the massive wealth you are capable of producing

5) Learning how to make intuitively accurate and prompt decisions

6) Creating a peer group of friends and associates who push you to be the best you are capable of being

7) Learning how to intelligently and healthfully share your wealth with the world

*Book three of the *Creating Cash Flow* series will focus on how to master all seven of these critical wealth skills. It will also teach you how to move into larger deals in commercial real estate so that you can do your wealth building with less time and energy. For information on release of book three of the *Creating Cash Flow* series, go to **www.QuickstartInvestor.com**.

"But we need to make sure we bring it back to ground level—Level One investing. You need to understand that you have to frontload your effort as you develop as an investor. It will take you hundreds of units of effort to succeed as a Level One investor and get your first few paydays. Later as a Level Two investor it will take you 10 to 20 units of effort to get your paydays. And finally as a Level Three investor it may only take one or two units of effort to enjoy a lifetime of paydays. But you've got to pay your dues at the start.

"Remember, it is the person you become along the journey through Level One and two investing that develops you into the person who can enjoy Level Three success.

"I have one more piece of good news for you. Although the average investor never makes it to Level Three because he or she doesn't even know it's possible, and those lucky few traditional investors who find their way into Level Three typically take 30 years or longer to do it, you can do it much faster. In fact, our goal in working together is to get you on the fast track to a Level Three life.

"Our Mentorship students typically take two to four months, sometimes as long as six to nine months, to reach the Level One finish line. Our Level Two Consulting clients generally take 18–24 months to begin reaping the rich rewards of Level Two success.

"And here is the best part! While the average investor who makes it to Level Three takes 30 years, our students are typically able to do it *seven to ten times faster!* My point is, just knowing this model propels you to the front of the pack. And by working together over time, you can succeed faster than you ever imagined. The path may be rocky and steep at times, but it's been charted, and we can safely guide you all the way to the top. I know that you are ready for this journey because, if you weren't, you wouldn't be here with us. In fact, if you weren't as committed to your financial and personal dreams as you are, you probably would never have been selected into the Mentorship Program to begin with!

"There are specific obstacles that you'll face as a Level One investor that stand in your way to success in real estate. The first obstacle is fear.

"Another obstacle that stands between you and your dreams is the host of false beliefs that you probably have about making money investing in real estate. These false beliefs range from 'it takes money to invest in real estate' to 'you need good credit to invest.' They are just not true. Over the past ten years our students have bought and sold over $1 billion of real estate, much of it without any of them using their own money or credit. How many of you in this very room have ever bought a property without cash or credit?" David asked. Sixteen students, nine of them returning Mentorship Graduates attending for a refresher course, raised their hands.

"Then there are the false beliefs about the market that make things so tough on many beginning investors. False beliefs like, 'this market is too hot,' or 'this market is too cold,' or 'this market is too flat, if only it was hotter or colder then I could make it work.'

"Where do these false beliefs come from? From the media and from all the

3 Ways to Overcome the Biggest Obstacle to Your Success

BRIGHT IDEA

In our experience of working with over 100,000 investors over the past decade the single biggest obstacle to your getting started making money investing is fear. Fear can manifest in many ways.

Here are three ideas to help you get past your fear and get started making money with your investing:

1) Take action right away. The single most effective way to break the bonds of fear is to repeatedly do the thing you are afraid to do, even while you are afraid to do it. Most fears dissolve when you get yourself to take action. The key is to not wait but to ACT NOW. Waiting *never* makes things easier. DO IT NOW!

2) Don't wait until you know it all. Many people say they will get started after they study and figure it all out. The problem is that the more they learn, the more they learn that they don't know! It's a paradox that keeps many would-be investors prisoners. You know enough the moment you get yourself to take action *knowing* that you'll never know it all.

3) Recognize that you are so much more than your fears. Many people falsely identify with their fear. That's just not so. You are not your fear. You are bigger and grander and so much deeper than your fear. So let your fear exist, and know that it is NOT you, it's just your fear and separate from you. Then take action while at the same time observing that your fear exists. Say to yourself, *"Isn't that interesting…here I am knocking on my first seller's door and I notice that my fear is acting up."* And as you say this, know that this fear is separate from you. Not only can you co-exist, but ultimately you will come to learn that fear isn't such a scary emotion to face and feel.

people around you who have never made any real money investing in real estate or from people who may have even lost money investing because they never got the training and support that you're getting.

"Isn't it ironic that most people get advice about investing from people who have utterly failed at it. Does that seem like a strategy for success? It's like the person who wants to be a star basketball player going to a local bar and enrolling five 'coaches' from the guys who sit on the stools watching the game and drinking beer but who never even played the game at the college level, let alone professionally in the NBA! How can they help you be a star when all they know is second- and third-hand nonsense that has never been tested in the only place that counts—on the court?

"Instead, doesn't it make sense to only listen to the best players and coaches who have a track record of helping other people get results? In fact, when you are selecting a mentor or coach, I believe that one of the best clues you can uncover about the results you can expect from working with them are the results their students consistently get. That's why Peter and I feel it's so important to have only coaches who are past Mentorship Graduates, because they embody the results and journey you'll be taking."

---

2 Keys to Choosing the Right Mentor for Yourself

1) Character is contagious.
Choose a mentor whose character you admire and respect—you'll probably catch it. How does this person treat other people? What does your intuition tell you about the way in which this person lives his or her life? Is this a person of high integrity? Do their words and actions match?

2) The success of the students is the success you'll enjoy.
Look closely at the results of your mentor's students. Can you see yourself taking the consistent action that their successful students have? Do their students who take action consistently get the results you want? Do you like being around their successful students? Can you identify with some of their successful students so that you'll have a clear image and role model to emulate?

"Getting back to these barstool investment advisors, they would have you believe, 'The only time to invest is when the real estate market is at the bottom of its cycle and on it's way back up again.' This is what they say, which by itself is harmful enough. But the real damage this idea does is that in the real world it scares new investors away from investing. They stay away from investing until they keep seeing the market going up and up and they fear missing out on the 'hot' real estate market. It's ironic that this is when most failed investors finally gather up enough courage to make the leap into investing by purchasing their first few properties— right at the height of the market frenzy. And they rarely have the education to buy intelligently in these markets, so they pay too much for the property, and do it with all cash—whether that cash is theirs or from a loan that they personally guaranteed from a conventional lender.

"Then when the market turns, as all markets eventually do, they don't have the cash flow cushion to ride out this down period, or they simply panic and sell. They buy in a foolish way at the height of the market, and then compound that error by selling at the worst time. Is it any wonder that they pass on the belief that real estate doesn't work? Do you think they say to themselves, 'Well it was really my own fault for jumping in for fear of missing out on the market gains, and doing my investing without any education or support from a knowledgeable mentor or coach'? Heck no! They say, 'Real Estate stinks!' and, 'You have to time the market just right to make money investing in real estate.' And another real estate naysayer is born.

"The reality was that these people were not real estate investors, they were real estate speculators. And there is a world of difference between the two.

Speculators versus Investors

Speculators are people who buy real estate at close to or even at full price as part of a cash deal, and then they hope-pray-gamble the market will rapidly appreciate so they can resell the property at a profit. The key distinction is that speculators haven't built a profit in for themselves at the time they purchased. Instead they are totally dependent on outside market conditions to produce a profit.

Sample Speculator: Buys a $500,000 house as a cash deal for $475,000 in a "hot" market, hoping that, if the market stays hot, the house will rapidly appreciate and in one year's time he'll be able to resell the house for $600,000 or more. But what if the market cools off? The speculator always runs the risk of getting stuck with a property that is a dog.

Investors are smarter than that. When they buy a property, they do so knowing that they are guaranteed to make a profit because of the way they purchased it. Either they have gotten great terms that make the property cash flow well, or they have negotiated a discounted cash price that ensures a profit when they resell. **The key distinction is that speculators gamble on outside forces to create a profit for themselves whereas investors negotiate the price or terms they need to build in their profit from day one—no matter what the market does in the short run.**

"So what eventually happens to these speculators? By a cruel twist of fate and with the most human of intentions, they evolve into the 'naysayers.' They are the ones who remind you that the sky is falling. They shout that real estate doesn't work. They whisper that it takes a ton of cash or great credit to make it as an investor. And they diligently recruit their friends and family and anyone who will listen to them to believe the same things they do. The saddest part is that they started as a naysayer with the best of intentions, to protect people. But ultimately their naysaying scares hordes of wealth seekers back to the 'safety' of life as usual—back to a path that for over 95 percent of our population leads to financial failure. Why would anyone choose known failure over a real shot to make it in real estate? Because they are scared. And fear is the single biggest roadblock to your investing success.

"You want to turn a real estate deal and net $25,000 in the next 90 days? You are going to have to face your fears and learn to dance with them. Remember, you'll never make your fears disappear completely, nor do you have to. I still get scared in my day-to-day life as an investor and business owner. But you will have to learn to do one key thing. If you can learn this one secret formula to deal with your fears I guarantee you can and will succeed with your investing. Here is that secret." David turned to the board and wrote:

Learn to act in the presence of your fears.

"Sounds too simple right? Well in my experience, and in the experience of thousands of other investors I've helped make millions of dollars investing in real estate, it is absolutely true. So often we think we need to blow through our fears, but we don't. We just need to make sure they don't stop us.

"You are not your fears. Your fears are separate from you. The real you lives an independent life separate from your fear. And you can learn to co-exist and take action while still feeling afraid. Now, after you learn this key lesson, guess what happens? Eventually fear's hold on your life diminishes. You start to stockpile a whole new host of references of how you are able to act while feeling afraid. And what happens to your experience of fear? You start to become less afraid of feeling afraid. And this leads to freedom and success in your investing and in your life.

It's my belief that it's the person you become in learning this key lesson that allows you to enjoy and share the wealth that you create.

"So who's scared about whether they can make their investing work?" David asked. Most every hand in the room went up.

"Good! That's normal. That's natural. How many of you are willing to take action knowing full well that you're going to be scared along the way?" Every hand went up this time.

"Excellent! The coaches and I are going to be reminding you of this promise over the next few months. Just know that when you are scared all you have to do is two things. One, do the best you can with what you've got at hand. If you're with a seller, do your best to negotiate the deal. Or if you're with a buyer, do your best to sell the property. Two, get onto the discussion board or on the coaching calls right away so that we can help support and guide you. You are not alone anymore in your investing. We are there by your side, doing it together step-by-step. The road you're traveling has been successfully charted.* Peter and I have done it. The coaches have all done it. Thousands of our students have done it. And you can do it too!

"You put in a good day's work and I'm proud of you. Two more days to go. I'll see you all in the morning," David said, ending the evening's session.

---

*Would you like a personalized action plan to chart out your course to your real estate dreams? Just log onto **www.QuickstartInvestor.com** and you'll be able to take advantage of our powerful online real estate business plan software, *The Strategic Investor Business Plan Creator*™. It's free to readers of this book!

CHAPTER EIGHT

The Final Day of the Training

Vicki sat talking with Mary while the rest of the students milled around. There was an excitement and tension in the room that could almost be touched.

"What did you think of that game we played to practice our negotiating last night?" Vicki asked.

"I thought it was incredible. It really pushed me to tie together all the different pieces of the Instant Offer System. I'm still a little intimidated about going on our real appointments to meet sellers today though. How about you?"

Vicki blurted back, "I'm terrified! Thank God that I won't be alone on the appointment. Knowing that I'll have Mark and Leon there is all that kept me from running this morning."

"Running?" Mary asked with a lifted brow.

"Okay, maybe I'm exaggerating a little bit, but I am scared. I feel like my head is so full of real estate knowledge. That helps. Especially all the time we spent yesterday going over the contracts and how to fill them out and explain them to the seller. If you would have asked me on Friday if I really thought I could do this, I probably would have said no. I just didn't think I would ever know enough. Scared as I am Mary, I am starting to feel like I know enough now to get started. Don't get me wrong, I don't think I know near enough to be a hot shot investor, but for the first time I think I know enough to at least get out there and get started. So for all my talk of wanting to run, the truth is I am ready to go. I'm just afraid that I'll get out there and the seller will ask me a question I can't answer and look at me and say, 'What kind of investor are you?' "

Mary smiled and reached out for Vicki's hand. "You'll do great today Vicki. If the seller asks you a tough question and you don't know the answer, that is okay. I wouldn't know the answer either. I told you on Saturday and I'll say it again, I know you are going to be great with this. It's just going to take you a little time to get your confidence level up."

Vicki's eyes started to fill with tears, but she held them back and gave Mary a long hug of gratitude. It was then that the morning's session started.

Peter smiled out at the room. "Good morning everyone! I trust you slept well. Who dreamed of motivated sellers and purchase contracts last night?

"This morning we are going to review what we've covered so far. One thing we've learned over the years is that this morning many of you aren't listening to a word I say." Peter smiled at this, then continued, "I understand that many of you have your minds on something else. Hmm, I wonder what that could be?" Around the room there was a lot of laughter.

"Once we're done reviewing the past two days then we'll spend the time on prepping you for your appointments and send you out to do the appointments. We'll meet back here when you're done to debrief the appointments and all breath a collective sigh of relief. Then the final session of the day will be spent on the 90-day action plan, with a strong focus on the critical window of the next two weeks. Any questions on that schedule?"

Tim raised his hand and asked, "Yeah, my group wanted to invite you or one of the coaches to come with us on our appointment."

The room started laughing when they heard the request. "Wow, it's nice to be wanted, but I'm going to have to decline your invitation. In fact, I won't let any of the coaches go on appointments with you either because if they were there with you what do you think would happen?"

Tim shouted out, "We'd sign up the deal!"

There was even more laughter in the room with that answer. "True," Peter responded. "But is the point of getting you out there to sign up deals? I believe that the real value of getting you out their meeting with sellers today is to show you that you can do it and survive. Today is not about signing up deals, although that would sure be nice. It's about getting yourself to do the thing that stops most wannabes cold, so that when you go home it's not so scary and you succeed. All the kidding and jokes aside, does that make sense?" Around the room heads were nodding. The students understood the point Peter was making.

"Okay, let's start our review."

CHAPTER NINE

The Final Session— Your First Two Weeks Investing

David stood up on stage and began the final session of the entire workshop. "Congratulations on your courage for going out on your appointments with sellers earlier today. As the coaches said when they led you through the debrief a short while ago, the most important outcome wasn't that two groups signed up deals. The most important outcome is that now all of you have been on appointments with sellers and you see how doable investing really is for you. As a result of this, when you go home you'll be much better positioned to go on appointments by yourself. It won't seem quite so scary anymore. I am proud of all of you for playing full out and going on your appointments.

"I see such growth in you all. When you walked in here three days ago you were a bundle of fears and overloaded with a mixture of investing strategies—some good, some bad. You've worked hard this weekend to face those fears, and along the way you've learned that they weren't so scary after all. You've also focused on the fundamental knowledge and skills you need to get started over the next 90 days to successfully launch your investing business.

"Right now I want to talk with you all about something of great importance to your success. That key is the critical importance of the next two weeks.

"Here you are, in the supportive company of your fellow investors who are at the same level you are at in the Mentorship Program, and it's been easy. The calls you've learned how to make to sellers and the Instant Offer System that you've learned how to use all seem so doable right now. And it is—right now. But how are you going to handle going out into the cold, cruel world as they say? How are you going to handle when real sellers say no to you on the phone? How are you going to handle when people you know, some with the best of intentions, tell you you can't do it?

"I put to you that if you look too far ahead the task will seem too big. My advice to you—just get through the next two weeks. That's it. You can be scared. You can have your tough moments. You just need to get through the next two weeks doing the things I'm about to share with you to do.

"One thing we've learned over the past decade of working with several thousand Mentorship students is that if you can just get through the first two weeks, then you've crossed the biggest barrier to your success. In life what does the average person do when they set they're dreams big and then get confronted with their first obstacle or their first rejection? They quit. And by quitting the average person is accepting known failure.

"Look, here's the truth of it. You are all at the edge of a cliff. Now the other side of that cliff is just three feet away. That's just 36 inches—barely farther than the length of three ordinary sheets of paper laid end to end. However, for the average person, the distance is just too far. The average person comes up that cliff where you are now standing and she says, 'that's too scary. I'm going to play it safe. I'm going to turn around and go back where I came, where they know me and I know them.' And she does. And in so doing she chooses known failure, because make no mistake about it, the results are known and the numbers clearly show that the average person who chooses this route ends up failing in life financially. That is one possible choice you have right now. You can leave here tomorrow morning, choose to turn from this cliff, and go back to the lives you led before you came here this weekend. If any of you choose this option, just know that you are choosing known failure. In essence you would be saying that you would rather fail comfortably than have the great chance to succeed but experience fear while doing it.

"Now the second choice you are faced with right now is to freeze at the cliff's edge. This is the person who delays making a choice to go forward or back. He stands there looking down at the gap between the cliff faces, looking back the way he came from, and over with desire at the dreams waiting for him on the other side. But he's too scared to make a choice, to commit to either of the two paths, either forward or back. Not only is this a known path to failure, but make no mistake about it, this is actually the most dangerous place of all. Imagine standing there at the edge of the cliff, with the winds swirling around you, and you being unsure, looking forward and back. If you choose this option you are at great risk for falling.

"The danger of losing your balance and falling into the gap increases with every passing moment you delay your decision. Better to turn back than live your life forever on the edge unwilling to make the final decision. Some of you who leave here might stay on that cliff face afraid to make a choice. It sounds like, 'Well, I'll do my dials tomorrow.' Or 'It's a busy week this week, so I'll just double up on the assignments next week.' Don't be seduced by the lure of keeping your options open. The truth is that to succeed in the early stages you must act on your dreams long enough to have built the momentum up to see you through any temporary setbacks that are sure to come your way.

"Your final choice there on the cliff face is to simply jump! To take a leap of faith. To step out and over and past the point of return. Now most people who come to the edge of a cliff know they want to go over to the other side but they beg, 'Please, isn't there some way we can inch our way across? Can't we incrementally commit to going to the other side?' The answer is no they can't, and neither can you. There are some decisions that you can't edge over—they require a leap of faith. Now, if you take that leap of faith, you'll have challenges waiting for you. You'll have temporary frustrations to deal with. And you'll have old and new fears to push past. But you'll also have everything you ever dreamed of having for you and your loved ones waiting there for you.

"This is the point you are all standing at right now. You are all on the cliff edge staring at one of three places. Either you are looking back at where you came from thinking how comfortable that old life was, and shouldn't you really give up all this silliness about wanting more and better for you and your loved ones. Or you're obsessed with the gap, with all you lack and all the reasons you may fail if you work to build a real estate investment business. Or you are looking across the gap to the other side, thinking about the positive impact committing to your investing dreams would have on your family and on your community.

"So what are you going to decide? Make no mistake about it: your very life depends on the answer you give right now—at this very moment. The way you answer this question now will determine the quality of the rest of your life. The way you answer this question now is how you will answer this question tomorrow morning when you are faced with the same choice. And it's the way you will answer this question the next day and the next. You will be asked this question each morning of each day of the rest of your life: how will you live this day? This day do you choose the 'security' of known failure? Or do you choose the freedom of working for your dreams.

"Which brings us back to the next two weeks. You are about to go home. And tomorrow morning you will wake up faced with this decision. The choice you make carries extra weight because for the next two weeks your dreams are fragile and your old life will try to pull you back. It's critical that each day for the next two weeks you make the right choice. I'm not asking you to think about the next ten years, or the next year. I'm not even going to ask you to think about the next 90 days. I am asking you to make the decision that, no matter what, for the next two weeks you are going to commit without excuses. There is only one direction and that is forward toward your dreams.

"Who is committed that no matter what you'll find a way to follow the action plan for at least the next two weeks?" David asked. Around the room every student firmly raised their hands.

"Now that we are all in agreement on the commitment, let's get into the specifics of what I want you to be doing with your days for the next two weeks. Please pull out your 90-day plans of action."

David then spent the next 45 minutes going over each specific assignment for the first 2 weeks after the training, including how the tracking and accountability systems worked. The feeling in the room had shifted. There was a sense of quiet determination and anticipation to get back home to put everything they had learned over the past three days into action.

With just a few minutes left to go in the workshop, Peter joined David up on stage and shared his closing thoughts to the students in the room. When he was done, the students all rose to their feet to give Peter and David a standing ovation. One by one the other coaches stepped up onto the stage to share in the applause.

And then it was over, and a fresh start began with all of the students investing. As Peter and David finished saying goodbye to all the students in the class, signing books, and posing for pictures, they each wondered if they had done enough, given enough. Who would succeed? Who would struggle? Who would give up? And who would persevere and create massive success? The next 90 days would reveal the answers, so for the moment all Peter, David, and the coaches could do is to wait and wonder.

PART TWO

THE REAL WORLD

CHAPTER TEN

Week 1—Vicki Gets Denied

When Vicki woke up on Thursday morning, she was excited and scared. She'd been home for three days since the training and she'd been making her dials every night after she put the kids to bed at 8:30 P.M. But today was different. It was her day off and she had her first solo appointment to go on since the training.

As she got caught up in the morning rush to get the kids off to school, she forgot all about her fear of meeting the seller at 11 A.M. Josh couldn't find his favorite action figure and had a meltdown when Vicki told him that he would have to go to school without it. Just when Vicki had calmed him down, Brittney had spilled her entire bowl of Cherrios onto the front of her dress and Vicki had to rush her upstairs to change into dry clothes for school. All in all, it was a fairly typical morning for a single mom, except that today, after she dropped the kids off at school she would have all the way until she went to pick the kids up at 3 P.M. to work on her investing.

Again her thoughts turned to how scary this all was for her. She just knew that the seller would see right through her. After all, she was just a mom and a nurse, not some fancy big shot investor. But she knew that she couldn't let that stop her. She knew that she had to make her investing work. It wasn't just the money she had invested in her mentorship tuition, it was her kids. It killed her that four days a week they went straight from school to day care until she could pick them up at 6 P.M. Sometimes it felt like her kids spent more time with strangers than with her, and this caused her heart to ache. She would do whatever it took to make her investing work. She was totally committed to earning enough money to leave nursing so that she could work from home and do her investing while the kids were in school. And if once or twice a week she needed to bring in a sitter to give her a few more hours to meet with a seller or to show a property, that was still so much more of her dream of being present in her children's life.

She turned over the property information sheet for the sellers she was going to meet later today. The sellers were a retiring couple who were moving to Arizona to have warm weather and be closer to their grandchildren who lived in Phoenix. Vicki had found the wife—Celia—when Vicki was doing her twenty dials two nights earlier. They had hit it off on the phone, and Celia had shared how their past real estate agent hadn't worked out and they were trying to sell it themselves.

Vicki had just followed the script and set the appointment to meet with Celia for today because it was her first day off. As she gathered her things to drive to the appointment, Vicki made sure she grabbed CD number 21 to play in the car as she drove over to meet Celia. This was the CD that had Peter and David role playing the Instant Offer System. Vicki had listened to this CD at least a dozen times over the last two months since she first signed up for the Mentorship Program and got her training materials. It was getting so she could say the lines with Peter as he negotiated with the seller in this role play. Vicki drew strength from this fact because she knew she wouldn't have either Peter or David, or any of the Mentorship Coaches for that matter, to be with her as she faced her fears and met with her first seller. Sure, she had gone on two appointments at the Intensive Training just three days ago, but that was with two other students, and somehow having them there with her helped her manage the fear.

As she pulled up to the house, the first thing Vicki noticed was that the sign in the yard was very small and hard to see. In fact, now that she thought about it, Vicki didn't remember seeing any for sale sign at the corner when she turned up the street. The bushes at both sides of the small two story house both needed to be trimmed back. But other than that the house looked quite nice.

Vicki rang the door bell and stepped back from the door. Her heart was racing and she almost turned and ran back to the car, but the faces of her two children kept her there. She knew that for her to give them all the things she wanted to give them, especially for her to be there in their lives more instead of working 50 to 60 hours a week, she would have to find a way to make this work.

Just then the door opened and a smiling woman in her late sixties said, "Hello?"

"Hello Celia, I'm Vicki. We spoke on the phone two nights ago."

"Oh yes, it is very nice to meet you Vicki. Come in, please."

Vicki stepped into the house and said, "Thank you for inviting me over Celia. Can you show me around?"

As Celia took Vicki through the house Vicki did her best to find things in common and to build rapport. It turned out that Celia's daughter-in-law was also a nurse out in Phoenix and one of the reasons they were moving was to be closer to her and her son and three grandchildren.

After they had finished going through the house Vicki asked Celia, "Where's a good place we can go to sit and talk this through?"

"How about the family room?" Celia said pointing the way. Vicki followed her into the family room and they both got settled into their chairs.

"Before we get started talking this all through Celia, I just want to make sure of one thing. I want you to know that if what we talk through just isn't a fit for you that I want you to let me know. Are you okay letting me know if something obviously isn't a fit for you?"

"Yes."

"Great. On the other hand, if what we talk through ends up being a fit for you, are you okay letting me know that too?" Again Celia agreed.

Vicki continued, "That's great. I promise you I'll do the same thing too. If things just aren't going to work for me I'll tell you that, and if things will work for me, I'll tell you that too. I promise that I won't keep you wondering where I stand. I'll let you know at the end of our time together. I am asking if you are willing to extend me that same courtesy—in other words, are you willing to agree to let me know at the end of our talk if you think we have a fit here or not?"

"Yes I'm willing to do that."

"Great, So what were you really hoping I could do for you here today Celia?"

"Well, I was hoping you would fall in love with the house and buy it."

"Okay. And how much were you asking for the property?"

For the next ten minutes Celia and Vicki talked through various options about how to find a fit, but it just didn't seem like Celia was that motivated. In the end, Vicki thanked Celia for her time and left. Vicki was feeling pretty low about it all.

In the training they had showed her how easy it all was, but this seller sure didn't seem to be very willing to budge on price *or* terms.

It was 11:50 when Vicki got home. The first thing she did was go to her computer and go online to check out the coaching call calendar for today. She saw that Stephen was leading a call at 1 P.M. She decided to use the extra hour she had until the call to order her I BUY HOUSES signs from the link to the vendor on the Mentorship Students home page. One of the things she liked best about the Mentorship Program is that it made things so easy to get access to the tools and connection she needed. It saved her many hours of searching and quite a bit of money. At 1 P.M. she logged into the coaching session.

"Hi everyone this is Stephen. How are all of your days going?" Vicki felt warmed by Stephen's infectious energy. She listened in as two other students asked questions about deals they were working on. In fact, Vicki learned a great technique from Stephen's answer to the second student. She jotted the idea down, but truthfully her attention was fixed on her appointment and wanting to get help on what she could have done better.

"Who else has a question about a deal they are working on?" Stephen asked.

"I do." Vicki took a deep breath and told Stephen all about her appointment.

"Vicki, as I hear you share about the appointment, a few things come to mind. First, congratulations on your victory on going on your first solo appointment. Heck, you just finished with the Intensive Training less than three days ago. And here you are out on an appointment in the real world. I know it can be scary, but you did it anyways. Second, great job on getting on this coaching call to go over and debrief the appointment together. This is so key for you to learn from every appointment you go on so that you can get what you want faster and easier. Also, you set an up-front agreement with the seller, and that is great. I'm sure it felt a little unnatural to do it, it usually does the first 10 or 20 times you use it. Just know that eventually it becomes second nature and habit."

Stephen continued, "Now I have two key coaching suggestions for you for next time. Actually, this will apply to everyone else on the call too. First, whenever you are dealing with a husband and wife or a property with multiple owners, you are going to want to make sure that both people are there at the property to meet with you. If you don't, you're chances to close a deal diminish."

"How do I get them both there?" Vicki asked.

"That's a great question. Here's what I usually say, 'Mrs. Seller, it sounds like a property I'm going to want you to show me through the inside of. When is a good time when you and Mr. Seller can invite me over to show me through the inside? We'll also need to plan on having a little time to sit and talk things through once you both show me around.' Now, if the seller says, 'Why do you need both of us there?' then just answer truthfully, 'Well Mrs. Seller, that is a great question. What I've found is that the properties I end up buying tend to be ones where I get the chance to sit and talk with both owners for a while. I guess it just makes me more comfortable to be able to sit down and meet with the owners before I'm willing to make the decision to move forward and buy their property. Boy, this probably sounds crazy and maybe a little old fashioned to you that having you both there makes me more comfortable to make the decision to buy the property, huh?' Did you notice the negative phrasing at the end there Vicki? How does that sound to you?"

"Wow! You make it sound so easy. Why couldn't you have come with me on the appointment!"

"You know what Vicki? I notice that newer investors like yourself tend to be really hard on themselves. They are so used to being excellent at what they do that they forget how long it took them to get there. For example, you're a registered nurse right?

"Yes," Vicki replied.

"Well how long did it take you to learn how to do your job well?"

"After the two-year training program, I'd say at least another three or four years on the job. I get your point. You're saying that I can't expect to be a great investor with all the right answers in three days."

"You can expect it Vicki, but it isn't going to happen," Stephen replied. "This goes to everyone on the call. Just relax a little and be kind to yourself. There will be a day when you look back at how far you've come with your investing and you'll be amazed. There is no pressure that it has to happen today though. For me, I remember this moment when I was talking with a bank about buying a property they had foreclosed on and I just noticed how I understood all the language of real estate and how confident I felt about negotiating with the lender. For a long time before that point I'd go on appointments and feel so scared that the seller would figure out that I didn't know what I was doing. But at that moment I realized how far I had come since my life in corporate America. You'll get there Vicki, just give it a little time.

"The second coaching point I have for you, and this also applies to everyone on the call: you can't force a deal if the deal doesn't exist. Vicki, the seller you spoke with was somewhat motivated, but maybe she wasn't quite motivated enough to strike a deal. The only way to really know is to ask. Which brings me to my final coaching point. One of the things that I noticed Vicki, you went straight from the up-front agreement to speaking about the money. That makes me wonder, did you maybe skip the motivation step?"

"Now that I hear you saying that Stephen, I realized that I did skip that step." Vicki said.

"I'm not sure how much good it would have done on this particular appointment, but it is a great lesson to learn for future appointments. The longer you can spend talking with the seller of the property about why he or she wants to sell, needs to sell, wants to sell and needs to sell to you, the more likely you are to get a great deal. The key words to keep saying to yourself over and over again are 'motivation before money.' Does that make sense?" Stephen asked.

"It sure does. That really helps me a lot. Thank you so much Stephen." Vicki listened to the rest of the call and picked up several new insights to help with her investing. When the coaching session ended, Vicki realized how useful it was to talk with other Mentorship students and especially with the coaches about her appointments, and she made a promise to herself that she would do this after each appointment that she went on.

Vicki looked at the clock and realized that she only had 45 minutes before she needed to pick the kids up from school. Looking at her 90-Day Plan of Action manual she saw that she had one assignment left for the day—doing 20 dials. Gathering her for sale and for rent leads, Vicki took a deep breath and picked up the phone and began her dials.

Just then she got an instant message popping up on her computer from Mary.

"Hi Vicki. I was on the coaching call too. Just wanted to tell you to hang in there. I believe in you and know you'll make this work. I'm so proud of you for going on your first appointment. Focus on this victory. You are doing something great for your kids, even if it's going to take some time to pay off."

Vicki's eyes filled with tears. She could almost feel the motherly, sweet presence of Mary. At the training she had felt a strong connection with Mary and Leon who were probably the same age as her parents. Vicki typed back, "Thank you so much for your support Mary. It means the world to me. I feel so lucky not to be doing all this on my own. Please give Leon a hug for me, will you?"

"Sure thing Vicki. Talk with you on our mastermind call on Saturday. Bye."

Wiping her eyes and smiling, Vicki got back to her dials.

The 36-Month Investor Development Plan

MONTH
1
▼

Dealing with initial fear of getting started and building momentum by establishing the behavior patterns of successful investors.

MONTH
2–3
▼

Focus on basic skill building in the following key areas:
- Get fluent with sellers and rental property owners over the telephone.
- Develop an intuitive sense for motivation to easily, quickly, and accurately sort through sellers to find those who are most motivated to sell.
- Basic understanding of the Instant Offer System & all five bridge questions.
- Basic understanding on how to fill out a purchase contract and lease option agreement with a seller.
- Learn about values in your areas of focus—both rental and resale.

MONTH
4–6
▼

Focus on your marketing efforts to consistently generate:
a) Part time – Three independent lead streams that each yield on average one quality lead per week.
b) Full time – Five independent lead streams that each yield on average one quality lead per week.

It's during this period that most of our students break out of Level One investing and into the beginning stages of Level Two investing by having completed their first, second, or third deal.

MONTH
7–18
▼

Early Stage Level Two—*Your focus is on improving your skill level and becoming a competent, skilled investor who can handle many types of deals.*
Key skills include:
- Deal Finding and Marketing Skills
- Deal Analysis and Due Diligence Skills
- Structuring Deals That Work for All Parties
- Negotiation Skills to Get Profitable Deals
- Real Estate Contracts & Paperwork
- Reselling and Leasing Skills

Level Two investors have created a net cash flow of $5,000 to $50,000 per *month*, and an increase in their net worth $250,000 or more per year.

MONTH
19–36
▼

Advanced Stage Level Two—*Your focus begins to shift away from yourself as a real estate investor to building a real estate investing business.*
Your focus is on building your real estate investing business so that it will help do the work for you and you start the transition into Level Three investing. During this time you put leverage and systems to work for you so that your business earns more while you not only work less, but you do those things that you are uniquely qualified to do and love to do and let your systems and team handle 75 percent or more of all the other things.

CHAPTER ELEVEN

The First Mastermind Meeting

When Saturday rolled around, Vicki woke up and got the kids their breakfast. Then she settled them down in the family room with their favorite video and asked them to keep quiet for an hour, promising to take them to the park to play right after her phone call if they could help mommy with her investing by being quiet little mice.

Vicki went upstairs to her bedroom and logged onto the Mentorship site for her mastermind meeting with her team from the Intensive Training: Tim, Nancy, Mark, Leon, and Mary.

When she was connected to the conference Vicki said hello, discovering that she was the second to last one to arrive.

"All we're waiting for is Mark," Tim said. "How are you doing Vicki?"

"I'm doing fine, a bit tired. It's been hard making the time to keep up with the action plan and working and dealing with the kids. But I'm committed to make it happen, so I've found creative ways to get it done. How about you all?"

Just then Mark joined the call, "Sorry, I'm seven minutes late. I have some great news to share. I just got home from meeting with a motivated seller and signed up my first deal!"

Vicki's first thought was, how did he do that? Why can't I do that? As she listened to the others congratulate Mark she realized how fear based those thoughts were and she joined the group in celebrating Mark's success. Besides, she thought to herself, he was one of the sweetest men at the training. She genuinely wanted good things to happen for him. And it made her realize just how doable this all is.

"Tell us all the details!" Tim asked.

"I had bought my I BUY HOUSES signs about two weeks before I came to the Intensive Training, but they didn't arrive until this past Tuesday. I spent about three hours on Wednesday night putting up 40 or 50 of them. Actually, I felt so foolish and embarrassed hanging them that I waited until 10 P.M. to start putting them out! I had a two-day route to fly on Thursday and Friday but was back late Friday night. I had checked my voice mail during my layover on Thursday night and had three messages. The first two were people from the areas complaining about the signs I had put up, I just deleted those, but the third one was from a seller who really sounded anxious to talk with me. I called him back and we spoke for about a half hour or so."

"What was his situation?" Nancy asked.

"He's this nice retired military guy who wants out of the area to move closer to his daughter and grandkids in Florida. We really hit it off. Heck, I learned to fly in the military so we had a lot in common. He's tried listing it with an agent for about five months, but the agent has just sat on the listing. We agreed that our deal would be contingent to the listing agent taking $500 to walk away from the listing, which we both feel is more than fair because the agent hasn't really done anything for the past five months to sell the house. The seller really didn't need his equity out; he just wanted to have it handled before he felt comfortable moving into his condo that he already owns down in Florida. So we agreed that he would let me lease option the house for up to five years at a price of $240,000 with monthly rent payments of $1,000 a month. I'm not totally sure of the values in the area yet, but my best guess is that the house is worth between $250,000 to $260,000 and it will rent for $1,200 to $1,300 a month. So the numbers at this point seem solid."

"What's the area like?" Leon asked.

"It's a fairly steady-growth medium market. I live about ten minutes away from his house so I know the area pretty well. My best guess is that homes are going up around 6 percent a year or so. As I said, it may not be a perfect deal, but it looks pretty solid to me so far."

"What are your next steps on it Mark?" Vicki asked.

"Well, the owner is going to call and talk with the listing agent later today. I am all set to meet the owner at the home tomorrow to get the agreement notarized, and then I'll go around the neighborhood and do my rent survey."

"Make sure you bring a big Rent to Own sign for the front yard when you go over there," Vicki reminded him. Mark thanked her for the idea and then went on to describe the details of the appointment.

BRIGHT IDEA

Power Format to Run Your Mastermind Meetings

Preparation for the Meeting *(Estimated time: 10–20 minutes)*

1) Create a bulleted list of the most important activities and events in your investing since the last meeting—key part will be the "Three Commitments" you made at the end of your last mastermind meeting:

- _____
- _____
- _____
- _____
- _____

2) What have you liked best about your investing activities since your last mastermind meeting? (Catching yourself doing things right and reinforcing those positives.) These are called your "Liked Bests:"

- _____
- _____
- _____

3) What one or two specific things will you do differently next time in your investing business that will have the greatest positive impact? (Notice that it's not, *"What did I do wrong?"* or *"What can I beat myself up over?"* but rather *"What can I do differently next time based on what I learned?"*) These are called your "Next Times:"

1. _____
2. _____

4) What two or three questions do I want to learn the answers to that will have a real impact on my development as an investor?

1. _____
2. _____

Meeting Outline
NOTE: the time must be evenly divided so that every member of the mastermind groups gets equal time to have the spotlight focused on them and their business. While this doesn't have to be to the second, if over time members feel an imbalance, they will be less willing to participate in the group.

(continued)

Power Format to Run Your Mastermind Meetings *(continued)*

Part One - Recap of investing activities and key results since the last meeting. *(Suggested Time: three minutes per member for (A) and 15–30 seconds for (B))*

A. Each member shares in turn the highlights of their investing business activities and results since the last meeting. This should go quickly since each member has prepared his or her bulleted list prior to the mastermind meeting. This recap should also include a quick report on what the member did on the "Key Commitments" he or she made at the end of the last mastermind meeting. Each member cam also share his or her top "Liked Bests" and "Next Times."

B. At the end of the recap, the member gives a quick description of how he or she is feeling about his or her investing business. It is important that this description is just shared, with no explanation or elaboration. (E.g. *"I'm feeling excited and proud about my consistency last week, but I'm a little nervous about being able to maintain this pace."*)

Part Two – The "Spotlight" Section.
Each member in turn will get five minutes of time focused on their investing business, with all the other members of the mastermind group focused on giving the person in the spotlight the very best coaching, support, and insight they can. A useful technique is for the person in the spotlight to prepare a question that will help harness the energy and brainpower of the mastermind group to create powerful ideas. (E.g. *"What can I do this week to immediately generate two more quality leads of motivated sellers to meet with?"* or *"What can I do today that will help me create another five plus hours to do my investing each week?"*)

Part Three – The Key Commitments Section.
At the conclusion of the mastermind meeting, the group will pause for 1–2 minutes while each member decides on three key commitments they are going to take on for the coming time between now and the next mastermind meeting. These key commitments are action items that the entire mastermind group will hold the member accountable to. (E.g. *"I commit to sending out at least 300 I BUY HOUSES postcards this week."* Or, *"I commit that by 9 P.M. tonight I will set a date with my husband sometime this week to discuss how he can best support me in our investing business."*) It is important that your key commitments be behavioral, observable, and measurable. What this boils down to is could a third party watch and observe you fulfilling your commitment? This is the essence of a powerfully formed key commitment and will provide rocket fuel to your investing business.

After the initial excitement of Mark's deal calmed, the group began going through the mastermind formatting that David had laid out for them at the Intensive Training. When it was Vicki's turn she shared her fears.

"I just get scared most days. There's so much to do and I worry that I'm not doing it right." Vicki was on the verge of tears.

Mary was the first one to respond, "It's okay honey, I know it's scary for you. But we all know you can do this and believe in you. It's just going to take some time, that's all. You just went on your first solo appointment ever a few days ago. And you've already learned so much. We're all scared, and none of us are doing things perfectly."

"Mark is. He just signed up his first deal!" As soon as she said it Vicki regretted it. She knew she was being selfish and that it was an awful thing to say, but it just slipped out.

"Vicki," Mark said in that soft baritone voice of his, "I just got lucky. I met with a seller who wasn't just motivated but was so easy for me to connect with. It could just have easily been Leon or Nancy or you who met with an ideal seller and signed up a deal. Don't be so hard on yourself. I was your role play partner a lot at the training and I know you're going to be great at this. Mary's right though, just give it a little bit of time."

"I'm sorry Mark, I shouldn't have said what I did. I really am thrilled for you. It's just that I'm scared. I put the training onto my credit card and I'm scared that not only won't it work, but that I'll have to face my kids and know that that money could've been used for their college funds, or to pay for braces if they ever need them."

"I understand Vicki," Mark said, "I've got two kids of my own. But if you don't go after your investing, what's going to happen?"

"Nothing."

"That's right, nothing," Mark said. "And how are you going to feel knowing that you let fear stop you from taking your shot and creating something special for you and your kids? I mean all you really have at risk is a few thousand dollars on your credit card. And if it doesn't work, you'll get it all back with the guarantee they gave us. But the important thing is that this is a real shot for you, for all of us. I know it will work—it already has started to. Just give it time."

"You're right Mark, I know you're right. It's just that I was so scared going on that appointment alone. It was one thing doing it at the training when you, Tim, and I went out to meet with those two sellers, but doing it all on my own, I just feel really alone."

Leon spoke up, "You're not alone Vicki. None of us are. Not only do you have all the coaches but you have all of us. We're here to support you Vicki."

"That's right!" Mary said. "If you get scared you just pick up the phone and call me and I'll be there for you."

"Yeah, and you only live an hour away," Mark said. "If you want to set up a time to go out on one or two appointments together, I'd be willing to drive down to go on the appointments with you to give you some support."

Vicki felt so lucky to have met these people at the Intensive Training. "Thank you all. I'm sorry I got all mushy on you."

Nancy spoke for all of them when she said, "Don't think twice about it Vicki. I admire your willingness to give voice to your fears. I was listening and realized that I'm scared too. But I was just too scared to tell any of you! I think you have a tremendous amount of courage."

The group went on to finish up their mastermind meeting and arranged for their next meeting to take place the following Saturday at the same time. As they logged off the computer, each of them realized how important and powerful this mastermind group was going to be for them.

CHAPTER TWELVE

Week 4—
Tim and Nancy
Make a Breakthrough

Tim and Nancy had been on the coaching call that Stephen was leading for about fifteen minutes when it became their turn to ask a question.

"Stephen," Nancy said, "Tim and I just went out on our fifth appointment with a seller today. I'm really struggling with this whole thing and I need your help with it."

"Sure Nancy. Tell me about the appointment," Stephen replied.

"Well, we found this seller who had a house he hadn't been able to sell for the past three months. He had a contract on the house that fell through two weeks ago for $469,000. He is moving in four weeks and wants it sold so he doesn't have to worry about it any more. We sat down and talked with him for about two hours yesterday. We got all the way through the Instant Offer System down through the What-If Step. In fact, he had even agreed out loud to our what-if offer of leasing the house for five years with a locked in price for us to buy it at $450,000. We agreed on a monthly payment to him of $2,200 per month which would cover his full payment, including real estate taxes and insurance. I think the house would rent for $2,300 to $2,500."

"Okay, Nancy, that all makes sense. Help me understand your question," Stephen prompted.

"After we reached agreement I went out to my car to get a blank contract. When I got back from the car I'd found that the seller seemed a bit cooler about the whole idea. And then, when we filled out the agreement just like we did at the Intensive Training, he got even more reluctant about working with us. Finally, the best we could get from him was an "I'll think it over and get back with you." So my question to you Stephen is what did we do wrong? I really think that should have been a great deal for both of us, but he backed away at the end. What happened, and how do we make sure it doesn't ever happen again?"

Stephen paused for a moment as he thought through the best way to answer the question.

"Tim and Nancy," Stephen started, "would you be okay if I asked you a series of questions to help me flush out what really happened on this appointment and perhaps on several appointments you've gone on? Before you answer I need you to know that I will be giving you specific coaching in a direct and straightforward manner, and some of what I tell you may not turn out to be what you want to hear at this moment."

Nancy responded right away, "Stephen, don't worry, you won't hurt our feelings; just tell us what we need to hear."

"Thanks for your permission to cut through all the surface stuff and get to the core as I see it. For those of you on the call listening to this, I want you to do two things. First, I want you to imagine you were me. Listen to the questions I am asking; listen to the answers that Tim and Nancy are giving. Then imagine you were their coach. What coaching would you give them? What do you think is really going on?" Stephen paused for a moment. "Second, I want you to listen as if you were Tim and Nancy and listen for specific insights and coaching that you can apply to your own investing. I already have a pretty strong intuition about what is going on with Tim and Nancy, and if my intuition is accurate, there will be several *very* important lessons that will come out of this exercise that will directly apply to your investing success. In fact, for a few of you at this coaching session the next five minutes will be the difference between success and failure as a real estate investor.

"Okay Nancy," Stephen said. "It sounds like the seller you met with was pretty motivated. Is that accurate?"

"Yes he was motivated. Actually he was the most motivated seller we had met yet. The other four sellers we've met with over the past four weeks since we've been home from the Intensive Training weren't very motivated," Nancy answered.

"That's helpful to know. Tim, share with me what went on while Nancy was outside getting the agreement. What were you and the seller talking about?"

Tim answered, "I did my best to make sure he didn't cool off while Nancy was out of the room so I started to explain to him all the benefits that he would get by doing this deal with us. I'm glad I did because with each benefit I shared with him he had lots of unanswered questions that may have killed the deal. In fact, my guess about why he backed out was that we hadn't handled all these potential objections earlier in the sales and negotiation process."

"That's really useful for me Tim," Stephen said. "Nancy, who took the lead in the negotiation, at least most of the time?"

"I did," Nancy replied.

"Great, and at the very end of the negotiation when you were filling out the Residential Lease Purchase Agreement, tell me more about that part of your meeting with the seller."

"Well, when I came back in with the blank agreement, I started to fill it out. It took me about five or six minutes to fill in all the blanks. When I was done, I gave it to the seller to read through and then sign. He took it from me and barely started to read through it before he began to ask me all kinds of questions about Tim and me, our background. He even wanted to revisit the price and start making it higher since the house would be more valuable down the road. Basically I guess you could say that it spiraled downhill fast from there. I tried to answer all his objections but he didn't seem like he was paying much attention at all to my answers," Nancy said.

Stephen then asked Tim, "While Nancy was filling out the agreement what were you and the seller talking about?"

"I was just there being friendly and building rapport so that the seller didn't back off any more than he already had. I was also trying to help him paint a very clear picture of what this solution we were offering would mean for him. I was just trying to make moving forward in the deal very compelling for him."

"Okay," Stephen interrupted, "You've given me what I need for the moment. Let me give you my feedback now. First off, my liked bests. I liked best how you have been going on appointments each and every week with sellers. I liked best that one of you took the lead at the appointment so that you wouldn't intimidate the seller. And my biggest liked best was that you got the seller to agree orally to a five-year deal with a price that was $20,000 below value and would have given you positive cash flow from day one. That is huge! I hope you feel great about that. Do you realize what growth that is? In one month you've come so far."

Nancy said, "Well I guess so, but it doesn't feel like growth, the seller still backed out of the deal."

"Fair enough," Stephen said. "But you've taken a deal all the way to the 10-yard line. Now all you have to learn is two more pieces: how to effectively close out the agreement so that the deal gets signed, and how to find your end user for the property, which in most cases is going to mean finding a tenant buyer for the property. So you are 90 percent of the way there and just have a few minor tweaks that I'm going to share with you right now to start getting your deals signed that will take you halfway through these final few paces. But the result you were able to generate is actually much harder to learn than the key skill of closing the deal. You've been able to find a truly motivated seller, qualify him over the phone, set up a meeting, go through the entire IOS, and get oral agreement on the deal. Celebrate that because if you could do it once that means you can do it a second time, and a third time, and so on. You are so close, Nancy and Tim. Let that sink in."

Stephen continued, "Now with that said, here are the specific coaching ideas you need to take it those final few steps to close the deal. I'll break down these ideas into three specific areas. The first area is in controlling the dynamics of the reluctant and eager parties. In any negotiation, especially at the very end, there is always going to be one party who is more eager to see the deal close and one party that is much more reluctant to actually let the deal close. Think of it like a battery—it has a positive end and it has a negative end. If you're not conscious of this dynamic, then you can often unintentionally find yourself playing the role of the eager party, which is the kiss of death to effectively closing the deal you've been working on."

Stephen paused for a moment and said, "Tim, as I listened to your side of the interaction, it became really clear to me that you had unintentionally put you and Nancy into the eager chair. If I remember correctly, your background is in technology sales right?"

"Yes, I've been in sales for over twenty years, and technology sales for the last ten years," Tim answered.

"This all makes sense in light of the high proficiency you have cultivated over the years becoming an effective sales person Tim. Your training as a salesperson has given you some great strengths like the willingness to ask people to do business with you, an ability to get along with people, and a disciplined approach to trust the numbers and not to take any one no as a permanent or personal statement. On the flip side, your sales background has given you one habit that you would do well to change. Don't think it's just you. I'm sure that over half the people on this call struggle with this very habit that I'm coaching you on. It's just really clear in your case. This expensive habit you have is that you are consistently selling the seller on the benefits of doing the deal with you. You are doing your best to lay out all the compelling benefits that will accrue to the seller if they do business with you."

Tim interrupted, "What's wrong with that? That's the essence of sales. Benefit! Benefit! Benefit!"

Stephen responded, "Tim, I understand your wanting to apply your sales skills to close with the seller, but the idea of using benefits to close the deal is not the best way to do it. Remember at the Intensive Training when Peter and David talked about how sellers are more motivated by the fear of making a mistake and getting taken advantage of than they are motivated by the desire to make money? What's happening is that at the end of the negotiation, the seller is feeling uncomfortable. All these benefits that you speak of not only automatically put you into the eager role, but they start to make the seller feel very unsettled, cautious, and skeptical of the deal you've negotiated. It just sounds too good to be true to him. He starts to think you're hiding something from him. Look, I was in sales for years before starting my investing, so I also had to make this same transition that I'm talking with you about. In sales benefit selling is very effective. In real estate investing when negotiating with sellers, establishing rapport, building motivation, and maintaining reluctant positioning is what closes the deal."

Stephen continued, "So what exactly do I suggest you do next time? The next time Nancy goes to the car to get the agreement to sign up the deal here's what I want you to say, 'Gee Mr. Seller, I'm not sure how you did it, but normally Nancy drives a much harder bargain than this. She's incredibly conservative in her investing, and I would have expected her to ask you for a minimum of six years, not five, and a price of around $430,000. But if that's what Nancy agreed to then she'll do it; she's like that. May I ask you a few more questions about the house? Are there any problems with the property that we should be aware of? Do the neighbors throw loud parties? What's crime and vandalism like in the neighborhood?' Not only does it prod the seller into the eager role by subtly invoking the fear of loss in the seller—which we all know is the single greatest spur to action for most people—but it also fills the time while Nancy is getting the agreement from the car in a way that keeps the seller very committed to the deal you just finished negotiating. Can you see how the seller would react better to this approach?"

Tim answered, "Yes, that makes sense. I should have complimented him to help him understand he did a good job negotiating, and then it would have been better for me to start to ask him questions that make him think he might lose the deal."

"Exactly! Now, if you don't think the seller did a good job negotiating then please don't say that he did. If that is the case, then just skip that part and move to injecting a little bit of doubt or hesitation into the deal. Do you think you can do that?"

"Yes."

"Good Tim. I have one more thing I'm going to ask from you, and then Nancy, it will be your turn. Tim, when you are trying to paint a clear picture of the deal and selling the seller, it starts to feel too good to be true to the seller. The seller wonders why you would even do the deal if it's so good for him and all you talk about are the good things he gets out of it. Instead, let the seller sell both himself and you on the merits of the deal. Say something like, 'Mr. Seller, while Nancy is out checking to see if she has a blank agreement to use, tell me again'—scrunchy face, voice getting softer and lower—'why was this deal such a good fit for you?' The seller will give you the benefits he gets. Listen to him and use selective hearing to get him to repeat himself here to reinforce the benefits he is selling himself on. 'I'm sorry Mr. Seller, you said that our making the payments would allow what?' You could even ask the seller a question like this one, 'Mr. Seller, if you were me, tell me again why would you think that this deal works for me?' Or, 'Mr. Seller, if you were me why would you feel this deal is even good enough that you would want this property over any of the other houses you had considered buying this week?' These last two questions subtly injects a lot of fear of loss into the negotiation and is like a tonic to close the deal. Does all this make sense to you Tim?"

"It does. It's golden stuff. I can hear how much better it is when I hear you role playing it a little. It's going to take some practice to remember to use it when

I'm sitting down with sellers, but I'll do it. But how were you able to pick up on what was going on so fast and have the cure so quickly?"

Stephen laughed. "After working with several thousand students over the years, we've gotten pretty good at being able to cut right to the core of most investing obstacles. I'm sure there will be other tweaks and refinements that you'll need over the next several months of the program, but the other coaches and I will be there ready to help you with them as the need arises.

"Now Nancy, it's your turn. Of course, it goes without saying that the idea of introducing doubt into the closing minutes of the deal is going to be one key for you and everyone else here on this call, but the most important shift for you to make right now in your investing is to let go of the need to be perceived as professional and expert. I know this one isn't easy to hear, but my intuition is telling me that this may just be the single most important shift you'll ever need to make to take a quantum leap in your investing. And I'm not just talking to you. My best guess says that over a third of the students on this call struggle with the same disempowering drive."

Stephen continued, "In the world of real estate investing, when you are meeting directly with the owner of the property, you need to help *them* feel smarter than you and to help *them* feel like they are in control of the conversation. Why? Because this lowers their fear of making a mistake and being taken advantage of, which in turn means that you can actually reach them with your ideas. If they have the shields up during the negotiation, then it's really hard for you to craft a win-win solution. I've even seen this dynamic get so bad that the seller has let the house go into foreclosure rather than work with an intimidating, know-it-all investor. Now, I'm not saying that you are even near that extreme. In fact, I think in your case it is only a small, easy-to-correct thing, but it is still something that you'll need to work on if you want to be the investor I think you can be."

Nancy said, "I can see how what you're saying is true, but I've worked so hard to be taken seriously in the world by the men I work with that it is really hard for me to give back all those gains I've made in how I'm perceived. The whole 'playing dumb' thing makes me feel uncomfortable because people won't take me seriously then."

"Nancy, that is so honest. I really admire your awareness of what's going on for you. Let's shift the way we language what I'm asking you to do. Rather than call it playing dumb, what we're asking you to do is to let the seller feel superior to you so that he or she is able to relax their ego-based defensive shields and really open up with you. Truth be told, if you are doing your investing the right way very little of the focus is on you. The focus is almost exclusively on the seller, which means he or she won't have any time to really wonder about you and your credibility. Motivated sellers just want two things. They want to have a specific real estate problem handled as quickly and painlessly as possible. And motivated sellers wants to feel safe and secure with the choice they made of working with you, the investor. I'm also guessing that there is a piece to all of this that I won't ever know first hand. I mean the part about how women in our culture have to be aware of how they are perceived in a professional setting in a way that many men don't. But I want to re-assure you that I've had lots of talks with our successful female students about this very thing. I've also watched my wife Susan struggle with it when she first negoti-ated with sellers and finally chose to do it the way Peter and David teach it to get better results and happier sellers. It just works. All I can say is that when you're at work, be professional. When you are meeting with motivated sellers, just be your-self and let them relax with you and feel like they are the ones in control of the process. How is this matching up with how you perceived the appointment with the seller?"

Nancy replied, "It really hits home for me Stephen, although I'm still a little unsure how to apply the insight to my investing."

"That's a great question Nancy. First, I'd say you are going to have to be a little less efficient and focused in your conversations with the seller. When you need a specific point to be made, see if you can't ask a question to get the seller to raise the point instead of you. One way to do this is by using the negative phrasing you learned at the Intensive Training so that the seller gets to be the one who mis-matches his way into eliminating his other alternatives, like working with a real es-tate agent or renting out the property. Also, when you get to the What If Step, make sure you make it their idea and give them credit for the idea. This might sound like, 'So if I'm hearing you right Mr. Seller, what you want me to do is make you payments on the property of $2,000 per month with a term of five years and a price of the full $450,000 we agreed on. Did I get what you wanted me to do right?' (scrunchy face). Then compliment them on the intelligence or creativity or practi-cality of their idea. One last way to let the seller feel powerful and in charge is for you to involve the sellers in filling out the agreement together at the very end of your negotiation. Ask them every easy question and then write down their answers.

Things like the date, the address, their names, are easy ways to let them feel important and in control by almost directing what you are writing on the agreement. This builds great momentum for the harder blanks on the agreement, like the purchase price or the date your first rental payment is due. Does this make sense to you Nancy?"

"It does, Stephen. It's not what I wanted to hear, but I can see it's exactly what I needed. Thank you for being so honest with me."

Over the next 45 minutes of the coaching call, Nancy and Tim listened in to Stephen helping six other students with deals they were working on. When they left the call one hour later, they both felt revitalized and ready to go meet with their next seller later that night.

CHAPTER THIRTEEN

Week 6—
Mark Signs Up His Second Deal

Mark turned and looked around the seller's small kitchen. He'd been sitting down talking with Sam, a motivated seller who had called Mark's classified I BUY HOUSES ad.

"So what were you hoping I could do for you Sam?" Mark asked.

"I want you to buy my house."

"What have you tried so far to sell the property?"

"I haven't done much to sell it. I really didn't want to sell it at first, but after I broke up with my girlfriend Kelly I needed to find a cheaper place to live. The payments on this place are too much for me to handle on just my salary."

Mark almost asked him what his payments were, but stopped himself at the last moment remembering what Peter had said at the Intensive Training—when the seller gives you an opening to talk about money too early in the motivation step it's a trap. Instead Mark took a deep breath and tried to keep himself calm and slow.

"Help me understand why you called my ad. I mean why didn't you just list the property with a real estate agent?" Mark asked.

"I wish I could do just that, but I don't have the time for a long selling period. The bank has only given me six more weeks before they say they'll sell my house at auction."

"Six weeks?" Mark asked with his face scrunched up, drawing the seller out just like John had coached him to do on the conference call yesterday when Mark had asked for help to prep for this appointment.

"Yeah, six weeks. I'm over four months behind on the payments and the bank's chomping at the bit to push the house to sale. I've already tried talking to them till I'm blue in the face, but they won't give me any more time to sell."

Mark took another deep breath and speaking slowly using the big eyes expression that was becoming second nature to him at this point, "Maybe if you talked with a different person at the bank?"

"No, I've tried that. No one will give me any kind of extension."

"I'm sorry?" Mark asked knowing that he had to help Sam break out of his "it will all be better in the morning" bubble he displayed when they spoke on the phone two days ago.

"I tried getting an extension and everyone I spoke with at the bank said no way. In six weeks the house goes on auction."

Mark spent the next 10 minutes talking with Sam about his options and situation, gently leading Sam to realize that he really did need some help to make the best of a bad situation.

Moving into the money step of the Instant Offer System Mark asked, "Well what did you conservatively think the house is worth if you only had some more time to sell it the *long* way?"

Quickly Sam answered, "It should sell for $350,000, if I just had a little more time."

"Yeah, that makes sense that it would sell for $340,000 to $350,000 if you had time to sell it the long way. What do you *realistically* think you could sell it for knowing that it has to close in four to five weeks to finish before the foreclosure auction?" Mark asked.

Sam thought about the question for a long moment before he answered. "I guess I'd be thrilled to get $330,000 cash for it and just be done with it all."

Mark held back his mounting excitement. All the scripting he had learned from Peter and David and the coaches was finally making sense to him. He could *feel* how all the other appointments in which he had struggled and worked so hard to get fluent with the language patterns were paying off. He really felt like he could make this deal work and help Sam at the same time. "Calm yourself down," he said to himself.

"That makes sense. Getting $320,000 to $330,000 that fast would be a great best-case scenario given the circumstances. Would you share with me what you owe against the property Sam?"

"I owe $290,000."

"Is that all on one mortgage or is it on two or more loans?"

"It's all on one mortgage with GMAC Financing."

"Okay, and what are the payments on that each month?" Mark asked.

"$1,800 per month. That includes the property taxes and home owners insurance though."

"Okay. And if I remember correctly, you told me the house was four months behind on the payments, was that right?" Mark scrunched up his face.

"Yeah. It will be five months behind in 10 more days."

"Have they sent you a letter saying how much it would take to bring the loan back in good standing?"

"If I sent them a check today it would be about $10,000."

"Wow, that much, huh? Have you asked them to see if you paid them a few thousand if they'd let you make payments for the rest of the back payments over time?"

"I thought about that but the most I can afford is about $900 or so a month. That's why I've been looking at two bedroom apartments to rent. There's just no way I can swing the $1,800 a month. Besides, where am I going to get the money to hold them off? No, I just need to sell the house."

"Oh, that makes sense," Mark responded. "You know, I was just thinking of an idea, which you'll probably hate, but what if I could convince my partner that we should put up the $10,000 to make up the back payments and make the loan current, and bought the house, and then each month after that we took over making the payments to the bank. Is that something we should even spend any time talking about, or probably not?"

Sam sat straighter, "Yeah, we should definitely talk about that. How would it work? How much would you pay me for the house?"

"Hang on there for a second Sam, I'm not too sure I'd even be able to get my partner to be willing to put up the ten grand to bring the loan current, which in a few more days will be up to $12,000. But if I could get him to agree to do that—make up the back payments and take over the payments each month after that—why would that even work for you?"

"It would stop the foreclosure and let me get a fresh start for myself."

Mark responded, "Make sure that I'm getting what you're telling me right Sam. If I'm hearing you right, the reason you want us to make up the back payments and buy the house, and take over the monthly payments is because it would stop the foreclosure and get you a fresh start. Did I get your reasons right?"

"Yes, you did. How much would you be able to pay me over what I owe?" Sam asked.

"That's a good question. I'm not so sure. May I ask you a question first?"

"Sure."

"If it turns out that my partner and I decide that we can't buy the property and make a conservative profit for our efforts, what's your plan B? Just in case we decide not to buy it, maybe I can give you some ideas to make your plan B a little better."

"What do you mean? I thought you said you wanted to buy it!"

"Slow down Sam. I want to buy the property, but before I can do that and get my partner to go along with it we're going to need to make sure we can do it in such a way that it fits your needs of stopping the foreclosure and our need to make a fair profit. Just in case we decide we can't do that, what's your Plan B?"

"If you don't buy it? I guess I'll just have to do my best to keep selling it and hope the buyer can close before the auction date."

"And if that doesn't work out . . . ?"

"Then I guess I won't have any choice but to let the bank sell it. I really don't want that to happen."

"I can understand that Sam. If it did turn out that way and the bank sold it at auction, how much do you think the bank will give you for the property?"

"Nothing. A friend of mine who is a mortgage broker explained that because I'll owe around $15,000 in back payments and attorney's fees, the bank would have to get over $305,000 at the auction, and that probably won't happen. I may get $5,000 or $10,000 but not likely. Why?"

"Well I'm just trying to understand what it is that you *really* want to have happen here. I mean, if we could just wave a magic wand here and make the foreclosure and the stress just disappear, but it would mean you walking away from the house for what you owe, is that something you would even consider doing, or you'd probably rather take your chances with the bank, huh?"

"Bottom line I just want this to end fast and I want to be able to walk away with five or ten thousand dollars in my pocket to get a fresh start."

"I can understand that Sam, and I want you to know that even if that means I may not be able to buy the property that it is totally reasonable of you. Heck, if I were you I'd probably want to be able to walk away from all this with a few thousand dollars in my pocket too. Here's what I'm struggling with . . . by the time we could close on the house it would still take about $12,000 cash to bring the loan current. Plus, we'd have to spend up to another $3,000 to $5,000 to get the place in showing condition. Add in closing costs when we buy and a few months holding costs before we find our next resident for the place, and it just won't work financially for us to pay any more into the deal. It adds up pretty fast. Boy, you probably hate the idea of just walking away from the place with a fresh start even if we can't give you any extra money, huh?"

"I don't hate the idea of it. Couldn't you even give me a few thousand dollars?"

"We may very well not be able to give you anything over the money it'd take to pay off all the money owed and for closing costs. But if we could arrange to get you a 'fresh start' gift of $500 or maybe even a little bit more, would you be able to wait for 6 months or 12 months for that money?"

"No, I wouldn't be able to wait for that money. I'd need it for me to move into another place. What about getting me an even grand at the closing? Look, I'm giving you a great deal on the house, and it's only $1,000 we're talking about."

Mark hemmed and hawed for a while, but in the end he gave in and agreed to pay Sam the $1,000 at closing and to buy the property subject to the existing first mortgage. It took Mark another 45 minutes to finish with all the initial paperwork to put the property under contract. When he left and drove back to his house, he was so excited. This was his second deal he had put together in the past six weeks. The first deal had been a straightforward lease option on a worn rental property. It had been nothing down and he'd collected $5,000 of option money from his tenant buyer two days ago. This deal was even better. He was buying the house for a price of $303,000 with $12,000 cash needed to make up the seller's back payments and bring the loan current and another $1,000 of money needed to pay the seller. Mark figured he'd need about another $1,000 for closing costs to make the deal work. But then he'd own the house, which was worth $340,000 and he'd have a great loan in place because he be taking over the house leaving the seller's existing $290,000 first mortgage in place. That loan was at a great interest rate and since he was taking title subject to that loan, he wouldn't have any loan costs or personal liability on the loan.

Mark got right to work when he got home on his due diligence checklist and mapping out his exit strategy for the house. The area was appreciating at only 5 percent, so he figured the most he could get on a two-year rent to own was $359,000. To be safe, he planned on getting $5,000 of up front money from his tenant buyer, which meant he'd need to feed the deal another $7,000 out of his own pocket. He wasn't thrilled about that, but he knew the house would rent for over $2,000 each month so it would give him good cash flow, and the equity in the house once he bought it would be about $40,000. It was a great deal. He could cover the $7,000, but he'd have to use one of his "emergency" credit cards to pull the money out on a cash advance to do it. He needed some input to see if there was a better way to do this.

He turned on his computer and hoped online. He went right to the bookmark he had for the Mentorship student web site. Logging onto the site with his user name and password, Mark jumped on the real estate discussion board. He posted what happened so far today, including all the terms and numbers of his deal, and then asked for ideas to make this good deal even better—especially for ideas on how to lower the amount of money he'd need to come up with out of his pocket to close on the house.

When he was done posting his message, he turned away from the computer and started on the next items on his due diligence checklist. The first thing he did was to fill out a "Memorandum of Agreement" for the seller to get notarized the next day so that he could record his contract so the seller couldn't back out of the deal. He'd made arrangements to meet Sam at 9 A.M. the next morning to get that document notarized at the local copy center.

After about an hour had gone by, Mark checked the discussion board and saw two replies to his post. The first was from a fellow Mentorship student he'd met at the Intensive Training who was congratulating him on his second deal. The second posting was from Emily, one of the Mentorship Coaches, who gave him the exact answer he needed.

> Congratulations and good work, Mark! Here is a potential way to do this without ANY money out of your pocket. Once you've got all the paperwork filled out with the seller, including: notarized and recorded Memorandum of Agreement, signed Agreement for the Purchase of Real Estate, and signed Authorization to Release Information, do a three way phone call with the seller and the bank. Here is what you do:

Get the seller to get a live rep on the phone and then coach them to say, "I have my friend Mark here with me. I don't get all this loan stuff, so I asked Mark to help me out and talk with you and he can explain it to me later. Mark, are you there?"

Then you talk with the lender and see if they'll let the seller (and you because you're buying the property subject to the existing financing) work out a "forbearance agreement". This is basically just a payment plan for the seller to make good on all the back payments. See if the lender will let you make up one or two of the back payments today, and make the next payment and all future payments on time, and then just spread the other back payments into 6–12 equal chunks. From there, negotiate the best payment plan you can.

My guess is that you'll be able to get them to accept two payments now, along with the current payment owed, and then to make two more payments each month until the loan is brought current. This will spread out the money you need to come up with up front and lower your effective risk on the deal. Make sure you get any arrangement down on paper signed by the lender.

There is one more key thing to remember: Do not send the lender any money until you have finished your due diligence, closed on the property, and *know* this is a keeper deal. This means that you've done your rent survey, got title insurance, and closed on the house. Remember, the more money you put into the deal up front, the more risk and commitment you have in the deal.

Again good work Mark and congratulations. I will check back tomorrow to see how you're doing on this deal. Get busy!

Emily
Mentorship Coach

Mark turned away from the screen. Of course, he thought. What a fantastic idea. He immediately began a checklist of things to cover with the seller when he met with him to get the agreement notarized. He was filled with energy. Worst case scenario and he'd have to front the money in the deal himself. With over $40,000 of equity from day one and long-term financing in place, he knew the deal would still be worth it. But he was very excited to see how much better he could make it.

CHAPTER FOURTEEN

Week 7—
Vicki Comes Face to Face
with Her Biggest Fear

Vicki rushed home from her meeting with the seller. She was feeling a rush of conflicting emotions. Excitement, fear, disbelief—all mixed inside her as though her world was spinning.

The first thing she did when she got out of the car was look again at the piece of paper in her shaking hand. There it was, plain as day, it was real. It really happened. There in her hand she looked at the signed contract on her first real estate deal.

She went inside and rushed right to her computer. She had 45 minutes left before she needed to pick up her kids. Just enough time to ask the coaches what in the world was she supposed to do now.

Vicki rushed over to her aging computer and turned it on. She logged right into the private Mentorship student web site. Once on the site, she began posting her questions about what to do next on this deal for the coaches to get her answers.

I did it, I think . . . I just got home from meeting with what might have been the first really motivated seller I've had an appointment with. The seller owned four rental houses when his business (he owns a local shop) started having problems. Not only did he need to raise cash to put into his business, but he just evicted one of his tenants and has another tenant who he thinks he'll have to evict soon. He sold two of the houses conventionally but decided he really just wants to dump these other two houses fast so he doesn't have to put any more time or energy into them. The first two he sold looked like they were the two that were in much better shape. The two that he still has left were fairly shabby—nothing structural but definitely need paint and carpet and some minor fixes (figure around $5,000 each.)

After following the Instant Offer System script exactly like you guys teach, the seller agreed to sell me his two houses for an all-cash price of $175,000 and $200,000 respectively. My gut tells me that after they are cleaned up a bit they are actually worth $270,000 and $300,000!

I didn't know what to do so I did just what you told me to do at the training—I put the houses under contract. I have 45 days (that's all he would give me) to close on them. He wanted me to give him a $10,000 earnest money deposit right there on the spot, but I remembered all the coaching you gave me on this so I negotiated with him to accept a $2,500 earnest money deposit after I have 10 business days to do my due diligence.

I used the contracts I got from the Online Forms Library* that came with the program, and he liked the fact that the Agreement to Sell Real Estate I used didn't have all kinds of weasel clauses in it about our agreement being subject to my partner's approval, etc.

So here's the thing—I know this a great deal—but what do I do now?!!!

I could come up with the $2,500 earnest money deposit by getting a cash advance on one of my credit cards, but I don't have the money to close on the houses. And I don't have a chance of qualifying for a loan for them from a lender (my credit is pretty lousy since just before my divorce, and I don't have the income to support the loan.)

To be honest, I'm scared to death. In fact, I'm more scared now than I was before I got the deal. I could handle the "no's," this "yes" terrifies me.

I will be on the coaching call later tonight at 9 P.M. Any help you have for me would be greatly appreciated.

---

*For more information on how you can inexpensively get investor friendly forms and contracts go to **www.QuickstartInvestor.com**.

Here are the financial details of the deal again:

	House one	House two
After Repair Value:	270,000	300,000
Amount of fix up needed:	5,000	5,000
My purchase price:	175,000	200,000
Cost to buy (my price plus fix-up):	180,000	205,000
Cost to buy divided by As Is value:	67% of value	68% of value

Thanks for any help you can give me.

Vicki

By the time Vicki finished her post she had to get her things together to go pick up the kids. On her drive over to daycare she couldn't stop thinking about her deal. She was so excited and nervous.

She arrived at the daycare center and picked up Josh and Brittney. The next several hours were a blur of activity—getting the kids their dinner, settling an argument they had that had ended with Brittney in hysterical tears and Josh looking innocent and wrongfully accused, and then finally getting them to bed. When all of that was finished, she realized that it was 8:30 P.M. and the coaching call started in half an hour. That was one of the things she had come to depend on about the Mentorship Program. With two to four hours a day of open coaching sessions with the 10 real estate coaches, plus online classes each week in a specific order designed to help students like herself learn at their individual pace, Vicki always felt she had the comprehensive support she needed to succeed.

Because she had half an hour before the coaching call, Vicki decided to check up on the discussion board to see if she had any answers posted for her. To her surprise she saw Emily had posted an answer for her.

Great work Vicki!

I am thrilled for you and want to acknowledge you for your courage and commitment. I remember the talks we've had during our coaching sessions over the past several weeks so I know how hard it's been for you to make the time to do your investing, what with being a single mom with no help from your ex. I also know how scared you were that while real estate might work for other people, it just wouldn't work for you. But you kept at it, with the best attitude you were able to generate. The biggest thing I've noticed is that you've been very consistent in your completion of your weekly assignments from the 90-Day Plan of Action.

As for this specific deal, here are my thoughts. If you have any questions about them I am doing the coaching call tonight at 9pm and will be ready to take the time needed to go over them with you.

1. The prices you locked up are good enough that you can do this deal without needing any of your own money (except potentially $2,500, but more on this below). You have the first house at 67 percent of value and the other house is at 68 percent of value. If these values prove to be accurate, then these deals look very good.

2. You have four main choices to close on this property outside of conventional financing. They are:

    a. Flip the deal to another investor—this means you find an investor who would love to buy your contractual right to purchase these two houses for such a great price. This investor would typically pay between 5–15 percent of the expected profits in the deal because, as a cash deal, the profits have a very high likelihood of working out. In this deal that would mean you assigning over your rights in the purchase contract with the seller for $10,000 to $15,000. If you had more time than 45 days, I think you could get as much as $20,000 to $25,000, but in this case I think you would do better to get a smaller assignment fee to make your first deal happen more easily.

    b. Sell the property to a retail buyer (this is the typical buyer of a home) for a great deal. In this case, you could sell it to your new buyer for the all-cash price of 80–90 percent of value. My favorite way to maximize profits from a deal like this is to sell the house with owner financing. If you choose this option, the coaches and I will walk you through the whole process step by step.

    c. You could get a hard money loan for the purchase price and close on the two houses. You would have to quickly fix them up and most likely sell them for cash because the hard money loan interest payments will be fairly high. But these prices are good enough for you to still make $50,000 to $90,000 even if you discounted the price for your next buyer to get them sold fast.

    d. You could bring in a money partner to fund the deal and split the profits 50–50. If you choose this option you have any one of a number of exit strategies. You could resell to a retail cash buyer after fixing the house up. You could sell on a rent-to-own basis. Or you could hold onto the properties long term as conventional rentals. Each of these exit strategies would work very well with the right money partner.

Those are some options you have. You'll need to decide your exit strategy soon. Each of the options have good and bad to them.

1. Flipping the deal gets you the easiest and quickest profit ($10,000 to 15,000) but it's also the smallest profit. If you choose this option you are trading speed and ease for a smaller profit.

2. Selling the house to a retail buyer at a discount or with owner financing (my typical favorite) will get you a large profit with a medium amount of work. The major downside of this option is that you don't have a lot of time to find your buyer before you need to close with the seller.

3. Hard money is a good option here, but you will need to be rock solid on the values and numbers before you choose this option because of the high interest rate eating away at your profit each and every month the house sits there before you resell it. This one can also be fairly stressful.

4. A money partner is great because they put up the money and typically don't get interest payments because they'll be an equity partner in the deal. This lowers your risk (much of which is passed on to the money partner).

You can tell me which options work best for you tonight on the call.

Here is your assigned action step: Go to the Deal Completion Wizard on the Mentorship web site and read through the summary of the 15-step due diligence checklist. For now, all I am asking you to complete are steps 1–3 within the next three days, and then check back with me on the discussion board or one of the coaching calls so we can go over the results you generated and your next steps after that. Congratulations again—you're going to make a healthy profit on this deal no matter which exit strategy you choose.

Emily

Mentorship Coach

Vicki not only read through the post twice, but she printed it out too.

Realizing the coaching session was just getting started, Vicki put down the print out and signed into the coaching session. Because Vicki had high-speed web access, she chose the option to get on the coaching call online rather than through the normal phone line. She liked the way the online version had the coaches "white board" for seeing the numbers and notes they were discussing, plus Vicki liked engaging in private chats with other students and even the coaches while the coaching call was going on.

"Hi everyone, this is Emily and I'll be leading today's coaching call." Emily's warm voice resonated the certainty that Vicki really needed. After having everyone briefly introduce themselves on the call, Emily started helping students with deals they were working on.

After about ten minutes it was Vicki's turn. "First, Emily," Vicki said, "I wanted to let you know that the coaching you gave to Sharon on that last deal was really useful for me too. One of the things I love about these coaching calls and the discussion board is how much faster I've been learning as a result of everyone else's questions. It's as though I am getting the benefit of ten times the number of potential deals and case studies just by hanging around and paying attention to all the quality questions and answers that are out there. Thanks for that Emily."

"Wow! That's a nice thing to hear Vicki. You're welcome." Emily laughed. "Now the pressure's really on and I have to give you a great answer to your question! I know the details of your deal, why don't you quickly recap your two deals that you have under contract and the conversation we've had on the discussion board. Not only will this bring the other five students on the call tonight up to speed on the deals, but it will also help me to make sure I was clear with my post to you a few hours ago."

Vicki took about five minutes and laid out the key details of her two houses under contract and the discussion she and Emily had had online. When she was done, she asked Emily her questions.

"Emily, your response was very clear and I'm ready to do the action steps you assigned me. My real question has to do with which exit strategy I should choose. I read through all four of the options you laid out. I guess my question is, which do you think is best?"

Emily answered in a quiet voice, "You know Vicki, I'm not going to give you the answer you want. I'm not going to tell you that you should absolutely choose option 1 or 2. None of us coaches are here to make your investing decisions for you. We are here to help you through the deal step by step, but our goal is to help develop you into a fully independent investor not a dependent one. So while I'll be helping you each step of the way, let me ask you: Understanding the benefits and downsides of each of the exit strategies, which of the options feels like the best fit for you?"

Vicki paused for a moment, obviously struggling with the question. "That's just it Emily. I don't know which one is right for me. Just tell me which is best!"

"I won't tell you which is best because that is impossible. Each of the four options has good and bad sides to it. Let's go at this a different way. What's most important to you, Vicki, out of these first two deals of yours? Is it to maximize long-term profit even if that means more work and a higher degree of uncertainty of the deal working out? Or is it to just get some quick cash now and build your confidence by getting your first two deals under your belt?"

"Well, when you put it that way I think that just getting these first two deals done and making some quick money is most important to me. If I could do that it would really make me feel more confident about myself and my investing. Plus, that way when my family or friends ask me about my investing I wouldn't feel so scared to tell them about it."

Emily responded, "Hearing that Vicki, it seems like finding another investor to sell your contract to might be the best exit strategy. Let's go with that one for now. You think it over tonight. If you still feel that's the way to go in the morning, then get to work on the steps I'll give you tonight. If you change your mind, just let me know and either I or one of the other coaches will walk you through the new option your choose. How does that sound to you?"

"That sounds great," Vicki answered.

"Okay, here is your plan of action to flip your deal to another investor."* Emily spent the next five minutes clarifying Vicki's next steps to flip the deal.

"Emily, this is Leon on the call and I just wanted to ask a question about Vicki's exit strategy."

"Sure thing Leon, what's your question," Emily responded.

---

*If you want to learn more about creating fast paydays by flipping deals download your FREE copy of the ebook, *Three Simple Steps to Flip a Deal For Fast Cash* by going to **www.QuickstartInvestor.com**.

"How can Vicki sell a house she doesn't own?" Leon asked.

"It sure seems strange doesn't it Leon. The fact is that Vicki is not selling a house to another investor. What she is really doing is assigning her right to purchase each of these two houses as laid out in the agreement she signed with the seller to this new investor for a fair fee. The way it works is that this new investor agrees to pay Vicki, let's say $15,000 to buy the rights to both contracts. This new investor gives Vicki a non-refundable earnest money deposit of $3,000 and agrees to pay the remaining $12,000 to Vicki within 10 days. When the new investor pays Vicki this remaining money, Vicki signs a simple Assignment of Contract agreement giving all her contractual rights to buy the property over to this new investor. Then this new investor moves ahead and closes on the two houses with the original seller."

"You can do that?" Leon asked a little hesitatingly.

"Absolutely. Any contract is fully assignable unless something in the contract expressly prohibits it from being assigned." Emily went on to explain. "Now Vicki, are you clear on the steps you are going to need to take over the next week?"

Vicki said she was, and then Emily had Vicki go back through the list one more time to make sure she was clear. The final half hour of the call went by in the blink of an eye. Vicki logged off the call when it was over and sat back in her chair. "*You can do this,*" she said to herself over and over again trying to hang onto the confidence she felt while she was listening to Emily's voice. But she couldn't quite hang onto the voice, and as it faded off it was as if a dark part of her was listening and began arguing back. "*No you can't. Who are you kidding Vicki. You'll never make it as an investor. You were never meant to be rich. You're just an average person. What makes you think you can do this? Who do you think you are? You're too stupid do this. You've never done anything like this before. This stuff won't really work for you.*"

Try as she might Vicki couldn't make that cruel voice shut up. She began to rock herself in her chair desperately working to hold back the wave of despair and fear she felt mounting like a river of water behind a shaky little dam. Just then she noticed she had an instant message invitation from another Mentorship student. She moved the mouse and clicked on the "Chat" button and the message popped up.

"Vicki. We haven't met. My name is Allison and I'm actually a Level Two Consulting client. I just happened to be on the call tonight because I needed to get Emily's help on a property I am refinancing."

"Yes, I remember you. You were one of the people Emily coached on tonight's call."

"That's right. Normally I don't participate in the Level One Mentorship calls like tonight's, but I really was desperate for a quick answer and Emily is always so great. But that's not why I wanted to talk with you. When I heard you on the call tonight, you reminded me of someone I knew when I first got started with the Mentorship Program over two years ago. She was a single mom with three kids under 12. She almost quit after her first week investing because a seller literally laughed at her and said she was wasting his time because she obviously wasn't an investor. But she hung in there and eventually four months later she signed up her first deal. It was actually a lease option, not a cash deal like yours, but she almost panicked and gave up on her investing. There was something in your voice tonight that reminded me of that student and I wanted to let you know what's possible for you."

"What do you mean what's possible for me?"

"With only five days left before her first payment to the seller was due this woman found her tenant buyer for the property who gave her $8,000 option money plus $1,900 first month's rent. She had to give $3,000 to the seller but the remaining money was what she needed to make her mortgage current. You see, while she was trying to get started with her investing, she had to cut back on the overtime she had been working, and that meant that she wasn't able to make her monthly mortgage payment for the past three months. She was right on the edge of losing her home when this first deal gave her the breathing space she needed to keep going after her dreams. Anyway the reason I'm telling you this is because if you're like this woman, you probably have all these fearful thoughts going through your mind right now about how you can't make this deal work and all that. I just want to reassure you that you can and will make it happen. Just do everything the coaches tell you, and when you get scared, breath . . . and keep going in spite of your fears."

By this point Vicki was in tears. "I can't thank you enough for your kindness and encouragement Allison. How can I ever repay you? I was so scared just a moment ago and sure I'd blow this deal, but now while I'm still scared, I think that just maybe I can do this."

"No maybe's about it Vicki! You can and will do it! The next time you even consider giving in to the fear, look into the eyes of your kids and know that you are not doing it for yourself. You're doing it for them. Then fight like crazy if you have to, but push on through the fear. Quitting is not an option."

"Allison? Whatever happened to this woman? Is she still investing?"

"Yes she is. In fact she's been a full time investor now for the past 12 months. At last count she's up to 16 houses in her portfolio, plus she's sold or flipped seven more. She's actually made more money in the last three months than she made in the last three years of her old job, which she hated by the way."

"That's incredible Allison. Thank you again for sharing this hope and strength with me. How can I ever repay you for your kindness? Is there some way I could thank this woman too, for being such an inspiration to me? How can I meet her?"

"You just have, Vicki. That student was me. Real estate has changed my life and it's changed my kids' lives. Hang in there Vicki. I believe in you. God bless you, and remember this moment and share it with someone else down the road. You'll know when the time is right."

CHAPTER FIFTEEN

Week 10—
Leon and Mary Learn
to Maximize Their Money

Leon and Mary had set aside the morning time to talk through their goals with respect to real estate. One of the big items they went over was what to do with their existing three rental properties. These were all properties they had purchased using traditional financing before they had joined the program and learned all the powerful deal finding, structuring, negotiating, and managing techniques.

After an hour of talking their situation through they had the makings of a plan, but they wanted to ask the coaches a few questions first to make sure their strategy made sense, and to find out the best way to actually implement it. This is when they got on the conference call this time being led by John from San Diego.

Leon and Mary patiently listened to all the questions from other students, taking notes on ideas they thought they could apply to their investing. When it was their turn they outlined their situation to John to get his feedback.

"Here's the thing John," Leon said. "Mary and I don't need any quick cash coming in right now. We've got my retirement income that covers all our living expenses, so we don't need current income from our real estate. Our goal is to generate a large portfolio of winning properties over the next 36 months that we can hang onto over time so that we can not only improve our lifestyle and make sure we're safe, just in case some economic problem happened, but we also want to be able to help create enough wealth so that we can eventually pay a large part of our four grandchildren's college expenses. Our thoughts are that if we can get a portfolio of homes in nice areas together, then not only will these homes boost our cash flow by $3,000 to $5,000 per month, but because they will be quality properties that will appreciate over the long term, we'll also be increasing our net worth over time too."

John prompted Leon, "That sounds like a very realistic and achievable goal Leon. What was it you needed from me?"

"Well, we know what our general plan is, but we've been struggling with a few things and would really appreciate your insight."

"Go ahead and I'll do my best."

Leon read through his first question from his list of questions. "We don't want to get stuck in the day-to-day management of a ton of rental properties if we can avoid it. That's one of the reasons we liked the idea of putting tenant buyers in our future properties who won't just be renters, but will also have the option to purchase these homes. I understand that by letting these tenant buyers rent to own the property they will not only give us an up-front option payment of 3–5 percent of the value of the property, but they will also take care of most, if not all, of the maintenance. But if we do this, doesn't that mean we are selling the property? And if we're selling the property, how are we building a portfolio for the long term?"

"You know Leon," John answered, "When I started buying properties in San Diego I didn't want any of my houses to sell. The market was going up over 15 percent each year, and I wanted them for the long term. Here's what I've found. Most tenant buyers will choose not to buy. For one reason or another, they will end up leaving the property after two or three years. This means we get the property back at the end and rarely had to do any real maintenance or fix up to the place during that time. When we get the property back, we put a little money into prepping it for the next tenant buyer and so on. I look at a property on a rent to own basis almost like a way of temporarily parking the property for a few years. The tenant buyer treats the house much better than the average renter and typically is much better about paying their monthly rent on time. On average, you'll find one out of four tenant buyers buying, with three out of four choosing not to exercise their option to buy."

Mary interrupted and asked, "That few end up buying?"

"On average, yes," John said. "Now you can increase that percentage so that as many as half of your tenant buyers will buy just by doing some specific things: match them up with a mortgage broker who will work with them about 12 months prior to the time they want to buy so that they can start cleaning up their financial act to be more able to get a loan to cash you out down the road; keep an eye on them every few months about what they'll need to do to get qualified to buy the house; possibly even carry back a small second mortgage to help them qualify more easily for their loan; and things like this."*

"So is it better for us to put renters in our properties as we pick them up or offer them on a rent-to-own basis to tenant buyers?" Leon asked.

"That is going to depend on you. The way I do it is I offer almost all of my properties on a rent-to-own basis. Over time, about two or three of them sell each year, and my portfolio grows over time. I also take some of the properties that are easiest to manage and sometimes just offer them on a straight rental basis, but usually only if they are a truly easy rental property. I know that Peter and David have a manager take care of both their rent-to-own properties and their rentals. Right now I manage most of my own properties, but it has been pretty easy since most are rent-to-owns. For me, the money generated from the rents each month, plus the money I get from the few that sell each year, produce a really good income stream for my family over time. Does that make sense?" John asked.

---

*To learn more about pricing strategies to increase or decrease the likelihood of your tenant buyer buying, log onto **www.QuickstartInvestor.com** and download the free ebook, *Seven Simple Steps to Sell Your Property on a Rent to Own Basis*.

"It does," Leon replied. "It's like you use the rent-to-own as a way of holding onto your properties over the long term, turning a few of the very best into straight rentals, and selling off a few of them each year."

"Exactly! And it doesn't hurt that when a tenant buyer chooses to buy, I get a very fair price for the property with no real estate commission or closing costs."

"John," Mary asked, "Our last question for you has to do with investing with cash. I know you talk about how to invest without cash or credit, and that all makes great sense, but Leon and I have a fairly good sized nest egg we've managed to save over the years. What's the best way we can leverage that money to accelerate our investing?"

"What a great question Mary. It's something that most investors have to deal with at some point. I think it's much easier to invest with cash and good credit, the only problem is sometimes it's too easy. I've watched investors put all their cash into one or two deals and then get stuck waiting for those properties to sell to get access to their cash again. In the meantime, since they only knew how to buy using their cash, they missed out on several very lucrative deals during the time their cash was tied up in the properties that weren't selling. My best advice to you is to use your cash wisely. Normally, this means not putting it all into one property but to spread it out over several properties. When I buy for cash now, I often will mix my money in with a private money lender. It gives me the flexibility to do more properties. Over the long haul this has been a real good strategy for me. Now, you might find you prefer not to do this, and instead choose to use your money to buy a fixer-upper. If you do this, just make sure you are ready if worse comes to worst to have your cash tied up for longer than you originally planned. Bottom line is that if you have cash to use in your investing that is great. Leverage it into several deals as best you can instead of dumping it all into one deal you are buying all with your own cash."

Leon and Mary thanked John and participated in the rest of the coaching session. When they got off the phone, they immediately pulled out their draft action plan and began improving their outline using the ideas John had shared. They were both very excited with the decisions they had made and were looking forward to meeting with their mastermind team in person in seven weeks on the Friday night before the Advanced Training they were both enrolled in.

7 Ways to Maximize Your Cash When Investing

Although it's all the rage to talk about doing every real estate deal with nothing down, there are times and situations where it makes smart financial sense to use your own cash in your investing.

Many of our students have a chunk of money, whether from their accumulated profits from investing or from other sources, to use in their investing and they want to get the best return on that money. We are in this situation too. Early on, we did all our investing with no money down because we didn't have any cash to spare. Later we continued to buy predominately with little or nothing down because it was extremely profitable. Now we still do much of our real estate investing without our cash or credit, yet we are willing to ante up our own money if the deal warrants it.

So how would we recommend you maximize the return on your capital when investing in real estate? Here are seven tips to help you make the best use of your cash...

1) Learn how to invest with little or nothing down first BEFORE you start to invest your own cash or credit. It's been our experience that too many investors will throw money into a marginal deal where a little more imagination, knowledge, and negotiation skill would have been the best way to go. Establish a strong foundation of investing skills and practice on a few nothing-down deals first. Then and only then put up your hard earned cash.

2) Value your cash. New investors often forget that their personal cash is more valuable than money they owe. $100,000 borrowed from a seller through owner financing or through a lender is not the same thing as $100,000 in your bank account, and they should not be equated as such. Anytime you take your liquid assets and use them in your investing, you need to make sure you are getting an incredible deal to make it worthwhile. Don't make the huge mistake of thinking that $100,000 of equity in a house is comparable to $100,000 of cash. Here is the spectrum of what form of $100,000 is most valuable to you:

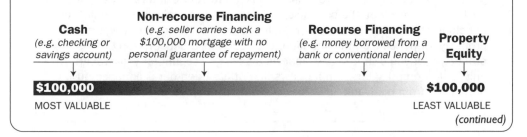

Cash *(e.g. checking or savings account)*	**Non-recourse Financing** *(e.g. seller carries back a $100,000 mortgage with no personal guarantee of repayment)*	**Recourse Financing** *(e.g. money borrowed from a bank or conventional lender)*	**Property Equity**

$100,000   **$100,000**

MOST VALUABLE   LEAST VALUABLE

(continued)

7 Ways to Maximize Your Cash When Investing *(continued)*

Notice that cash is most valuable in the spectrum, and equity is least valuable because it is the least liquid form of wealth.

3) Leverage your cash. One of our favorite buying strategies is to leverage our cash in a deal by mixing it with some form of owner financing. For example, we find a seller who is willing to carry back most of the financing if he knows we're committed to the deal and he gets some of our money up front. Perhaps we can use a down payment of 10 percent with the seller carrying back the balance. This differs from just putting a down payment down and using conventional financing for the balance because with seller financing you can often get incredible deals on the terms of the seller financing. We've negotiated seller financing with interest rates half of what a conventional lender would have given us. We've also negotiated interest-free loans where all our monthly payments have gone to pay down the principal balance of the loan. Plus, with owner financing you'll almost never have any loan costs or qualifying paperwork to deal with.

4) Use your cash to bail out sellers in foreclosure and take over the property subject to the existing financing. Here is a specific application to leverage your cash with sellers in financial distress. This is one of the single most lucrative ways to maximize your cash in a deal, so we highlighted it as it's own tip. An example: We found a seller who was four months behind in her payments and about midway through the foreclosure process. We agreed to make up her back payments and give her some cash for her equity in the property in exchange for her selling us the house subject to her existing financing. All totaled, it took us about $20,000 to get the house, but we ended up with over $80,000 of equity from day one and a positive cash flow of over $350 per month. One of the coaches in our Mentoring Program came up with the ratio of 1 to 4. For every $1 of his cash he is willing to put in a deal, he wants $4 of immediate equity. The benefit of this technique is that it allows you to take your $100,000 of cash and leverage that into five or more properties instead of sinking it all into one. This will exponentially magnify your wealth producing rate of return.

5) When you use your cash, clear your money from the table as fast as possible. When buying with your cash, make sure your exit strategy will get you back your money from the deal quickly. There are two main ways to pull your principal from a deal right away—reselling the property or borrowing off the property. Depending on the situation, both can make sense. Don't use a property that you own free and clear as a savings account for your wealth. Not only is it a tempting target in any lawsuit, but it's been our experience buying properties from motivated investors that when you need the cash most will

(continued)

7 Ways to Maximize Your Cash When Investing *(continued)*

invariably be the moment you struggle to get the cash out of the property. This has forced many investors to sell for dramatically less than they could have had they only had more time. The best course of action when you use a large chunk of your cash to buy a property is to either resell or refinance that property to recoup your investable cash.

6) Leverage your cash in marketing. The best deals always come when you have found a highly motivated seller. We strongly recommend that you take a portion of your capital and invest it in marketing activities to find motivated sellers. This could be classified ads, or direct mail campaigns, or simply hiring outside help to put out 100 I BUY HOUSES signs per month. The bottom line is that money invested in intelligent marketing will reap a huge return.

7) Leverage your cash in training*. We saved this one for last on the list because we believe it is the most important. We strongly council you to invest a portion of your capital to get the best investor training possible so that you learn through the accumulated experience of other people's painful experiences. There is no greater form of leverage than that of other people's knowledge and expertise properly harnessed and directed.

*For a suggested reading list of books, home study courses, workshops, mentoring and consulting programs to help you succeed as a real estate investor, log onto **www.QuickstartInvestor.com**.

CHAPTER SIXTEEN

The 90-Day Checkpoint—
The Mastermind Reunion on
the Eve of the Advanced Training

Vicki was nervous as she walked down the hall of the hotel. Here it was just 90 days after her rocky start investing in real estate and she was getting together in person with her mastermind group. They had all said the timing couldn't have been any better since the Advanced Investor Training just happened to fall the day after they had wanted to meet in person for their 90-Day Check-in.

She reached the meeting room they had reserved at the hotel to hold their mastermind session and walked in.

"Vicki!" Mary rose immediately from her seat and came over to give Vicki a warm hug. "It's so great to see you!" More hugs from everyone else followed, and the next half hour was simply a chance to connect with her friends, for that's what they had truly become. For the past 90 days they had each supported and encouraged each other. And when it was needed, they had even given each other a kick in the pants to get back to work. Now was their chance to mastermind on all they had accomplished and learned, re-evaluate their goals, and adjust their action plans to be even more effective and productive.

"Well, you all chose me to lead today's mastermind session," Nancy announced in the middle of all the separate conversations and laughter. "So I suggest we all take our seats and get started. We've set aside three hours for our mastermind meeting, and then we have reservations at a great restaurant for dinner that is just a short ride from here.

"The first thing on our meeting plan is to go around and each take three to five minutes to give a summary of our investing successes to date, the major lessons we've learned in the last 90 days, and finally, how we are feeling about our investing at this moment in time. Who wants to start?" Nancy asked.

Mark volunteered to go first: "For me things in my investing have just happened so quickly, it's almost overwhelming. Since the Intensive Training I have done five deals. I purchased three houses subject to the existing financing and I picked up one house on a four-year lease option. All have tenant buyers in them. These four properties generate about $800 per month of positive cash flow at this point, they netted me $12,000 in option payments from my tenant buyers, and I have over $90,000 of back-end profits waiting for me. The fifth deal was a duplex that I put under contract and flipped to another investor for an $18,000 profit.

"I finally feel comfortable using the Instant Offer System when I meet with sellers, and I think I have a real good sense of knowing who's motivated and who isn't when I talk with sellers over the phone. I've got two really solid lead generators consistently going in the form of my classified I Buy Houses ad and my I Buy Houses signs. My ad generates about two or three calls a week, of which four or five of these calls per month are good leads. My signs generate more calls, but when all is said and done, it delivers about the same number of good leads per month as my ad.

"My biggest challenge has been time, which is something I'll bring up later in the mastermind session when we get to the 'challenge solution' session. But I do have an important announcement to make. Originally I had planned to transition into investing full time over the first 24 months, but with all that's happened and the growth I've experienced as part of the Mentorship Program, I've decided to make that transition over the next three months. I think this has been my biggest lesson, that in order for me to really grow as an investor I am going to have to make the leap of faith into doing my investing full time. That's one of the reasons I am so excited about the Advanced Investor Training this weekend because it will help me make the transition into being a Level Two investor much easier and faster.

"As for how I am feeling about all this, I guess I am feeling incredibly grateful and excited. I'm grateful for how quickly things have been working out for me and that I can see how, within the next year or two, I'll have the time to volunteer to lead a middle school or high school music program. I'm excited about how much fun it's been putting myself out there and jumping into my investing with both feet. I've always been a challenge motivated person and you all and the Mentorship Coaches have really pushed me, and I am very appreciative and thankful for that support."

They all congratulated Mark on his success and all that he had accomplished over the last 90 days. Next it was Leon and Mary's turn: "Well we have a small surprise to share with you all. You know how three weeks ago we signed our first deal—that five-year-lease option on the townhouse in the downtown area of where we live? Well, two days ago we met with our tenant buyer for that property and collected a nonrefundable deposit of $1,500 to hold the property, and we'll be meeting with her the day we get home from the Advanced Investor Training to collect the other $7,000 she agreed to pay as option money! We are so excited to have done our first *whole* deal.

"Also, now that we have seen how easy it is to find a tenant buyer when you follow the action steps and coaching laid out in the Mentorship Program, we have made the decision to convert two of our rental properties into rent-to-own houses over the next month. We have a great tenant in the third property so we are going to leave that one as a straight rental for the time being. We figure that we can increase our cash flow by over $500 per month by switching the other two properties into rent-to-own.

"Our biggest lesson has been to finally understand what it means to buy a property for cash and how we need to value our money more when we're investing. We just never really understood this before we got started with the Mentorship Program and we realize that this caused us to pay too much for two of our three rental properties. We now plan to take a chunk of our nest egg and use it over the next nine months to buy eight more houses subject to the existing financing. Plus, we have decided to put a part of the money into our marketing campaigns to generate motivated sellers. The final lesson we learned has been how valuable it's been to get on all the coaching calls and actively participate in the program. We've learned so much both from our own efforts and from listening in as the coaches help other students."

Tim and Nancy went next with Nancy beginning. "It's been hard going for us. We really struggled for the first month or two with our biggest obstacle being ourselves. Tim had to really work hard to retrain himself out of many of the sales habits he had acquired from all the years he's spent in sales. I've been so proud of his work ethic and diligence doing this. He makes his dials every day and meets with at least two sellers every week, no matter what.

"At first I was so hard on him and negative about whether this investing would really work. I kept saying things like, 'this stuff won't really work in our area.' And he never got mad at me for all my complaints. I have to say that the biggest challenge for us has been me. When we finally signed up our first deal but couldn't find a tenant buyer for the property, I was like, 'See, I told you this stuff doesn't work.' But something happened to me about week ten. I guess it was watching all of you blossom and getting that weekly input from the coaches. I finally realized that it was working for all of you and that the only difference was that I had had such a horrible attitude through the process. I finally understood that I was the reason we weren't being successful. My attitude needed to change or we wouldn't make it. Tim and I had a long talk about it, and we came to the conclusion that if it takes us another three months or three years to make our investing work, it doesn't matter. We are totally committed and know that this will happen for us. I feel like even though we haven't done a deal yet, we are already into the beginning stages of Level Two investing because we *know* this will work for us. It's just going to take a little more time."

Tim was uncharacteristically quiet as Nancy shared all this. The group could see his eyes get moist as he reached out and took Nancy's hand in his. "I've let go of my timeline for needing this to happen," Tim said. "I have decided to just trust and keep myself focused on the behaviors and actions I can control. I feel so blessed with the changes Nancy has gone through. Forgetting all this real estate stuff, it's made a dramatic difference in our marriage. I've always dreamed of being loved the way she loves me know. I feel so content right now. The real estate stuff is almost a side benefit, you know?"

They all looked at Tim and Nancy and marveled at their growth and courage. Then quietly they turned and waited for Vicki to take her turn.

"I've got a confession to make," Vicki began. "I've been keeping something from the group. You all have been so important to me over these past three months. You've seen me when I felt terrified that I couldn't do this investing and you've encouraged me when I felt overwhelmed taking care of my kids, working at the hospital, and then fitting in my investing around both those other things. You've been so great that I feel really guilty that I haven't been honest with you.

"You know how I had locked up those two houses from that one seller under contract to purchase as cash deals? The first week with those houses under contract I felt paralyzed trying to find another investor to flip the deals to. I was scared that I wouldn't be able to do it, and I was even more scared of what it would mean if I *was* able to do it. It would mean that all the excuses I'm made throughout my life were just that—excuses—and that the only one responsible was me." Vicki looked around the room and saw the concerned and caring faces of her friends.

"I feel like I shouldn't have kept this from you all, but . . ." Vicki paused. "Well four weeks ago I actually flipped one of the two contracts to another investor who paid me a $12,000 assignment fee!" Everyone was stunned. They knew what this money meant to Vicki who was struggling to raise her family on her nurse's salary.

"But you never told us!" Mark interjected.

"I know I didn't. I wanted to keep it as a surprise for this reunion. And I have two more things to share with you all." They all looked at her expectantly. "I guess getting that $12,000 cashiers check in my hand gave me the boost of courage I needed to know I could do this or something, but I approached my sister who is an attorney in Chicago. I explained to her about my two deals and how I had just sold one contract to another investor and that I had one more house left but that I needed to cash the seller out in 4 more weeks. To make a long story short she agreed to be my money partner on that deal. We actually closed on the house three weeks ago and immediately did all the cosmetic fix-up work and put the house back on the market. We decided to sell it ourselves at a discount, and nine days ago we found our buyer! The escrow is set to close in three more weeks, and when all is said and done my sister and I will split a check for $58,000!" They all went crazy with this news, cheering and celebrating.

"But you said you had two more things to tell us." Mary interrupted. "What's the second secret?" At this the whole room grew quiet and all eyes went expectantly to Vicki.

"Well I've made the decision that when I get my half of that $58,000 I will take a leave of absence from the hospital and start my investing full time. That means I'll have more time to do deals and because I can arrange most of my investing around my schedule I'll have more time with my kids."

At this point they all got up and hugged Vicki. They were so happy for her success and in awe at the growth she had shown in the past 90 days since she got started with her investing. After letting the celebration continue for a while, Nancy got them back into their mastermind meeting. They finished the meeting and truly celebrated that night over a fine dinner. As they all went to bed that night, they wondered what the next day would bring. Just 90 days ago none of them had imagined how much real estate, the Intensive Training, and the Mentorship Program would change their lives nor how quickly. They went to bed that night with a strong feeling of positive expectancy for what the Advanced Investor Training would bring for them.*

---

*Would you like to "attend" that Advanced Investor Training and find out what's being taught to help these six investors successfully transition into Level Two investing? Then make sure you get a copy of book two of the *Creating Cash Flow* series, *The Real-Estate Fast-Track! How to Generate a $5,000 to $50,000 per Month Real Estate Cash Flow*. In it you'll learn exactly what it takes to master the five core investor skills and how to build a successful investing business. For details on the publication date for this second book in the series just go to **www.QuickstartInvestor.com**.

YOUR TURN!

CHAPTER SEVENTEEN

Seven Real-Life Success Stories to Get You Fired Up

Patty

If you're wondering if you can really make these ideas and strategies work for you, take one of our recent Mentorship Graduates, Patty. When she first got started with our program, she had just been laid off. Not only did she have to deal with all the normal emotions of losing her job as her old company made massive cutbacks, but for Patty this was even harder because it had be the highest paying job she ever had—earning $45,000 per year.

Patty actually had to borrow the tuition to participate in the Mentorship Program from her mother. But she got started with her investing, which is one of three critical steps to being a successful investor. Her first nine months were tough. Because she didn't think she had the money to do her marketing, she cut corners with following the 90-Day Action Plan we had laid out for her. Still, even though she drastically "modified" the action plan, she was still able to complete her first deal within 90 days of getting started. But over the next six months of doing it her way, she didn't close any deals. It was during these six months that Patty demonstrated the second critical step to succeed in your investing—she persevered. She could have quit on her investing and looked to find another "dream job" earning $45,000 per year, but she didn't. She recognized that the only real chance she ever had to be the one in control of her financial destiny was for her to stay with her investing. It was at this point that she took the third, and ultimately the most important step of her investing—she opened herself up to doing it exactly like we coached and mentored her, without any more "modifications."

The first thing she did was attend one of our advanced investor trainings where she focused on how to better execute her marketing efforts to find motivated sellers. When she went home from this training she put into action three of the deal-finding strategies that she had learned, which only cost her $150 to implement. Using these three techniques she found three subject to deals, two foreclosure deals, one lease-option deal, and two rehab deals. And she did these all within four months!

When she sold four of these properties she ended up putting $195,000 into her bank account! Plus, she still had five other properties in her portfolio. Patty's courage to take those three critical steps helped her net almost *five times* more money then she had ever earned in one year before. Best of all, she now knows that she is the one in control of her own financial life.

Sasha

Or take Sasha, one of our Mentorship Graduates from Colorado. During his first 18 months Sasha literally signed up a dozen deals, only to have all of them fall apart. He was doing his investing part time, with his full time profession being a talented physical therapist. As you can probably imagine, Sasha was working against himself, and without realizing it he was pulling apart his own deals. It was during these 18 months that the support of his mastermind group of fellow investors he had met at the Intensive Training became so critical. He saw his mastermind partners, Kevin and Stephanie, go on to do many deals during that difficult period of his investing. This proved to him that the system worked, it was just that he was sabotaging his own deals.

The turning point for him was when Kevin asked him if he wanted to be the money partner on one of his deals, providing money needed to fund a down payment on the purchase of a house. Sasha agreed and became a fifty percent owner of the property. This proved to be one of the most important decisions he ever made. It allowed him to finally make the shift to seeing himself as an investor. Over the next 10 months, he picked up 10 deals, all of which were successfully closed, and he generated over $200,000 in profits. In fact, he recently came back to our Advanced Negotiation Workshop and shared with the entire class of 180 investors that he had quit his job as a physical therapist and was now a full time investor. At that point, his portfolio was generating $2,000 per month cash flow from his rents and he had over $250,000 in back-end profits. It took great courage on his part to remain true to his decision to make his investing work no matter what, but again and again we've seen the truth, that if you persist in your dream of successfully becoming a real estate investor, if you consistently take action, and if you learn from the best, then you can and WILL succeed in your investing.

Jeff

After spending six years overseas as a missionary, Jeff and his wife returned home to Iowa with a net worth of only $50,000. It was at that point Jeff began his investing career by joining our Mentorship Program (that was five years ago). In his first two years of investing, Jeff slowly picked up four houses and built up his roofing and carpet installation businesses.

After attending a Level Three Investor event we held, called The Maui Mastermind,* Jeff made some ambitious plans for his investing. During the next 12 months after leaving that Level Three event, he picked up 18 single family houses, 3 four-plexes, 3 duplexes, and 20 manufactured homes on an urban infill lot!**

Over the course of five years, Jeff was not only able to increase his net worth by over several million dollars, but more importantly he finally uncovered his real

---

*To learn more about the Maui Mastermind event just go to **www.QuickstartInvestor.com**. Each year we hold this one-of-a-kind event in conjunction with our mastermind partners to help our very best clients become Level Three investors.
To watch an interview with Jeff where he and his business partner Scott share how they sold 84 houses in one day just go to **www.QuickstartInvestor.com.

passion—helping other people succeed financially. Jeff and his business partner Scott now specialize in purchasing and packaging blocks of investment properties and installing management teams and systems to make them cash flow well, and then selling these blocks of properties to outside investors. They now package and sell well over 100 properties a year and feel great about the income they've helped their investor clients generate.

Juli

Juli was a holistic healer from the Seattle area. When she got started with our Mentorship Program, she had just started to invest in real estate after being inspired to get out of the rat race and create financial freedom for herself after reading, *Rich Dad, Poor Dad*. At that point, she and a partner had purchased one rehab property, but her partner had literally quit on her leaving her on her own.

That's when she found our book, *Making Big Money Investing In Real Estate Without Tenants, Banks, or Rehab Projects*. After four months of trying to do it on her own without any success, she called our office and spoke with one of our experienced Program Consultants. After completing the 45-minute Strategic Investors Consultation, Juli was laser clear and focused on the exact next steps she needed to take to get started with her investing. It was also at this time that Juli joined our Mentorship Program. Fast forward by 24 months and Juli has now completed over ten deals with over $300,000 in profits.

On just one of her deals she had found a seller who was making double payments and just wanted to dump her old house. As Juli relates the story, she walked away from the closing table after reselling that house with $26,000 in cash for the 10 hours of work she had in the deal.

The best part of Juli's story is how she has dedicated a part of her time to work with others in her local area, helping them learn to be financially free. In fact, she recently collaborated with a community college math professor so that his class of students could actually run the numbers and projections for a mobile home park on which Juli was negotiating. This project became a tangible way for a classroom of young adults to learn about investing in real estate.

Nate and Maggie

Five years ago, Nate and Maggie were struggling with debt and financial turmoil. They were the typical story of a dual income American family whose lifestyle exceeded their income. What made them different, however, was that Nate and Maggie did something about it. Four years ago they joined our Mentorship Program and began buying single family homes. In fact, one of Maggie's early foreclosures deals was so good it became a case study in our third book, *Making Big Money Investing In Foreclosures Without Cash or Credit*. After their first year of investing, Maggie continued to invest in single-family houses while Nate began buying commercial buildings. It took them a little over two years to reach Level Three with their investing. To hear them talk about their success, you'd learn that what they are most grateful for is the time they have to enjoy each day. But Nate and Maggie wouldn't be able to enjoy any of the wonderful fruits of investing if they hadn't stepped out from the crowd and committed to their investing four years ago.

Understand that when Nate and Maggie got started they were scared and unsure. But they took that critical first step of *deciding* to get started and they took action by joining our Mentorship Program. You can be successful investing in real estate if only you do what Nate and Maggie did—take action now!

Angela and Jeff

Imagine the sweetest young couple you've ever met, and you've got a clear picture of Angela and Jeff, both from the midwest. Two months after they went through the Intensive Training they found their first deal—a lease option on a nice single-family home. After not being able to find their tenant buyer for three weeks, Jeff and Angela ended up giving the property back to the seller.

But the seller kept calling them wanting them to buy the house. Eventually they agreed on a discounted cash price of $280,000 (the house had an as-is value of $400,000). Jumping through some hoops, Angela and Jeff arranged conventional financing and purchased the house. Five weeks later, they had resold the property for a $54,000 net profit. You might wonder what their burning why was that kept them moving forward in their investing. It was their beautiful two-year-old daughter Emily. Who is there who is counting on *you* to succeed in your investing?

Rick and Rob

It never ceases to amaze us how quickly the floodgates of wealth can open up for a new investor. Take the example of Rick and Rob, two Mentorship Graduates of ours who have recently partnered up in their investing. Rick's first deal was with a seasoned investor who had several rental homes his son had mismanaged and let deteriorate. Rick met with this owner and put together a deal for twenty of the houses. The houses were within five miles of Rick's home, and all of them on the same street! Rick structured the deal in blocks of five homes at a time which he felt was more manageable then taking possession of all twenty at one time, and sold each of the homes on a rent-to-own basis. Each house required that he put one dollar down and netted him over $20,000 each. In fact, by the time he was done, Rick ended up making over $400,000 on this one deal.*

But the story goes on from there. About 18 months later, the owner that Rick had bought the homes from called him up. It turns out that he had 95 condos in Arizona that he wanted to sell to Rick. By this point Rick had partnered up with Rob, and the two of them flew down to Phoenix to check out the deal. After negotiating with the owner for a few days they agreed on a deal in which the owner financed the whole purchase. The deal generates over $10,000 of positive cash flow each month and will end up netting Rick and Rob several hundred thousand dollars. Rob is so excited about his investing that he actually joined our team as one of the newest coaches in our Mentorship Program.

We hope you realize that if these investors can make their dreams come true with real estate, then you can too. It's going to take consistent action and a willingness to learn along the way. We know you can do it, but the real question is will you decide and commit to making it happen?

---

*To listen in to an exclusive interview with Rick, where you'll get to watch him share the detailed story of how he found, structured, and closed on this amazing deal, just go to **www.QuickstartInvestor.com**.

CHAPTER EIGHTEEN

It's Decision Time

We're fast approaching the end of the book. Although we hope you found the story of these six beginning mentorship students both entertaining and educational, we don't want it to end here. We've brought you as far as we can in the pages of this book. Now it's going to be up to you to make your choice. Remember, in the beginning we shared the analogy of you standing at the edge of a cliff with all the success and financial freedom you've ever dreamed about just a short space away on the other side. Now it's time for you to face your three choices and make a decision.

Choice number one is to close this book and to turn back to the life you have been living. We understand that when a chance for their dreams is made real, some people are going to get scared and slip back into the old, known, tolerable life they used to lead. The saddest part is that although this choice leads to *known failure*, some people will still choose it and thus settle for less than they are capable of instead of making the decision to create the life they and their family truly deserve.

Choice number two is to freeze at the edge of this cliff. As you have already learned, this is *the most dangerous place of all*, forever exposed to the whipping winds and lost equilibrium of standing frozen in such a precarious place. This is the choice of the deer caught in the headlights of change.

Choice number three is to **step out on faith and commit to make it happen**. We've never known one of our students who has stayed the course to have regretted their decision to make this leap. Of course you are scared, just as you are excited too. Let's take the next step together to make your investing success more certain.

We've designed a comprehensive, online Quick-Start Real Estate Success Program to help you turn the ideas in this book into tangible results for yourself. There are details about how readers like yourself can qualify and take advantage of this $1,595 program for free in Appendix A of this book.

We are going to assume that you have chosen your dreams and possibilities and not your fears and limitations. We are going to assume you have chosen choice number three. It is with that understanding that we have created a detailed plan of action for you to help launch you in your investing as fast and effectively as possible. However, only turn the page to read this action plan if you are truly committed to making your investing happen, no matter what.

CHAPTER NINETEEN

Your 90-Day Action Plan

Your 90-Day Action Plan*

Step 1: Log onto www.QuickstartInvestor.com and register for the Quick-Start Real Estate Success Program.
Your entry password to register is **"dreambig777."** Once registered, take 10 minutes to complete the *Wealth Factor Test*™ to see if you really have what it takes to succeed as an investor. You'll learn how to leverage your strengths and to overcome your weaknesses to create the wealth and freedom you desire.

Enter your name here →

Your password is "dreambig777"

Connect to 'www.quickstartinvestor.com' as:

Your Name:

Password:

Realm: Protected Area

☐ Remember Password   Cancel   OK

Step 2: Uncover your "Burning Why."
Who else besides yourself is counting on you to succeed with your investing?

What is the real cost you will pay if you give up? And how would it make you feel if you gave in to your fears and gave up?

What are the three biggest rewards you will enjoy by succeeding with your investing? And how will you feel when you get to enjoy these rewards in your life?

*Log onto **www.QuickstartInvestor.com** and register for the *Quick-Start Real Estate Success Program* for a more detailed online version of this 90-Day Action Plan to follow. In addition to comprehensive online assessments for you to tap into, you'll find more detailed audio and video training to get you started with your investing.

(continued)

Your 90-Day Action Plan (continued)

Step 3.
Clarify Your Dreams and Goals
❐ Create a dream list of 101 things you want to be, do, and have in your life below or complete this exercise online at **www.QuickstartInvestor.com**.

❐ Go back through your list of 101 dreams and put a rough date by which time you want to accomplish or enjoy each of those dreams. (E.g. now; 1 year; 3 years; 5 years; 10 years; 20 years; etc.)

❐ Choose the two or three most important or appealing dream in each category and transform this dream into a "well-formed goal." A well-formed goal is a specific outcome in affirmative, first person language with a definite time by which you will accomplish it.

Financial Dreams	Date	Well-formed Goal
Example–Make a million dollars.	3 yrs	By December 31, 2012, I have created a $1,000,000 net worth.

Real Estate Dreams	Date	Well-formed Goal
Example–Build real estate portfolio for passive cash flow.	5 yrs	By January 1, 2010, my real estate portfolio earns me a net, positive, passive cash flow of $15,000 per month.

Health & Physical Body	Date	Well-formed Goal

(continued)

Your 90-Day Action Plan *(continued)*

Step 3. *(continued)*

Relationship Dreams	Date	Well-formed Goal

Learning & Adventure	Date	Well-formed Goal

Possessions & "Toys"	Date	Well-formed Goal

Personal Qualities & Character Dreams	Date	Well-formed Goal

Giving & Legacy Dreams	Date	Well-formed Goal

(continued)

Your 90-Day Action Plan (continued)

Step 4.
Take stock of where you stand.
Score yourself on a scale from 1 to 10 (1 = weakest score/least resources or knowledge and 10 = strongest score/most resources or knowledge)

	WEAKEST 1	2	3	4	5	6	7	8	STRONGEST 9	10
Business Experience	❑	❑	❑	❑	❑	❑	❑	❑	❑	❑
Financial Resources	❑	❑	❑	❑	❑	❑	❑	❑	❑	❑

Real Estate Knowledge
Acquisition Strategies:

	1	2	3	4	5	6	7	8	9	10
– Buying for Cash	❑	❑	❑	❑	❑	❑	❑	❑	❑	❑
– Lease Options	❑	❑	❑	❑	❑	❑	❑	❑	❑	❑
– Subject To	❑	❑	❑	❑	❑	❑	❑	❑	❑	❑
– Owner Carry	❑	❑	❑	❑	❑	❑	❑	❑	❑	❑
– Foreclosures	❑	❑	❑	❑	❑	❑	❑	❑	❑	❑

Exit Strategies:

	1	2	3	4	5	6	7	8	9	10
– Selling/retail cash buyer	❑	❑	❑	❑	❑	❑	❑	❑	❑	❑
– Flipping a deal	❑	❑	❑	❑	❑	❑	❑	❑	❑	❑
– Selling/rent to own	❑	❑	❑	❑	❑	❑	❑	❑	❑	❑
– Renting	❑	❑	❑	❑	❑	❑	❑	❑	❑	❑
– Selling/owner financing	❑	❑	❑	❑	❑	❑	❑	❑	❑	❑

Fundamental Investor Skills:

	1	2	3	4	5	6	7	8	9	10
– Negotiation	❑	❑	❑	❑	❑	❑	❑	❑	❑	❑
– Managing people	❑	❑	❑	❑	❑	❑	❑	❑	❑	❑
– Contracts and paperwork	❑	❑	❑	❑	❑	❑	❑	❑	❑	❑
– Finding Deals	❑	❑	❑	❑	❑	❑	❑	❑	❑	❑
– Due Diligence	❑	❑	❑	❑	❑	❑	❑	❑	❑	❑
– Cultivating Funding Sources	❑	❑	❑	❑	❑	❑	❑	❑	❑	❑
– Creating Business Systems	❑	❑	❑	❑	❑	❑	❑	❑	❑	❑

Step 5.
Major Obstacles that Stand In Your Way
On a scale of 1–10 how big are the following obstacles standing in your way (1 = not at all and 10 = almost insurmountable)

	SMALLEST OBSTACLE 1	2	3	4	5	6	7	BIGGEST OBSTACLE 8	9	10
Lack of knowledge	❑	❑	❑	❑	❑	❑	❑	❑	❑	❑
Limiting beliefs	❑	❑	❑	❑	❑	❑	❑	❑	❑	❑

(continued)

Your 90-Day Action Plan (continued)

Step 5. (continued)

	SMALLEST OBSTACLE							BIGGEST OBSTACLE	
	1 2 3 4 5						6 7 8 9 10		

Lack of time   ☐ ☐ ☐ ☐ ☐ ☐ ☐ ☐ ☐ ☐
Lack of money   ☐ ☐ ☐ ☐ ☐ ☐ ☐ ☐ ☐ ☐
Lack of support   ☐ ☐ ☐ ☐ ☐ ☐ ☐ ☐ ☐ ☐
FEAR   ☐ ☐ ☐ ☐ ☐ ☐ ☐ ☐ ☐ ☐

If you were being totally honest with yourself and let go of all your excuses, what do you think is the real obstacle standing in your way of real estate success?

_____

_____

Step 6.
Committing to Your Action Plan
Market that you'll be doing your investing in...
_____ *Median price of home* (E.g. $400,000)
_____ *Average rate of appreciation* (E.g. 4%-5%)
_____ *Conservative profit per deal you anticipate* (E.g. $30,000)

Financial Target:

	Dollar amount	# of deals/year to target	deals/month to target
Example Year	$120,000	4	1/3
Year One			
Year Two			
Year Three			
Year Four			
Year Five			

The number of hours per week you'll set aside for your investing: _____
_____ hours per week for your marketing activities.
_____ hours per week in study and review.
_____ hours per week meeting with sellers about their properties.
          (meet with ___ sellers/week x 2 hours/meeting)

Budget: *Approximate money you've budgeted for each of following areas...*
$_____ Business overhead (phone line, web access, etc.)
$_____ Marketing (signs, ads, etc.)
$_____ Real Estate Training and Mentoring

(continued)

Your 90-Day Action Plan *(continued)*

Action Commitments:

_____ Date by which you'll have tested out three lead sources.
_____ Date by which you'll have met with your first three sellers.
_____ Date by which you'll have found the **right mentor**.

Step 7.
Action and Ongoing Weekly Feedback*
It's time to work your action plan. Each Sunday evening, sit down with your calendar and schedule in your investing sessions for the following week. Also review the prior week.

> *What went well?*
> *What will you do differently next week as a result of what you learned this week?*
> *What questions will you find the answers to?*

The key is for you to consistently take tangible action to further your investing goals each and every week. Strive to do something for your investing at least three days out of the week. We've found that by spacing out your investing activities rather than loading them all into one day, you will greatly enhance both your learning and ultimate success.

Step 8.
Your 90-Day Review
Take out your calendar *right now* and schedule in the specific date and time of your 90-Day Review. You will use this focused two- to four-hour session to review and update your real estate action plan based on what you've learned to that point in your investing.

Ask yourself questions like what went well, what would you do differently next time based on what you learned this time, and what do you need to learn in order to progress in your investing?

Date and Time for 90-Day Review: _____ *at* _____ A.M./P.M.

*To access your "Online Real Estate Success Journal" to track your success over time, simply log onto **www.QuickstartInvestor.com**.

CHAPTER TWENTY

Final Thoughts

For most of this book we've focused almost exclusively on creating financial wealth through investing in real estate. Never forget that real estate is just one piece in the whole of your life. Although it's important because it will enable you to become financially free, don't make it more than it really is—a part of wealth, and a small part at that.

If you were to ask us what one key ingredient would do more than any other ingredient to help you create massive wealth for yourself and your family, we would boil it down to one word. This word is so critical for you not because it will help you create wealth, but more importantly because it will help you recognize and enjoy the wealth you already possess. That word is *gratitude*.

We each have so many blessings in our lives right now. Take a moment to reflect on the people, things, and opportunities you are thankful for in your life. What are you grateful for? What *could* you be grateful for if you just allowed yourself to be?

In our modern world of rushing, hurrying, and scurrying, it's too easy to forget how simple and easy feeling wealthy really is. Everyone of you who is reading this book has more money, more opportunities, and more hope for an even better life than over 90 percent of the world's population. It's so easy to forget; that's why we have to consistently remind ourselves.

When times are tough with your investing, which will happen to all of you at some point in your investing, count the blessings you do have and know that over time even more wealth will flow into your life. When times are incredible with your investing, the habit of gratitude will help you enjoy the massive wealth you are creating.

We believe in you. We are here with you and so is our coaching team. In fact, the entire staff of Mentor Financial Group is committed to helping you succeed in your investing dreams. You can borrow our faith in you and in real estate any time you need it. We know that together we are going to touch a lot of lives, buy a ton of real estate, and make a great deal of money. Thank you for the trust you placed in us and choosing us to be your mentors and reading this book We trust that you now know that it wasn't an accident that you chose this book. It's time for you to get to work making your dreams real. We wish you great wealth and abundance along the way.

Peter and David

The Quick-Start Real Estate Success Program—Your FREE $1,595 Gift from the Authors!

Dear Reader,

Do you truly want to turn the ideas and strategies in this book into enough money for yourself so that you can enjoy the time and freedom you've always dreamed of having?

If you answered yes then we urge you to take the next step and claim your free $1,595 bonus for reading this book.

To register all you'll need to do is go online to **www.QuickstartInvestor.com** and use the access code: "**dreambig777**."

When you register online you'll get immediate access to this comprehensive 30-day online investor business start-up system. It's designed to help investors like you quickly and easily launch your investing business right away so that you can make the money to create the freedom you've always wanted for yourself.

A Surprising Secret That Few Readers Know

You may not know this but the original manuscript of this book that we turned in to our publisher was 20,000 words too long! It was heartbreaking to cut out so many powerful investor strategies and techniques, but we had to do it anyway.

But we found a "compromise" solution that worked . . . we simply put all that extra content up on the Web as part of this valuable bonus! (Actually, we took it one step further and turned much of that extra content into online investor training courses that you get for free, but more on that in a moment.)

What You Get As Part of This Valuable *Free* Bonus:

- Powerful *investor software and planning tools* that will help you make sure you are building your investing business on a solid foundation.

- Exclusive footage of **private interviews with 20 successful investors** who have applied the ideas in this book to make hundreds of thousands and millions of dollars. You'll hear one new investor share his story of buying 20 houses from one investor and making over $400,000 on his very first deal! And how another investor sold over 50 homes in one day! Plus you'll hear what they learned along the way and how they found their real estate mentor and much more.

- Access to the *Quickview Market Evaluator*™! Would you like to know what type of real estate market you are investing in? And how to leverage this understanding so that you make your profits with less risk? Then register right away so that you can get access to our proprietary real estate market analysis software that will help you determine exactly what type of market you are investing in. Plus you'll learn how to boost your profits and use the best strategies for your specific market conditions.

- And much, much more!

You'll learn:

- How to find the right real estate mentor to guide you to your investing goals.

- How to inexpensively secure investor friendly contracts and agreements.

- How to escape the three biggest pitfalls that keep most "wannabe" investors broke.

- What are the steps you need to take to be successful investing in real estate.

- And much more!

Plus You'll Also Get *Five* Free Online Investor Training Courses:

Course One: Buying Foreclosures Without Cash or Credit!

Course Two: How to Buy Homes in NICE Areas with Nothing Down!

Course Three: Upside Leverage: How to Intelligently Invest with Cash to Make More Money with Less Risk!

Course Four: 7 Secrets to Negotiate Profitable Win-Win Real Estate Deals!

Course Five: How to Generate a $10,000 per Month Cash Flow Investing in Multi-Unit Properties!

Who Is the *Quick-Start Real Estate Success Program* right for?

It was designed for three groups of people:

Group One—**Brand-New Investors**

People who have always wanted to get started investing in real estate but in the past lacked the tools and support to make their investing dreams happen. For those of you in this group, we urge you to register immediately. This is the single most important thing you can do to make sure you will succeed with your investing.

Group Two—**Part-Time Investors**

New investors who've just gotten started with their investing but need more clarity and direction on exactly what steps to take and how to avoid the costly mistakes other investors have made in the past. For those of you in this group the biggest thing you'll get by registering right now is the certainty and assurance of *knowing* that you now have a definite, concrete, and winning real estate business plan to follow so that your success is *guaranteed*!

Group Three—**Experienced Pros**

Experienced investors who want to take their existing investing businesses to the next level. You'll get a powerful framework to help fine-tune and turbo-charge your existing investing business and make it ten times more profitable. The biggest danger you face is allowing your thinking to get closed off and to let your dreams stay too small. That's why it's critical for you to break past these self-imposed limitations and use the Quick-Start Real Estate Success Program as the spark to help your success skyrocket to the next level and beyond.

The bottom line is that this valuable bonus is for readers like you who want to actually get started making money investing as fast as possible and are willing to take action.

Whether you're completely new to investing and this is the first real estate book you've ever read or you're an experienced investor with dozens of properties in your real estate portfolio, the *Quick-Start Real Estate Success Program* will help you take your investing to the next level.

The Real Reason We Can Give You This $1,595 Bonus for FREE

Let's face it. We live in a cynical world. Some skeptics are wondering how we can give every reader such a valuable bonus for the price of a $20 book. It just sounds too good to be true . . . unless of course you understand our two motivations for giving you this $1,595 package for free.

First, we both feel it's our mission in life to help people reach the level of financial freedom and success that everyone deserves. Real estate has totally transformed our lives. Remember Peter was once an auto mechanic earning $10/hour and David was once an amateur athlete living on $6,000 a year of income! We feel compelled to share this gift with as many people as we can.

Second, we know that by sharing our knowledge and insights as openly and freely as possible, the right students will find our company and get started in our Mentorship Program. And since we split profits on deals with our students in the beginning of our work together, this is one way we can pick up hundreds of properties every year to add to our portfolio. We think this is the ultimate win-win. Our students get our hands-on, step-by-step guidance and coaching, and we get a portion of their first two real estate deals. As an aside, if you're interested in interviewing to become one of our Mentorship Students you can apply at **www.QuickstartInvestor.com**.

Here's How the Quick-Start Real Estate Success Program Works!

Step 1: Go online to **www.QuickstartInvestor.com** to register using the password **"dreambig777."**

Step 2: Take the *Wealth Factor Test*™. In less than 10 minutes this proprietary success assessment will help you identify the biggest wealth traps that are keeping you from earning all you want to earn. The *Wealth Factor Test*™ will also give you an individualized printout with specific steps for you to take to leverage your wealth strengths so that you can start to make money investing in real estate easier than ever before.

Step 3: Use the *Strategic Investors Business Plan Creator*™ to map out a personalized real estate business strategy that will take you from where you are to where you want to be with your investing. It will help you focus all your investing efforts so that you can succeed as quickly as possible. Plus, you'll be able to sidestep all the frustrations most new investors struggle through because we'll be guiding you along proven investor highways so that your journey to financial freedom is smoother and easier.

Step 4: Tap into the other powerful investor tools and online training so that you can increase your investing skill level and get started right away.

Step 5: Take your breakthrough learning and new insights with you into the real world as you get into immediate action buying real estate.

Warning! If you don't think it's worth all the hard work and effort in the first few years of your investing so that you can enjoy a **lifetime** of financial freedom, then please do *not* register for this bonus. The powerful information and clear action-oriented strategies and tools would only frustrate you.

Only *register right now* if you understand that to make money investing in real estate takes energy and action, especially during the start-up phase.

If you want to make millions with zero work and zero effort we suggest you buy a lottery ticket. If, however, you are willing to invest the time and energy in the early years to build an investing business that will pump out consistent cash flow and create windfall profits for you to years to come, then *register right now*.

10 Reasons to Go Online and Register Now!

1. This special bonus offer is only available for a limited time and may be withdrawn at any time. You'll kick yourself if you miss out on this opportunity!

2. The sooner you log on and get access to all the powerful information and investor tools, the sooner you'll start making money investing!

3. Real estate is one of the most certain paths to financial freedom!

4. The *Quick-Start Real Estate Success Program* will help you get out of the rat race and become financially free!

5. We just may come to our senses and start making people pay for this valuable bonus!

6. The sooner you start making money investing, the sooner you can start sharing your good fortune with other people!

7. It will help you take your investing to the next level!

8. It will inspire you to get into instant action!

9. It will help hold you accountable so that you make money, not excuses!

10. You'll build so much momentum by reading the book and logging on now you'll literally be propelled to your next real estate success!

Register Right Now and Get the Following *Five* eBooks—FREE!

When you register right now you'll also get our five most popular ebooks—absolutely free! These books are:

- *Seven Simple Steps to Sell Your Property on a Rent to Own Basis*
- *The Hidden Secrets of Seller Financing*
- *Three Simple Steps to Flip a Deal for Fast Cash Profits*
- *Short Sales-Making Money on Foreclosure Deals with Little or No Equity*
- *The Nine Essential Contract Clauses When Buying Real Estate*

Exactly How You Register to Get This Powerful Bonus—Free!

To claim your free bonus package simply go online to **www.QuickstartInvestor.com** right now and complete the enrollment form. When prompted for your pass code simply enter "**dreambig777**." It's literally that easy!

Again we thank you for reading our book. We wish you a lifetime of success and happiness and know real estate will help you achieve this. Enjoy your "graduation gift" of the *Quick-Start Investor Success Program*!

Our very best to you,

Peter and David

P.S. To get your free Quick-Start Real Estate Success Program ($1,595 value), simply go to **www.QuickstartInvestor.com** and register using the password "**dreambig777**."

P.P.S. We urge you to register right now because this offer is for a very limited time only and we'd hate for you to miss out!

Ambassador Number: _____

The *Creating Cash Flow* Series!

We hope you've enjoyed Book One of the *Creating Cash Flow* series. As you've learned in the book there are three investor levels.

Level One investors are just getting started and need to prove to themselves that real estate can and does work for them.

Level Two investors work both to develop and fine-tune their investor skills, but also to begin to build a real estate investing *business* instead of just settling for being a real estate investor.

Level Three investors have transitioned out of the day-to-day operations of their investing business and have the freedom to enjoy the incredible Level Three lifestyle that setting up their investing business the right way has provided for them.

The series is designed to teach you how to start as a Level One investor and grow to become a financially free Level Three investor as fast as possible.

Soon to Be Released!

The Real Estate Fast-Track:
How to Create a $5,000 to $50,000 per Month
Real Estate Cash Flow

Ever wondered how to tap into the amazing world of real estate investing to make enough money to create the time and freedom you've dreamed about? Then join Peter Conti and David Finkel, two of the nation's leading real estate investment experts, as they take you by the hand and show you exactly how to build a profitable real estate investing business.

You'll learn how to master all five of the Core Investor Skills:

1. Marketing—How to Create Systems to Consistently Find Great Deals!
2. Analysis—How to Determine If a Deal Is Worth Pursuing In Five Minutes or Less!
3. Structuring—How to Structure Win-Win Real Estate Deals!
4. Negotiation—How to Get the Other Party to Say "YES" to the Deal You Want!
5. Contracts—How to Write Up Money Making Real Estate Deals!

Plus you'll learn advanced secrets to buying real estate without cash or credit like:

- How to tap into the six forms of leverage
- 5 fun, easy systems to find deal after deal
- A simple 3-step system to safely evaluate any real estate deal
- 9 Advanced deal structuring strategies to unstuck even the toughest of deals
- 12 Advanced negotiating techniques to make up to an extra $25,000 on every deal
- How to avoid the 10 contract pitfalls that trip up most investors

Available Fall 2006!
Book Three of the *Creating Cash Flow* Series

Are you ready to "go passive" with your investing? Level Three investors have learned to transition into passive profits with their investing business so that they can enjoy the freedom and security of a Level Three lifestyle.

In Book Three of the wildly popular Creating Cash Flow series you'll learn how to supersize your profits by investing in commercial real estate. You'll also learn how to master the 7 Critical Wealth Skills of The Super Successful Investors! And much more.

Ex-auto mechanic turned real estate multimillionaire **Peter Conti** and ex-Olympic level athlete turned real estate multimillionaire **David Finkel** are two of the nation's leading real estate experts. Over the past 10 years their more than 100,000 students have literally bought and sold **over $1 billion of real estate**.

Conti and Finkel have co-authored 15 real estate courses together and three other real estate bestsellers, including the *Wall Street Journal* and *BusinessWeek* bestseller *Making Big Money Investing in Foreclosures Without Cash or Credit!* Both their last two books were selected as among the top ten real estate books of the year by syndicated real estate columnist Robert Bruss. Their first book, *How to Create Multiple Streams of Income Buying Homes in Nice Areas with Nothing Down*, was selected as one of the all-time top three investing books by the American Real Estate Investors Association.

Their company, Mentor Financial Group, LLC, has been helping new investors get on the real estate fast-track and build a profitable real estate investing business so that they can enjoy the time and freedom they deserve. Over the past decade the 5,000 graduates of the Mentorship Program have gone on to buy thousands of properties all across the United States and in the process gain financial freedom and security.

Conti and Finkel are the co-hosts of the nationally broadcast *Real Estate Radio Show*, one of the most popular investing shows of all time. Their how-to investor articles have been featured in over 4,000 newspapers and periodicals across the country, including the *Wall Street Journal Online* and *Miami Herald*.

Conti and Finkel have had their hands in thousands of real estate deals and are both still active investors with investment companies that buy residential and commercial real estate across the United States.

Each year thousands of investors attend their Real Estate Success Conferences. To find out more about these powerful investor events or Mentor Financial Group, simply visit the company web site at www.resultsnow.com.